BEING DISCIPLED BY THE HOLY SPIRIT

MARK JUDY

AN INTENSIVE, TRANSFORMATIONAL APPROACH TO WALKING IN THE SPIRIT

ISBN 978-1-66787-731-0

CONTENTS

A PERSONAL WORD TO THE READER

Hello, dear Child of God~~~the fact that you are holding this book is not by coincidence, nor is it by chance.

I don't know how many times it has happened to you before, but there have been many times in my walk with the Lord that just the right book, with the right message, came to me at just the right time.

Each of those times was a crucial turning point in my walk with God....

A turning point where I needed a miracle; I needed an answer from heaven; I needed miraculous, spiritual provision from on high—and then those cries were answered.

Perhaps you are already feeling the same way....looking at the cover of this book, new Hope has been ignited in your heart....

Perhaps you have been crying out for a desperately needed deliverance, and as your eyes fell upon the man walking between parted waters on this cover, you felt a renewed surge of hope, that your own prayers for deliverance have been heard—and they are about to be answered....

Perhaps you have been wandering through a wilderness place for a very long time, and the God that was once very real to you, has seemed distant and far away, and you're not sure how that happened....Perhaps you are wrestling with feelings of unworthiness, thinking maybe you don't deserve to be close to Him like you once were....

Or, perhaps you are one of many who has seen heartbreaking changes in our world that have caused you to hunger and cry out for a Living, Real connection with the God that you've heard talked about in churches....and yet you hear their words, but there's no Life.

Maybe you've gone into church after church after church, seeking more of Him and His Reality, His Life, His Power....and yet every time, you leave disappointed and further away than before....I know how that feels, beloved—I've been through that same place....

But I am here to tell you, by the Spirit of the Living God, that today is Your divine appointment—Because the book you hold in your hands is the Beginning of a New Journey between you and the Holy Spirit, and He's been waiting for you...He's been waiting to minister a great many things to you....

And today, it begins—for You....

Now, I don't know anything about your spiritual walk, but I hope you'll feel comfortable later on sharing with me through email, or social media, or however you feel comfortable, about where you are in your walk with the Lord, and where you hope to go. Consider this an open invitation that you may take advantage of any time. I am grateful for this opportunity to join you on this new journey.

Just so we can get to know each other a little bit better, I'll be sharing my personal testimony with you shortly.

You see, this book is a journey for me as well.

I've been in the Lord for over 44 years, and my precious wife Roopa was in the Lord for over 22 years, before she went home to be with the Lord 21 months ago.

Roopa was unwaveringly and gloriously devoted to the Lord through all of her battles with chronic illness, right up until the Sunday night she went home. True to her nature, she was always trying to encourage everybody else, including me....and one of the last things she said to me was to not give up, to not let grief take over, because the Lord had a job for me to do.

And now, He has called me back into active duty—for You.

The apostle Paul was not so much focused on writing letters to his churches, as much as he was focused on writing on their Hearts.

He said to the Corinthians, "You yourselves are our letter, inscribed on our hearts, known and read by everyone. It is clear that you are a letter from Christ, the result of our ministry, written not with ink but with the Spirit of the living God, not on tablets of stone but on tablets of human hearts." (2nd Corinthians 3:2,3).

And I am interested not so much in writing a book, but in the Holy Spirit writing a book through me that is in turn going to write on your heart….Writing the things on your heart that the Holy Spirit has personally for you.

DEDICATION TO MY BELOVED WIFE, ROOPA

My darling wife battled post polio syndrome and chronic lung disease for 16 years, and in all that time, I never saw a more devoted follower of the Lord. Her sincere love and gratitude for the Lord never wavered, although she suffered more than anybody I've ever known in my life. We were married for just over 19 years, when she passed away in November 2020.

Before she went home to be with the Lord, she said to me so many times to not allow the coming battles with grief too overwhelm me.

She said, "Mark, you have to remember the Lord has a job for you to do".

Roopa had given me over 19 years of the most unconditional love I've ever had in my life, and then it was gone....But the one thing that began to bring healing to me in the midst of overwhelming heartache, was stepping out in faith and coming back into my first true love— discipleship ministry.

The Lord led me to launch Vigilance for the Endtimes podcast in September 2021, and the huge number of people who have written me to tell me how much it has transformed their spiritual life, has now led me to turning the podcast episodes into a discipleship manual.....One that I believe has the potential to radically deepen every believers relationship with the Lord, in ways they never imagined. I know that it will, because the things that I write about and teach, I've walked out and experienced in my own life.

"A wife of noble character is her husband's crown" (Proverbs 12:4)

DEDICATED TO MY DEVOTED LISTENERS & FOLLOWERS OF VIGILANCE FOR THE ENDTIMES PODCAST, WHOSE SPIRITUAL HUNGER & DEDICATION TO THE LORD WERE THE INSPIRATION FOR THIS BOOK

Vigilance For the Endtimes Podcast Listeners Share How Their Spiritual Lives Are Being Transformed

"Wow! I just listened to Episode 28: "Dreams, Visions, & Warnings—Preparing the Last Days Believer". I'm going to need a transcript of this one. What a provocative message to close out a powerful day. This was a true eye opener. God bless you brother. Your ministry has been a powerful help in my life, and is reaching others through me, and I'm sure many others who hear it! I have a renewed vigor for walking in the Spirit. Why this isn't being preached from every pulpit is beyond me."

{Matthew Yockey}

"Hey there, Mark! I just wanted to let you know how your podcasts have been blessing me. Thank you again for obeying the Holy Spirit's lead. You're a treasure and a blessing for sure. I am so encouraged by your podcasts, I have learned so much about the Holy Spirit. I am always so encouraged by the wisdom and passion He pours into you. Thank you for obediently walking in unison with Him."

{Shannon Cox Howell}

"Hi Mark, just got done with Episode 29, "Serving as Priest & Prophet of Your Home, Through Intercession & Praying in the Spirit, & Ministering the Living Word to your Family". As always, I'm completely blessed and blown away. So many gems in this one, it really hit home! I took four pages of notes, thank you Mark, really lit me up, that was fire! I feel so blessed that God is using you so mightily, and I'm fortunate enough be an eager student, it's humbling, inspiring, and empowering all at the same time. God bless you! Love you brother, I'm so grateful for your sharing this wisdom"

{Danny Poleto}

"I really appreciate your ministry, and I know God is doing something in me. I am just thankful for coming in contact with you, because your messages are really challenging me in my walk with Christ to desire more."

{Faith Guzman}

Listener Review on Episode #16; A Spiritual Warfare Mindset, Part 2: Letters from the Battlefront —

"Mark, I'm so thankful for your obedience to the Holy Spirit. Brother I'm so engulfed in the Spirit right now after hearing this message. I haven't gotten to #17 yet, but I'm at a point spiritually that I've never been before.

Hearing episode #16, I wept, I was taken away. I can't describe where I was. I'm wondering how can anyone read these scriptures and not understand the Kingdom of God and the expectation of that. *We need to go from superficial to supernatural quickly.*

As I wept, I felt the love of God overwhelm me. Like how could I know someone's hurting so bad, yet I have every excuse to not do what I'm called to do. I'm convicted not condemned. I agree, we've been playing church while Satan is playing his game of killing and destroying. This isn't a game. After listening I prayed in tongues like never before. I'm being honest, I don't claim to be some pillar of faith, some spiritual superhero. What I do claim is I'm there, I'll grow, I'll get bolder, I'll lose any unbelief. I'll be ready and obedient. Thank you my brother. God has certainly brought you to me for edification and encouragement. I was walking the walk of faith, but I've been complacent. I needed to wake up. I thank God for the impact you've had on me. It's you, but I know spiritually, it's God working through you to me. I praise the Holy Spirit for this awareness I'm getting."

{Danny Poleto}

Listener Review by David Clifton on Apple Podcasts;

"Just listened to #18...you were on point the entire episode...your best yet.... when you have time, please email me the transcript. Very, very deep and profound episode 18. Thanks so much!

Listener Review by Jason Taylor on Apple Podcasts;

"I really like this brother! I know God connected us spiritually for such a time as this. I know some of his anointing and wisdom has been imparted due to his wife's passing last year. We grow tremendously spiritually if we abide in Christ when we suffer and he has. It's very rare to come across someone who is Spirit-filled, wise, humble, compassionate, empathetic, patient, not pushy, trusting of God and others, and Biblical."

Review & Word of Appreciation From Kim Greco;

"Hi Mark, first off, I thank you again for serving us in a time of where your soul is still dealing with the loss of your wife Roopa. I would like to say things will one day get easier for you, but I'm not too sure that day will come until you are home with the Lord. Roopa was a gift of a lifetime. My prayer is that Lord renews His strength in you daily, so that you may continue on with His work because I know your heart desires this. I just listened to Episode 11."

Review by David Clifton on Episode #11;
Subdue the Flesh, Renew the Mind, Exercise the Spirit;

"Looking forward to this one Mark. There is general confusion among believers about the difference between the soul and the spirit. Scripture appears to conflate the two at times, and then other times, clearly shows soul and spirit to be distinct from one another. I read the pre-Nicene church fathers, and found they were as confused as modern believers on the spirit/soul relationship. I'm really interested in your teaching on this."

Listener Review From Julie Lewis;

"Hi Mark, I have listened to all your podcasts, and they are helping me a lot to understand many things. I have felt very far away from God.... Yet I clung to him when I had extremely aggressive cancer and he healed me 13 years ago.....But hearing your podcasts brought me a longing for fellowship with Him. Thank you so much!"

Listener Review From Neil Hosken;

"ABSOLUTELY Outstanding, Exceptional! Praise be to the God and Father of our Lord Jesus Christ!"

Review by George Mitchler;

"I'm up in the morning now walking my dog before daybreak and then sipping my first cup of coffee while reading His Word at my desk. I top it off with a dose of Spirit guided wisdom from Mark while my bride listens from adjacent room too. It's been an amazing start to a glorious week."

Review by Patrick and Char Flanagan on Episode #10; Spiritual Clarity — Seeing with Kingdom Eyes;

"The Holy Spirit has been strengthening many of us through your teachings, and through your obedience the same Spirit will heal your heart from pain and grief as He heals and equips others to work His fields. God always has His remnant... There is much fruit that the vine is bearing! I believe the Holy Spirit has turned up the flame of intercession with many here! God Bless!"

Review by Danny Poleto on Episode #11; Subdue the Flesh, Renew the Mind, Exercise the Spirit;

"Powerful message Mark, I have known some of these things but quite honestly haven't always done the greatest job at keeping it foremost in my walk. I keep pushing. I haven't attained the power God wants to anoint me with. I know my heart is right, and I diligently seek him. Your teachings are really inspiring me so much. I want it and I know Jesus will give me what I need to grow spiritually. The Holy Spirit will guide us all. It's a serious matter. Thank you Mark"

Review by Matthew Yockey on Episode #21; Temples of the Holy Spirit, Drawing Close to the Father;

"I want to share a praise report with you, as your ministry has had a profound effect on my walk with the Lord. I met with my pastor today to discuss the battle that is being waged around me, and this desire for the baptism of the Holy Spirit. He and I talked in depth about what I've learned from your podcast as well. Thank you so much for listening to the leading of the Spirit and producing these podcasts. They've been invaluable to me and the renewal of my connection to our Holy Father. I wholeheartedly believe that every interaction that has happened over the past few months is leading to a new level of connection with God. I'd love to chat with you sometime and describe this all and more detail. I just wanted to thank you for now!"

INTRODUCTION

As a Spirit-Filled believer for more than 39 years, and having been involved in multiple forms of ministry since the early 1980's, I have observed that most so-called discipleship programs focus heavily on change from the Outside In, with an emphasis on activities that are supposed to "make" you a disciple—Memorizing scripture, structured prayer, and a myriad of other religious activities.

Because True spiritual liberty is born of the Holy Spirit, and sustained by walking in the Spirit, then spiritual liberty can only be derived from and experientially received through the Holy Spirit.

Just the Word of God alone in a believer's mind will not produce spiritual liberty, apart from the indwelling presence of the Holy Spirit, and the illumination of the Holy Spirit upon the Word of God.

True New Testament discipleship is only born out of a deeply personal, One-on-One relationship with the Holy Spirit, where you are guided, taught, led, and discipled by HIM, the Spirit of Truth.

This is strictly a "from the inside out" spiritual lifestyle, where you learn to live from your spirit, not merely religious intellect.

The result is a Spirit-empowered Lifestyle, where *personal fellowship with and through the Holy Spirit is what shapes & guides your life*, not religious activity. *Your life becomes progressively transformed by the power of the Holy Spirit & the Living Word of God, and you in turn are able to be a vessel used of the Lord to dramatically transform others.*

This book will be a tremendous and powerful resource for any believer who is honestly committed to walking in the Spirit and growing in the Spirit. For decades now the Western church has been full of head knowledge about God, and head knowledge about the Holy Spirit, but head knowledge does not impart life, and head knowledge certainly does not empower anyone spiritually—"head knowledge is dead knowledge".

Jesus said, "The Spirit gives life; the flesh profits nothing. The words I have spoken to you are spirit and they are life" (John 6:63).

The apostle Paul expounded upon that principle, when he said, "My message and my preaching were not with persuasive words of wisdom, but with a demonstration of the Spirit's power" (1 Corinthians 2:4).

This book points the way for any believer who is earnestly desiring to walk in spiritual liberty and spiritual power, and if you are ready to leave behind dead head knowledge, and enter into a true walk with the Holy Spirit, this is your first step.

Take that from your brother who has been a believer for over 44 years, and was baptized in the Holy Spirit over 39 years ago. I have lived what this book is sharing with you, and I have proven it day after day, in all kinds of ministry and life situations.

Together, Child of God, we will intensively focus on guiding You into a New Testament Lifestyle where the Word of God is ALIVE, and where the Holy Spirit is Ever-Present with You to Guide, Direct, Counsel, Comfort, and Empower You. This is Not "religion"; This is His Life & Power Flowing Through You, and His Abiding Presence With You and IN You, Every Single Day, Till He Comes Again.

My Vision For the "Being Discipled by the Holy Spirit Intensive Discipleship Manual"

In seeking to identify and clarify the various focal points for this discipleship book, I matched them up with the focal points of the apostles Paul and Peter—specifically with reference to *Desiring the Spiritual Gifts*, *Functioning in the Spiritual Gifts*, *Developing our Faith in utilizing those Spiritual Gifts*, and *Being Stewards of the Gifts*.

Those focal points that I just mentioned all fit under 2 headings:

1. Our personal fellowship with the Lord and our personal growth with the Holy Spirit;

2. Ministering to our fellow believers.

The Main heading for all of this, then, could be simply described as *Growing in Spiritual Functionality*, or, *Growing in Spirit-led Functionality*.

In other words, you are not becoming functional in natural gifts or man-made talents; ***you are growing and developing functionality in abilities and giftings that are derived directly from the Holy Spirit Himself—*** *which means the Holy Spirit is the main element and focal point for all of this.*

And with the Holy Spirit as the main element and focal point, the Sub-Points under that would include:

*   Receiving the baptism of the Holy Spirit;

*   Functioning in your prayer language;

*   Growing in receptivity and sensitivity to the Holy Spirit—out of which comes all the rest, the overflow and the outflow.

I remember the Lord showed me many years ago in Lake Worth, Florida, while walking and praying through John Prince Park, that He was going to utilize me as a sort of college professor of the things of the Spirit, much like a professor teaching on how the human body works, or a psychologist teaching about how the mind works.

The Lord showed me that I would be doing in-depth teaching about how the Spirit works, and how the things of the Spirit work, because it is every bit as much a science—even though this is a spiritual science—as anything else in all of God's creation. In other words, the realities of the Spirit are every bit as real as physics or any other natural law, because everything originates from God Himself, Who IS spirit.

God has an order to everything, and not just in the physical realm.

God has an order to everything in the spirit realm—things have an order, things have their own function, that we need to learn how to flow with and cooperate with.

Paul said, "Now about spiritual gifts, brothers, I do not want you to be uninformed." (1 Corinthians 12:1), and most people are simply uninformed of how spiritual things work and operate, therefore they never learn how to operate in spiritual things; they never learn and study how they can flow in spiritual things, and how God designed us to flow and operate in things of the Spirit.

Jesus did just that with His disciples—He first Demonstrated that the Kingdom of God was Real, then He commissioned THEM to demonstrate that same spiritual Kingdom Reality.

Here in the West, we have only focused on MENTAL transference of spiritual truth, without Demonstrating Spiritual Realities—and Appropriating & Demonstrating Spiritual Realities is the whole intention, vision, and purpose of this discipleship manual —to enable you to become proficient in the things of the Spirit.

It's the same thing if you enroll in a career college to learn draftsmanship; you can expect very specialized, intensive training in becoming a draftsman. We need to treat the things of the Spirit as that intense and specialized, and worthy of our utmost respect and attention.

PART 1:

THE BAPTISM OF THE HOLY SPIRIT: THE SINGULAR GATEWAY TO TRUE SPIRITUAL LIBERTY AND MATURITY IN THE LORD

CHAPTER 1

THE SPIRIT OF ADOPTION: SPIRIT-LED SONS AND DAUGHTERS

Much of this book will include testimonials of things that I have learned by walking in the Holy Spirit; specific experiences that I learned from, because "....the kingdom of God is not a matter of talk but of power" (1 Corinthians 4:20), so *we must move beyond the theoretical, to the actual & experiential outworking of spiritual truths and concepts*.

Part of this will simply be learning to practice walking in the Spirit; practice learning how to cooperate with the Holy Spirit, and ALL of this requires an honest investment of an individual's time.

It is not something anyone's going to learn by reading a book—it will only be learned by giving of ourselves over to the Holy Spirit's timetable, and trusting that He indeed Wants to lead us, guide us, and teach us.

Jesus went beyond simple teaching, where His disciples were concerned—He engaged them out in the real world, demonstrating the power and authority of the Kingdom, where they learned to participate with Him; so it will be with us and the Holy Spirit, in the very same way.

Just as there were almost no two situations alike as the disciples participated with Jesus, so it will be with the Holy Spirit—He will lead us out of our comfort zones mentally, spiritually, and physically, so we will need to be yielded and trusting continually. There is no way around it; all of us are heading into completely and totally unknown, uncharted territory that will most probably test us to our very limits mentally, emotionally, spiritually, and perhaps even physically.

That means that we must go through as much spiritual preparation and training through the Holy Spirit Now, while there is still time—and I personally don't know where we are on the clock.

Now, I want to share something that will hopefully change for the better *How you come to the Word of God.*

In other words, your mindset as well as your heart attitude when you approach the Word of God—*what is that mindset based on?*

What I'm about to share with you now will totally change how you read your Bible—especially the New Testament—because **it will change how you Read it, and it will change how it Speaks to you.**

Here is what I mean.

The letters of the New Testament were exactly that—*they were letters.* They didn't have numbered chapters and numbered verses so that people could intellectually dissect the different letters of the New Testament, as though we are analyzing them under a microscope.

The epistles were not written by some religious professor in a seminary somewhere, seated at his solid oak desk in his study.

These letters were written from the front lines of a spiritual battlefield, by an apostle who said, "to this very hour we hunger and thirst, and are naked and have no dwelling place of our own"!

Picture in your mind the movie Saving Private Ryan, and you're on the front lines trying to write letters of encouragement and faith to your fellow soldiers in the other fox holes!

I'm speaking to so many of my brothers and sisters today, and many of you are in your own spiritual foxholes right now, facing different battles on enemy lines, and part of my job as God has designated it, is to do my part in helping you have clear communication lines with the Head of Command, the Holy Spirit—*Because out here on the battlefield, His voice is all we've got, and if that communication gets cut off, we're done.*

Sunday school chitter chatter won't cut it—*we have to have clear lines of spiritual communication from the Spirit of Truth, Who was sent to lead us and guide us into all truth*—He was sent to be our guide, our comforter, the one of whom it is written, "He will not allow your foot to slip; your Protector will not slumber." (Psalm 121:3). We serve and love a God Who is ever vigilant over each and every one of us.

Part of My job is to see to it that those who are feeling cut off from the ranks and isolated do not lose heart, but instead, are able to see *these were personal letters, written by a Spirit-led, persecuted apostle to Spirit-filled, persecuted believers.* He was writing letters of encouragement; he was writing letters to inspire their faith, to confirm and ground them in the spiritual realities of their faith.

Paul wasn't sitting in a prison cell waiting to be executed, while writing to the Philippians "chapter 1 verse three". When was the last time we wrote a letter to a loved one and divided our heartfelt personal letter into chapters and verses????

Such a thing would never occur to us. And yet, it was done to the very heartfelt, personal, Spirit-inspired letters of Paul to all the churches, and to every other book of the Bible that was inspired by the Holy Spirit, and written by men moved upon by the Holy Spirit...***Very personal writings from a God who wants to reveal Himself to us, to mankind, and to reveal all that He has provided through His character, His nature, and the sacrifice of His only Son***—but we have turned it into a book of chapters and verses to debate, critique, analyze, to subject it to our human reasoning faculties—but almost Never is it truly and honestly treated as something profoundly personal From a God Who Wants to Dwell with Men.

To the degree that we do Not approach the Word of God as a Living Word from the heart of God himself, to That degree we rob ourselves of its life-giving power.

I absolutely cannot stress that enough—the Word of God mixed with faith is what brings spiritual life.

The Word of God mixed with human reasoning profits nothing, just as Jesus said—"The Spirit gives life; the flesh profits nothing. The words I have spoken to you are spirit and they are life." (John 6:63).

From Genesis to Revelation, the Word of God is a whole, complete, living thing—*it is an extension of the very heart and life and nature of God Himself, and to the degree we comprehend that, and truly receive that into our hearts—to THAT degree, we will walk in the life and nature of God, as the apostle Peter said—"His divine power has given us everything we need for life and godliness, through the knowledge of Him who called us by His own glory and excellence, that through these He has given us His precious and magnificent promises, so that through them you may become partakers of the divine nature".*

This is not a philosophical or intellectual exercise; *this is drawing upon the very life and nature of God Himself through His Spirit-breathed Word, by the revelation of the Holy Spirit.*

Just by way of stark contrast to drive this Truth home, NO ONE with just an intellectual grasp on Scripture EVER cast out a demon, but someone fasted & prayed up in the Holy Spirit DID.

THAT is THE Difference between a book with a nice leather cover, *and a spiritual weapon that also gives Life.*

I remember babysitting for a friend back in 1990 at a church in West Palm Beach Florida, and I used to take this little boy to the beach a lot. I always rode with my New Testament on the console of my car, and I remember this incident like it was yesterday. I was driving over a bridge going from the beach, and the little boy, out of nowhere, pointed at my little New Testament and said, "Kills bad spirits!" I was so amazed at his spontaneous & powerful perception!

I replied, "Yes, it DOES!"

He wasn't even four years old, and he had more spiritual sense than most of the adult professing Christian population!!!

That is precisely the mindset and the state of heart we have to walk in 24 hours a day, seven days a week—if demons tremble at the name of Jesus and His Word, how dare we tolerate any man or woman who condescendingly treats it as anything less.

We have Christian television channels absolutely choking with a plethora of so-called Bible teachers who are as dead as the stage they stand on, with an audience full of people sitting there like a little mannequins receiving more mental input that they'll never act upon in power, because it's not being imparted with any power—it's being imparted from a mind, an intellect.

In my younger days, I used to drive with a little pewter sword on my keychain, to remind me every time I looked at it that the Word of God is the sword of the Spirit, and it is alive and powerful.

If we do not look at the Word of God even subconsciously as a Living thing, it's not doing us any good at all—it's a paperweight sitting on a desk or a table.

And whatever we have to do to keep and maintain that mindset, is what we have to do—because we've never lived in a time like this before that demands such a state of heart, and mind, and spirit.

If we can just simply take this one truth and meditate on it, and dwell upon it, and let it soak into our spirit, I believe the results will be overwhelmingly miraculous in all of our situations.

Just stop and think about it for a few minutes—the Pharisees had the very same scriptures that Jesus read from in the temple, but they were dead, lifeless, whitewashed tombs—even though they stood up in the temple before the people and read from the same exact scriptures Jesus did, and no one was ever healed; no one was ever delivered; no one was ever raised from the dead; no one ever said, "Wow, they speak with such divine authority".

Jesus takes the scroll of the book of Isaiah, stands up to read it, and the next thing you know people are saying this man speaks with such authority and power—look, even the demons obey him!

He even healed in the temple where He was reading the very Word of God.

In both situations, it was the same scriptures being read, the same scriptures from the same God—but the ones who read it as a legalistic, religious document produced only death and cold hardness.

Jesus, as the Living Word, reading from the Scriptures that his Holy Spirit had inspired in the beginning, brought forth life & deliverance from that same Word!

There are multitudes of professing believers treating the Word of God as a religious book to debate, analyze, and critique—there are actually social media groups dedicated to debating the Bible!

So the Pharisees are alive and well today on social media everywhere, and in all of these white washed institutions we call churches, where the Word of God is primarily treated in much the same way—a book with chapters and verses, all divided up into sections like a dead corpse on an autopsy table.

My heart's desire has been for over 40 years to see the Church of the Living God treating His Word as the Living thing that it is, as He always intended for it to be.

When the Pharisees arrested and beat Peter and the rest of them, they said they were ignorant and unlearned, *but they spoke as men who had been with Jesus—**Because the words that they spoke were full of His life, His authority, & His power.***

No Sunday school Bible lesson will do that to you.

And honestly, it really isn't going to help anybody to create all kinds of videos and podcasts and every other sort of social media outlet for teaching the Word of God, if the Reality is never communicated and taken to heart that the Word of God is alive and powerful.

I would rather die right where I sit than to ever try to engage people in a merely intellectual exercise around the Bible! We have had decades of that, and we have more denominations than ever before—all of them having more conferences and meetings than ever before, and yet the institutional church at large is deader than it's ever been, in spite of the feverish, never ending striving of men to make it bigger and better and shinier and more entertaining. We just keep putting newer make up and newer clothes on the same dead corpse with the same dead results.

But treat the Word of God as a Living thing, and by the Power of the Holy Spirit, He will speak to you all day long, making His Words come to life, speaking to your situations, to your hurts, your difficulties...

At night, He will speak Peace and Comfort, as Holy Spirit-inbreathed scriptures gently float up from your spirit, washing and renewing your mind, replacing thoughts of doubt with overwhelming assurance and confidence....Replacing thoughts of sorrow and loss with Comfort and Hope.....

Any and every single thing that has ever transpired in my life of a miraculous nature, was because the Word of God is alive and powerful.

And if, when I stand before Jesus, I can hear Him say to me, "Thank you, Mark, for helping My Word to come alive for so many of my brothers and sisters", then I can truly go into Eternity as a very blessed and happy man.

CHAPTER 2

THE BAPTISM OF THE HOLY SPIRIT: THE GATEWAY TO GOD'S GOVERNMENT IN HIS CHURCH

"But whenever anyone turns to the Lord, the veil is taken away.
*Now the Lord is the Spirit, and where the Spirit of the Lord is, there
is freedom.* And we, who with unveiled faces all reflect the glory of
the Lord, are being transformed into His image with intensifying
glory, which comes from *the Lord, who is the Spirit...*"
(2 Corinthians 3:16-18)

*The baptism of the Holy Spirit, in it's primary sense, is the
manifestation of God's governmental authority in
His Church on the earth.*

That sums up the very first thing we should understand about the baptism of the Holy Spirit when we refer to it.

It is not merely "a charismatic experience", since many would like to put it in that box, so they can then take that box and set it aside as irrelevant to themselves.

It most certainly is not an antiquated experience that no longer has any relevance to what we call the church today.

It is not just "an optional doctrine" or belief that we can choose to accept, or set aside, or ignore, or Debate.

The baptism of the Holy Spirit is in very fact the establishment of God's Authority, His divine Power, and His Government, within His Church. Even a cursory reading of the Book of Acts reveals that to be the truth. Virtually every action on a human level in the Book of Acts was done by the empowerment, the direction, and guidance of the Holy Spirit.

Hebrews 6:4, 5 says that we who have been partakers of the Heavenly Gift of the Holy Spirit, have also tasted the goodness of the RHEMA (the Spoken, revelatory Word of God), and the POWERS (Greek word is "dynameis") of the Age to Come. That LAST phrase is All-important.

When you Experientially receive the Holy Spirit, you are receiving into your spirit The Third Person of the Eternal Godhead, sent by the Father, from the Heavenly Places to dwell within YOU.

The Holy Spirit's presence within you is actually a Supernatural, Heavenly depository guarantee of the Kingdom you are going to inherit—And, you are enabled to begin "tasting" of it— appropriating it experientially in your life—Right Now

You have Also "tasted" of the POWERS of the Age to Come—and THAT is precisely WHY the Holy Spirit wants to minister His gifts through us, to DEMONSTRATE the Reality of His Kingdom, Here and Now, in Real Time, to the Glory of God. These things Testify to the Undeniable Reality of the Invisible Kingdom of God that Rules Over EVERYTHING....even while flesh & blood men act like they will always be in charge—but right now, there are rocks & mountains just waiting for the Day when these same men run to them for shelter from the Ancient of Days.....

The Lordship of Jesus, who is now in Heaven at the right hand of the Father, Continues to Operate through the Holy Spirit—" Now the Lord is the

Spirit, and where the Spirit of the Lord is, there is freedom." (2nd Corinthians 3:17).

Probably the most far-reaching and dynamic aspect to This truth, is that to truly be referred to as an expression of His Church, we must be under the Lordship of the Holy Spirit—And the New Testament does not give us any alternative to that.

I don't believe there's a professing Christian alive who would question the Lordship of Jesus or His authority.

However, those same professing believers many times have no problem whatsoever disregarding the authority and the Lordship of the Holy Spirit, treating Him like some kind of optional spiritual accessory, and not the third person of the Godhead.

Let's take a look at one verse that I believe speaks volumes to this truth.

"Until the day He was taken up to heaven, after giving instructions through the Holy Spirit to the apostles He had chosen." (Acts 1:2)

Now, the Greek word for "instructions" is ἐντέλλομαι ("entellomai"), and it's strongest meaning comes through loud and clear in all four Gospels as the word "Command" (see Matthew 17:9, Matthew 28:20, Mark 13:34, and John 15:14).

So when we read Acts 1:2 with that Greek key word in mind, this is how it looks: (*my paraphrase using the Greek word for "instructions"*) 'Until the day He was taken up to heaven, **after giving Commands through the Holy Spirit** to the apostles He had chosen.'

The most fatal assumption the professing Church could make at this point (and make no mistake, it's been operating under this assumption for a very long time, here in the West especially) is that since the last apostle passed away, that authority went with them.

But that is a completely hollow assumption that flies right in the face of Acts 1:2.

Those orders that Jesus relayed to the apostles from the Holy Spirit *were orders regarding governing the Church—and that Church is still HERE, and so is the Holy Spirit*—And, there is no way you could say with your lips that Jesus is Lord, unless you are likewise submitted to the Lordship of the Holy Spirit—and it is high time to accept that spiritual fact.

Notice that at the very outset, the Holy Spirit came upon 120 who were gathered in the upper room, *as per the direct orders of Jesus Christ to wait until they were endued with power.*

The Word of God never shows us what might've happened if they had been disobedient, and instead of waiting in the upper room had scattered and gone their own ways—But you can probably rightly assume that it would not have gone the way that it did.

But the apostle Peter makes the statement in Acts 5:32, "We are witnesses of these things, and so is the Holy Spirit, *whom God has given to those who Obey Him.*"

You will never walk in the authority of God, unless you are willing to be Submitted to the authority of God—And no one would dare be so foolish as to assert that the Western professing "church" is truly submitted to the authority of God…not if they aren't submitted to the authority of the Holy Spirit. We are living in a world of religious self-deception, presumption, and rebellion.

And make no mistake about it—

God is going to pour out His Spirit on His people in this in time, but it will only be upon those who are completely and totally submitted to His authority, and to the authority of the Holy Spirit.

The prophet Joel and the apostle Peter both said the same thing—He will be pouring out His Spirit upon *His bond servants and maidservants,* and *servants do not consist of those who are running their own lives, or have their own agendas.* In this Endtime, the lines are not only clearly drawn—they are carved into the very earth, and it is time to pick a side!

This is not a new revelation—Not in the least.

In fact, there was one individual who saw it clear as the noonday sun, and Jesus was so amazed and captivated by this individual, that he said he possessed greater faith than anyone in Israel.

That man was a Roman centurion, whose words to Jesus clearly revealed that he completely grasped the reality that Jesus was a man functioning under the delegated authority of God, and therefore whatever Jesus commanded, would be done.

Let's take a fresh look at what took place between Jesus and the centurion, and allow the Holy Spirit to show you the power of that interaction!

"When Jesus had entered Capernaum, a centurion came and pleaded with Him, "Lord, my servant lies at home, paralyzed and in terrible agony." "I will go and heal him," Jesus replied.

"The centurion answered, 'Lord, I am not worthy to have You come under my roof. But just say the word, and my servant will be healed. *For I myself am a man under authority, with soldiers under me. I tell one to go, and he goes; and another to come, and he comes. I tell my servant to do something, and he does it.'*

"When Jesus heard this, He marveled and said to those following Him, 'Truly I tell you, I have not found anyone in Israel with such great faith!" (Matthew 8:5-10)

*And for hundreds of years now, the church has seemingly lost all concept of God's delegated authority—**And the spiritual principle is, you only possess authority to the degree you are submitted to it.***

Failing to recognize, respect, and honor the Holy Spirit's divinely delegated authority robs you of blessing, robs you of walking out and fulfilling your heavenly calling, and robs you of being a vessel and a channel of God's life and power.

Didn't Jesus say, "Whoever receives a prophet because he is a prophet will receive a prophet's reward, and whoever receives a righteous man because he is a righteous man will receive a righteous man's reward"? (Matthew 10:41)

Didn't Jesus say, "He who receives you receives Me, and he who receives Me receives the One who sent Me."? (Matthew 10:40)

"And the King will reply, 'Truly I tell you, whatever you did for one of the least of these brothers of Mine, you did for Me"? (Matthew 25:40)

Our actions betray us, regardless of what our lips speak.

We say His name, but we live as though we are completely detached from all that He is. We do not live and act as those who are *extensions of their Lord, their KING*—And that is because our consciousness has been one of religiosity and religious conditioning….and yes, even religious brainwashing….

We don't think Kingdom thoughts; we think 'churchy' thoughts.

We don't think Kingdom Authority and power; we think church influence or church programs.

But the one who walks with a Kingdom Authority consciousness, and of being directly connected to the Head, Jesus Christ, and empowered by His Spirit, has no reservations or qualms about casting out demons or laying hands on the sick.

And the division is being made even now, and the gulf between the religious-minded and the Kingdom-minded is only going to become wider and deeper.

CHAPTER 3

THE VOICE OF THE KING: A TOTAL EXCHANGE OF DIVINE PERSONS

For any professing believer to have an incomplete understanding of the relationship we are called to have with the Holy Spirit, is a guarantee that they will probably never reach spiritual maturity—and that does not have to be the case.

I'm going to read you the very words of Jesus, as He Himself is setting the stage for us to understand the relationship the Holy Spirit was intended to have with us, and that this relationship was decided by the Godhead—not by seminary professors.

In John 16:7, Jesus says these words (pay very close attention please);

"But I tell you the truth, *it is for your benefit* that I am going away. *Unless I go away, the Advocate will not come to you*; but if I go, I will send Him to you."

Do we truly comprehend what Jesus is saying here???

He is saying, Just as I have been with you, when I go, I will send the Comforter, and HE will be with you.

It is a Total Exchange of Divine Persons.

Jesus has been physically present with His disciples, and He is saying that the Holy Spirit will come to take His place with us.

Now, if that does not drive home the vital importance of embracing a wholehearted, fully committed relationship with the Holy Spirit—just as we would do with Jesus himself—I don't know what will.

Jesus also took great care to fully explain the Ongoing ministry that the Holy Spirit was going to have with us and initiate with us upon His arrival.

"However, when the Spirit of truth comes, He will guide you into all truth. For He will not speak on His own, but He will speak what He hears, and He will declare to you *what is to come.*" (John 16:13).

THAT refers to the ongoing revelatory ministry of the Holy Spirit to the Church in Each and Every Generation until the End of the Age— which fulfills Jesus' covenant promise to be With us Even to the End of the Age, through the Person of the Holy Spirit.

Jesus also takes care to completely lay out the multi-faceted ministry of the Holy Spirit to us. He calls the Holy Spirit the Spirit of Truth; the Counsellor; the Comforter; and the Advocate. (John, chapters 14,15,16)

Jesus said to the disciples concerning His departure, "I will not leave you as orphans; I will come to you." (John 14:18)—*And He comes to us in the ministry of the Holy Spirit whom He has sent.*

Jesus' present ministry is now that of being our High Priest and Intercessor in the Heavenlies, according to the Book of Hebrews.

* * * * * * * * * *

The Holy Spirit's ministry here on the earth to believers is to be our Teacher, our Counsellor, our Comforter, our Guide.

* * * * * * * * * *

Part of His ministry to the Body of Christ is to show us things to come, or things that are coming that we as the Church need to prepare for.

And to reiterate once again—the Holy Spirit's ministry to us, to the church, is predicated upon us being baptized individually in the Holy Spirit.

If the Holy Spirit is not residing in us, His ministry to us is profoundly limited, and this is clearly reflected in Paul's extensive teaching on the gifts of the Holy Spirit—we cannot minister the gifts of the Holy Spirit to one another, if He is not already in us.

The fact that the apostles Paul and Peter both clearly taught in a very focused way on the Body ministering to itself via the supply of the Holy Spirit, is clear and present proof that the Body is dependent upon the Spirit.

This is precisely why the apostles took great care to ensure that all new believers received the baptism of the Holy Spirit; this is seen three times in the Book of Acts ("By the mouth of two or three witnesses let a thing be established").

The Holy Spirit gives us access to the Father (Eph. 2:18);

"For through Him we both have access to the Father by one Spirit."

In Ephesians 2:22, it also states that we, the Body of Christ, are built into a holy habitation of God through the Spirit; "And in Him you too are being built together into a dwelling place for God in His Spirit."

So, no matter where we turn in the New Testament, the subject of the Holy Spirit indwelling us, empowering us, and working in and through us is inescapable.

Just as Jesus is Lord OVER the Church, the Holy Spirit is meant to be Lord WITHIN the Church! The Lordship of Jesus manifests, as the Lordship of the Holy Spirit is allowed to be Preeminent. There is no alternative or substitute for that.

In reframing the baptism of the Holy Spirit and speaking in tongues, it is important to keep the focus on One thing—where the Spirit of the Lord is, there is liberty.

Now, in the Greek, that word "liberty" has several different meanings, but *the predominant meaning is that of **emancipation from slavery & from bondage—Which is a very powerful truth about the nature of the third person of the Godhead, the Holy Spirit.***

Where it says the "Spirit of the Lord", that word "Lord" in the Greek also has some very powerful meanings attached to it.

The Greek word for 'Lord' is "Kuros", which means "Supreme Authority"—And if more people read it with that meaning in mind, they might be slower to disrespect the things of the Holy Spirit, who is 'Supreme Authority', as in, "Lord"!

Remember when Jesus stood in the temple reading from the scroll of Isaiah? Remember the passage that He read from?

Isaiah 61:1;

"*The Spirit of the Lord GOD* is on Me, because *the LORD* has anointed Me to preach good news to the poor. *He* has sent Me to bind up the brokenhearted, to proclaim liberty to the captives and freedom to the prisoners". *See that??? **The Spirit of the Lord was Upon Jesus; The Spirit of the Lord Anointed Jesus; The Spirit of the Lord SENT Jesus!!***

Now, just look at the many ministries of the Spirit of the Lord—the Holy Spirit—in just this one verse:

1. He anoints us to preach the Word that sets people free; it is anointed preaching, anointed by His presence and His power;

2. To preach good tidings to the meek…So many times, it is those who are gentle and humble in heart who have been through the most rejection, mistreatment by others, feeling unwanted, unworthy, and so on.

The Holy Spirit brings good tidings that you are accepted in the Beloved; that you are chosen by the Father to be a part of His family; that you are uniquely gifted by Him for a special purpose.

You may be hidden away from society, overlooked, and thought of as someone of not much importance; however, *the Holy Spirit's estimation of you is totally different from man's.*

3.   He has sent me to bind up the brokenhearted—*Again, the Holy Spirit always deals with the heart, and the issues of our inner person, to bring healing and freedom.*

4.   The Holy Spirit's ministry of proclaiming deliverance to the captives, and the opening of the prison for those who are bound— This speaks directly to the ministry of deliverance and, I believe, even inner healing.

Deliverance from demons is pretty straightforward, but if anyone has a question, feel free to reach out to me. I have had lots of experience with that, so I won't dwell on it here. Inner healing is closely related, because most of the time it deals with emotional hurts and bondages.

For example, I have ministered to those coming out of the occult, cults, and the stronghold of Catholicism—and I can assure you, even after dealing with the evil spirits associated with those things, there is still many times emotional and inner healing needed.

One young lady I spent many weeks ministering to had finally come to the place of realizing the spiritual bondage of being in the Catholic Church, but there were many very deep emotional roots that had to be dealt with.

For one, leaving the Catholic Church meant being ostracized by her family. Secondly, it had been a part of her identity for a very long time.

But I have to tell you, when Christine finally made the step of faith to walk away from that world, she experienced a joy, a deliverance, and a freedom that I have never seen in anyone before. The change was more drastic than any deliverance I have ever seen before, and I am happy to report that the results were lasting, as she later went into ministry to other women, leading them into the same liberty.

The Bible begins with the operation of the Spirit of the living God, and the Bible ends in Revelation with the speaking of the Spirit of the Living God.

The Lord has me on a mission to awaken believers to the absolute truth and necessity of the Holy Spirit, and to provide intensive discipleship in the things of the Holy Spirit. That is my calling; that is what is with me every single day, and every single night.

After over 44 years as a believer, I am completely and totally convinced that there is no more vital subject for the believer than that of learning to walk with the Holy Spirit, being led and guided by Him on a daily basis. No one would dare question or diminish the disciples walking with Jesus, so why would we dare question or diminish walking with the Holy Spirit????

Jesus referred to the Holy Spirit directly 56 times in the gospels

One of the most notable places where Jesus calls attention to the Holy Spirit is a major feast where Jesus went in secret.

Initially, Jesus had gone to the feast concealing His identity, but, "On the last and greatest day of the feast, Jesus stood up and called out in a loud voice, "If anyone is thirsty, let him come to Me and drink." (John 7:37).

Jesus is saying for those who thirst spiritually, to come to Him and HE will give them the Holy Spirit to drink.

So, those who minimize the Holy Spirit are minimizing Jesus Himself.

The gospels make One thing clear—that Jesus and the ministry of the Holy Spirit are to be revered and respected in precisely the same way.

If you want to know what the New Testament believers' attitude must be toward the Holy Spirit, look at Jesus.

Carefully meditate on every single thing that Jesus spoke concerning the Holy Spirit, and then gauge your heart attitude by His words— Because it is the words of Jesus concerning the Holy Spirit that you will be accountable for, not mine.

It is time every believer who professes the name of Jesus Christ on their lips, to wage holy war against every religious stronghold that minimizes or diminishes the authority and power of the Holy Spirit.

No believer in their right mind would demean the Father or the Son, so why then do we think it's OK to do that to the Spirit????

I'll tell you why— it's because the enemy has done a bang up job in making the Holy Spirit look like a stepchild in the family of the Godhead, and he has caused believers to look upon the Holy Spirit as LESS than the Third Person of the Godhead—the Eternal Godhead! Jesus put the Holy Spirit's ministry on the same level as His own—and slightly higher, because He said He will be IN you!

Jesus also said very poignantly, "But I tell you the truth, it is for your benefit that I am going away. Unless I go away, the Advocate will not come to you; but if I go, I will send Him to you…. However, when the Spirit of truth comes, **He will guide you into ALL truth**. For He will not speak on His own, but He will speak what He hears, and He will declare to you what is to come." (John 16:7,13)

What have WE done???

We have amassed to ourselves hundreds and hundreds of shiny little Bible teachers, hanging on their every word, and we quote them more than we even quote Jesus!

We have elevated their intellect above the mind of the Holy Spirit Himself—and I have never met anyone who was truly discipled in the Word, that was not also truly discipled in the Spirit.

My heart and soul for this book and the podcast ministry is to provide my fellow believers with the most Word-based, Holy Spirit-led discipleship possible anywhere. But there's just one catch—I cannot be with you 24 hours a day; *the Holy Spirit can.*

And everything that I am pouring out of myself to those of you taking the time to read & listen is out of a well—a very deep well, that the Holy Spirit Himself dug & filled, over 44 years.

And I can honestly say that if it were not for the Holy Spirit having been in my life all these years, I would have nothing profitable to share with you.

The Word says that the mind of the flesh is at odds with God, and is not subject to the things of God. *One critical area believers need to be aware of, is that when you were born again, your mind did not get saved.*

If you've been alive for 40 years and just got born again, your mind is still the same mind you've had for 40 years.

Your spirit man has been reborn, absolutely. Your mind has received some illumination, yes.

But your lifelong thinking and reasoning patterns are still basically the same, until you learn from the Word of God how to think the way God thinks.

The trouble is, most believers begin using **their own reasoning** to size up the things of God *in their unrenewed mind.* It's not a conscious thing, I know. Nonetheless, it's not a thing easily grasped at the beginning, and it's not something that is consistently taught.

Most believers are pretty much left to their own devices when it comes to what happens next when they get saved.

The most common belief is that they have to "plug into a church" somewhere, and from there, they learn everything they're supposed to know. **That's the worst thing that could possibly happen to a new believer.**

Why? *Because 9 times out of 10, no one is going to assume spiritual responsibility for you and disciple you one step at a time, one day at a time, and help you renew your mind in a concerted, Spirit-led way.*

But until then, if you make a habit out of assigning to the things of God your own mental assessment, nine times out of 10 you're going to be off.

Until your mind is sufficiently renewed by the Word of God, you'll be at a disadvantage when it comes to assigning the proper value to spiritual things.

You'll end up listening to Pastor so and so, or some shiny popular teacher, and then you'll just end up with a head full of stuff that has to be unlearned.

Now, everything that I just said—this is precisely why the apostles took great pains to make sure that ALL new believers were baptized in the Holy Spirit.

I'll say it again for Effect—this is Precisely why the apostles that Jesus hand-picked Himself, took great pains to make sure that All new believers were baptized in the Holy Spirit.

First of all, they were obeying Jesus's Explicit command that He gave initially, to wait to be endowed with power from on high, before they set 1 foot out of that upper room....The FULL command that Jesus gave, including His reason for giving it, was to wait to be clothed with power from on high, and THEN they would be witnesses for him.

Jesus never recalled that order; He never cancelled that command; He never gave an alternate directive.

If you understand that you belong to a Kingdom from on High, then you know full well, just from common sense, that you do not have the right to disobey a direct order from the King; you do not have the right to modify or alter a direct order from the King.

The Reality that we are under a King, is something we need to get our heads around, and I am just someone that the Lord has tapped on the shoulder to call His people back to attention to Him and to His Authority—because as long as you are willing to follow men, you will most likely be at odds with your King.

Jesus' final directive given in the Book of Revelation is, "Let him who has an ear, hear what the Spirit says to the churches" (Revelation 3:6).

Your ears better be tuned to One Voice, and one voice only, if you have your heart and soul set on being among the Overcomers.

No Pastor is responsible to hear the voice of the Holy Spirit for you.

No teacher is responsible to hear the voice of the Holy Spirit for you.

YOU are responsible to hear the voice of the Holy Spirit for yourself. Get that firmly settled and embedded in your heart, and you will be OK.

People will hire a personal trainer for their physical fitness, but yet they don't avail themselves of the Holy Spirit who will be with them every single day, and be their spiritual Mentor, Guide, Counsellor, and Teacher?

Again, the resounding exhortation in Revelation is, Let him who has an ear, HEAR what the SPIRIT is Saying to the CHURCHES. THERE IS NO HIGHER PRIORITY RIGHT NOW.

Our King of all the Earth is coming... and Now is the time to learn to hear His voice—so shut out every other one.... whatever it takes.

Remember, there is only One Voice we will answer to when He sets up His Kingdom here on this earth—so get used to walking under His authority Now. Every single knee is soon to bow before King Jesus, so begin living under His Rulership right here and now, right where you are.

I guarantee you, when we all begin walking under One banner, listening to One voice, we will be His testimony in the earth—as He said, "And THIS gospel of the kingdom will be preached in all the world as a testimony to all nations, and then the end will come." (Matthew 24:14).

This is the message that I have been commissioned to bring—that everyone in the Body of Christ, regardless of our outward stature, is called to be under One King—not under men who have tried to build their religious kingdoms here. So let us walk side-by-side as brothers and sisters answering to the voice of King Jesus, the voice of His Holy Spirit, as we watch for the Kingdom He is soon bringing....His Kingdom, and Ours....

Don't be a 'Christian'—be something far, far greater than that...You know as well as I do that every time you hear someone call themselves a Christian, it means something different to them than it does to the next person who calls themselves a Christian.

The definition of the word "Christian" changes constantly depending on who you're talking to and who's calling themselves a Christian...No, be greater than a Christian...

Be a Kingdom follower of King Jesus; Let the King you follow and His Kingdom be what defines you...

No longer will you be a "Christian", who defines themselves by what Bible teachers they listen to, by what scriptures they believe and what scriptures they choose Not to believe (Because if we're honest, That is the description that best suits Western professing Christianity, and you know it's true)

When we are all following the King, and walking under HIS authority, and seeing ourselves as royal subjects of His everlasting Kingdom, we will ALL look the same...

Following the one true King, hearing and obeying His voice, is what unites us—not wearing the label "Christian"...And if we truly and honestly believe we are receiving a Kingdom that cannot be shaken, then let us Begin Now living and acting as citizens of the Kingdom...*Because if we believe in its Future reality, then we need to Live in its Current reality....*

What is my hope for this book, these podcasts?

My hope is to make the Kingdom of God so real to you, that when you walk out of your house in the morning, the hair on your arms stands up because you feel it's that close....If I fail at that, then I have not done my job...

I want you to be like Elijah's servant, to see the chariots of God all around you, with your eyes having been opened...To be like Stephen, looking up and seeing the heavens opened, and the Son of man standing at the right hand of God...

CHAPTER 4

IDENTIFYING & OVERCOMING HINDRANCES TO FELLOWSHIPPING WITH THE FATHER, PART 1

In communicating with many fellow believers over the last couple of years, I am convinced that this is a topic of utmost importance, as so many believers are truly hungry, even desperate, for a more intimate relationship with our Heavenly Father —*and yet, for many different reasons, they feel blocked or hindered, and simply don't know what to do about it.*

I do not believe that there is a more all-important subject for us right now at this time in history, than that of truly growing in and experiencing spirit to spirit, heart to heart fellowship with the Lord in every respect that He intended, and in every respect that He has provided for.

It grieves me and it breaks my heart to know that there are believers who are struggling in this area, and who cannot seem to find the answers that they need to bridge this invisible gap between them and the Lord.

God's original design was to have fellowship with Man, and in the Garden of Eden, He walked with Adam, and talked with Adam, one on one in fellowship and communion.

God and the man He made, walking & talking together in a garden.

There were absolutely Zero barriers to communion and heart to heart fellowship—and this is why Man was originally created, so that God might have fellowship with His own creation, someone like Himself.

So, with everything that we have in our minds about God—about our relationship with Him, about all of the different things that our mind might dwell on when we're thinking about the Lord, I think it would be profoundly helpful to each one of us—especially in this day and time—to remember that the ONE thing that we were created specifically for by the Lord himself, is to Fellowship with Him; not to just do ministry or religious tasks or duties, none of that. When God originally made us, it was just Him, a garden, and the man He created.

Think about it......

There were no pastors acting as mediators or go-betweens; there were no church buildings, there were no church programs....

There were no worship teams to create "the right atmosphere" for Man to fellowship with God...

There wasn't a "proper religious setting" for fellowship to take place...

Too many times, the religious trappings take the place of intimacy with Him, because those religious trappings are sort of like our Church-shaped Figleaf—we feel incomplete perhaps, or naked without it...

Fallen man has a history of covering his nakedness and his sense of unworthiness to come before the Lord, so we come up with all kinds of things so that we feel "more worthy" to come before Him, more "suitable" to come into His presence....so instead of a figleaf, we have all these religious things to cover ourselves with, so we can be "more presentable to the Lord his Majesty Almighty God".

Part of our fallen, unrenewed nature (and this is where renewing the mind continues to be a focus), has reservations about getting "too close" to the One who already sees us as we are, and knows everything about us—but we want to somehow look away from that, as though it weren't entirely true... That we can still kind of cover up areas of ourselves that we might be embarrassed about, or feel uncomfortable about.

*I honestly believe that **that** is one of the main hindrances to believers receiving the baptism of the Holy Spirit—although I am sure that no one has ever really thought of it that way before.*

The first thing the Lord needs to make real to each one of us individually, is that His First desire for every one of us, is to have very personal, one on one fellowship.

We are, in our fallen nature, still inwardly squeamish about Him being too personal with us, about being too accessible to Him—we don't want our souls to be laid bare before Him (even though they already are).

* *

Right here is the perfect place for a piece of my testimony—which I had planned on sharing at some point, but here we are in this part of our conversation, and I think it's profoundly fitting for this context—That being, our innate reticence of being too intimate with our Heavenly Father and "too accessible".

Something happened to me in the Summer of 1980, 2 years after I was saved, that speaks directly to our subject.

Ever since I was a boy, I habitually took walks and talked to God even before I got saved. I knew He was "up there", I knew He existed; He had made everything that I could see. My mind never even thought to question it.

So, on this particular Summer afternoon, as I was walking to work, I could feel a divine nudge— And intuitively, I could sense what the gentle nudging from the Lord was speaking to me—I could most definitely feel that His nudging was His way of saying to me that He wanted a more intimate relationship with me.

As I walked down the street that afternoon, and I felt the Lord's nudging, that he wanted to be closer to me, I found myself saying, "Lord, I know that you want to be closer to me, but right now I'm not comfortable with that, but maybe later".

Immediately, I felt a sense of Him backing away, and a momentary twinge of sadness—even disappointment.

I've wished 1000 times I could go back to that afternoon and say, "Lord, I feel that you want to be closer to me, and I don't know how you wish to do that, but I trust you completely and I say Yes, I am open to that".

Afterwards, a spiritual wave of attacks began that were relentless, to the point that even when at work I felt overwhelmed. I probably went to the men's room dozens of times every day just to sit in the bathroom stall, and open my pocket New Testament to the Psalms, which I would read for comfort—and that relief was always very short lived. As the Winter of 1982 approached, the oppression seemed impossible to bear.

Around the same time, there were customers coming into the grocery store where I worked at, that always seemed to have a light in their face, and I remember thinking to myself so many times, "Here I am a Christian, and yet I'm so oppressed, and fighting anxieties and panic attacks, and I have no joy and no inner freedom whatsoever".

The repeated visits of these joyful, lit up Christians caused me to cry out to the Lord for answers as to what was missing, and why did I feel like the God that I belong to is so far away. No matter how much I pray, no matter how much I read my Bible, the distance never lessens, there doesn't seem to be any way to close that gap.

I finally said, "Lord, I know that there is something I am missing, something that other Christians have, and I desperately need to know what it is. I will do whatever you want, I just need you to show me what I am missing". I constantly felt like I was chained to myself, even though I was a

Christian and was not in any sin, I still felt the weight of me being chained to Me—if that makes any sense.

The next thing I knew, every time I turned on the radio, some preacher or somebody was talking about the Holy Spirit; anytime I walked into a Christian bookstore, all I could see were books on the Holy Spirit.

I said, OK God, I understand what you're trying to tell me now. I need the Holy Spirit; but what do I do?

By divine appointment, I ended up meeting a really nice Christian brother named Jim—married, had kids, and was another one of those joyful, lit up Christians that I'd been running into.

I shared with him everything that I had been going through, going all the way back to that Summer in 1980 when I felt the Lord's nudging for a closer relationship, and he lovingly explained to me that that was the Holy Spirit I'd been feeling. I'd never been told about the Holy Spirit before, and he gave me some scriptures to read, and said that he would be blessed to pray for me but wanted me to have some understanding of the Word first.

So I went home, and over the course of a couple of weeks, I spent a lot of time in the Word seeing what Jesus had to say about the Holy Spirit, what Paul had to say about the Holy Spirit—but my moment of truth and liberation came when my eyes fell on that passage in the book of Luke.

And this time as I read, I could feel the familiar, kind nudging once again—the nudging that I had so foolishly turned away from in that Summer of 1980.

As I read Luke 11:13, I could feel the same gentle, loving pull that I had felt what seemed like a lifetime ago; "So if you who are evil know how to give good gifts to your children, how much more will your Father in heaven give the Holy Spirit to those who ask Him?"

I began to weep, because it was like I had been on a long, long journey—a painful one that took me far away from the God that I loved...and now here we were, back together again, and with tears streaming down my face and my eyes closed, I said, "God, your Word says that you want to give the Holy Spirit to those who ask you, and I have never asked; but I'm asking now, please give me Your Holy Spirit".... and as I cried and lifted up my voice to the Lord in my bedroom I suddenly felt a warm sensation coming over me, and as I prayed, I felt words begin to come that were not English— but yet not completely foreign either, and as I continued to pray and speak to God in this language that my mind didn't understand, all I could feel was me getting lighter and lighter....as though I was being washed clean of all the oppression and fear and anxiety, and all of the spiritual battles from the past two and a half years—And then suddenly, my mind & my head felt light and clean, and even pure...I felt like I had been baptized from the inside out!

And I had an appetite for the Word of God that was like a raging inferno, because every time I opened my Bible, it was like the Holy Spirit was talking right to me right there on the spot, it was like every word ministered to me.

It was like reading the Bible for the very first time in my entire life.... It was like it was actually Alive!

But the most profound transformation that took place, was that I felt the nearness of the Lord no matter where I was or what I was doing—that God "way out there beyond the fog", was now right here sitting next to me.... and not Next to me; He was IN me.

Suddenly, all of the passages where Jesus was pouring out his heart to his disciples, his followers, and those around him about the ministry of the Holy Spirit—suddenly, all of those passages were totally for me.

I would find myself walking the streets in the afternoons and evenings, praying and talking to the Lord—but now as I took my prayer walks, praying in the spirit, I found myself experiencing a closeness and intimacy with the Lord that I never had believed possible before....and it was a two-way intimacy, it wasn't just me being intimate with him. I could feel him responding, if that makes any sense.

He wasn't necessarily responding with words, but with a closeness and with an overwhelming awareness that transcends my ability to even put into words....an awareness that he was In me, not just "with" me, not just "around" me—but actually dwelling in me. So, if there was hope for ME being "healed" and delivered of barriers to fellowshipping with the Lord, then there is for you too.

The true starting point for each of us to have real, honest, true fellowship with the Father, is through the Holy Spirit.

Ephesians 2:18 declares, "For through Him we both have access to the Father by one Spirit"

So, our access to the Father is by the Holy Spirit. Now, that verse actually says, "We BOTH have access to the Father by the Holy Spirit—who is "both"?

There are verses in 1st Corinthians, Ephesians, and elsewhere that tell us who the "both" are, but let's look at Acts chapter 10, to see this "both" in its proper context, where this "both" actually happened.

Sorry for the bad grammar, just play along.

So, Acts 10:44-47; "While Peter was still speaking these words, the Holy Spirit fell upon all who heard his message. All the circumcised believers who had accompanied Peter were astounded that the gift of the Holy Spirit had been poured out even on the Gentiles. For they heard them speaking in tongues and exalting God. Then Peter said, "Can anyone withhold the water to baptize these people? They have received the Holy Spirit just as we have!"

Now, to our Western minds, the gravity of this does not really register, but in verse 28 Peter tells Cornelius that it was against their Jewish law to come under a Gentiles roof.

Doing something of that nature would render a law-abiding Jew as ceremonially unclean.

However, God had already spoken in the Old Testament, saying that He would make the two people one—that He would call a people who had not been His people.

And God's ordained way of doing this, so that everyone would understand it was HIS divine initiative and HIS divine working, was This: the Gentiles received the Holy Spirit in the same way the Jewish disciples did—With signs following (the signs being speaking with other tongues and prophesying and worshipping the Lord).

Now, let's look at how the Holy Spirit helps us in overcoming hindrances to fellowshipping with the Father.

Let's start with the fact that because you were born again, your spirit man has been made alive—That means you now have the capacity to know God, and to know that you are His. Romans 8:10 says, "But if Christ is in you, your body is dead because of sin, yet your spirit is alive because of righteousness."

Paul also says in verse 14, "For all who are led by the Spirit of God are sons of God" (Romans 8:14).

Remember, as we have discussed in previous chapters, the apostles took great care to ensure that new believers received the baptism of the Holy Spirit, just as they did in the beginning themselves, and with the Gentile believers starting with Cornelius and his household, and again in Samaria after Philip the evangelist preached the gospel with signs and wonders following. Peter and John afterwards laid hands on the new believers to receive the Holy Spirit. The apostle Paul did the same thing with new believers in Acts chapter 19.

This is the New Testament pattern and precedent, and we have nothing in Scripture that indicates that ever changed.

So, with the baptism of the Holy Spirit firmly in mind, and how the Holy Spirit indwelling us gives us a brand new capacity to fellowship and commune with the Father, let's look at Romans 8:15;

"For you did not receive a spirit of slavery that returns you to fear, but you received the Spirit of sonship, by whom we cry, "Abba! Father!"

Read simply and plainly, this means the Holy Spirit is the Spirit of adoption which enables your spirit to now know, comprehend, and intimately relate to God as your father, Abba, which is a very intimate Middle Eastern term meaning "daddy"—In other words, He is no longer the God away up there, just beyond your reach. He is your loving Father, right here with you and in you by his Holy Spirit—*the Spirit of adoption, the Spirit of Sonship.*

As I mentioned earlier, as a young fatherless boy, I took walks at night and talked to the God up in the stars, because he was the only father I'd ever known—and even though at the time I did not think of him as my father or a father, I knew he was someone I could approach and talk to about anything. ***But after I was baptized in the Holy Spirit, the feeling of profound acceptance and sense of belonging was something that never left me.***

For those who have had similar life situations, growing up with the ache of a missing parent —specifically a missing father—I can assure you by my own experience, that *the Holy Spirit will bring definitive, deep healing to those areas of your heart.*

> *He is the Spirit of adoption that brings the reality of your being a true child of God to life in your heart.*

Of all the hindrances to fellowshipping with the Father, I believe rejection and abandonment rooted in childhood issues is the biggest one, and I have plenty of experience with all of that.

I have also experienced abundant healing on a level that I cannot even put into words that would not have been possible at all without the baptism of the Holy Spirit.

This is where the baptism of the Holy Spirit is not a doctrinal issue; it is not a denominational issue; it is not a charismatic issue—it is a Bible issue.

It is the Father giving the Spirit of adoption to those who are His children, and every way in which that Spirit of adoption, the Holy Spirit, wants to manifest and act on our behalf with the Father's love in mind, is the Operation of God Himself. He is not confined to a doctrinal or denominational belief.

Having said that, *understand that the religious spirits that existed in Jesus day exist now, and they hate the Spirit of Adoption, because they do not want you to be truly free from them; they do not want you free from the religious systems that they control; they do not want you walking free from them in any way, shape, or form.* "It is for freedom that Christ has set us free. Stand firm, then, and do not be encumbered once more by a yoke of slavery" (Galatians 5:1).

When it comes to true fellowship and communion with the Father, you will never find true freedom, true spiritual liberty in any denomination or any religious system; you will only find it through the Spirit of Adoption, the Holy Spirit.

I recently had the most profound honor of sharing with a sister in the Lord, many of the things that I have shared in this chapter today.

She is someone that has been a real friend to our family, and I have not known very many Christians who seek the Lord the way she does.

And yet she has struggled with wanting to feel closer to her Heavenly Father, but just not quite sure how to bridge that gap.

And it is my deepest heartfelt desire, one that I cannot put into words to do any justice to it here in this chapter, but just let me say to those of you going through the same struggle that I have felt intimately what you are going through myself, and I want to be of all the spiritual help that I can be to you, so I ask you to please reach out to me via Facebook, or email, or whatever it takes, but don't go through this alone.

Remember the testimony I shared earlier of what I went through, and know for a fact that your Heavenly Father wants intimate fellowship with you more than you want it, because He has provided for it abundantly.

He gave His only Son, he sent His Holy Spirit, and Jesus said, "So if you who are evil know how to give good gifts to your children, how much more will your Father in heaven give the Holy Spirit to those who ask Him?"

(Luke 11:13)

He wants to give you—in fullness—His Holy Spirit, the Spirit of adoption—the Spirit that links Your spirit to Him, for that intimate, heart-felt connection and communication.

Paul the apostle said it best when he said, "For he who speaks in a tongue does not speak to men, but to God. Indeed, no one understands him; he utters mysteries in the Spirit." (1 Corinthians 14:2). In other words, talking to my Heavenly Father spirit to spirit.

That is the ONLY thing that will quench your hunger for your Heavenly Father's love, and it is the only way that He can pour out His Fatherly love to you, directly into your spirit ("And hope does not disap-point us, because God has poured out His love into our hearts *through the Holy Spirit, whom He has given us*"; Romans 5:5).

Please spend some time truly reading and meditating on John 14, where Jesus speaks at length about the ministry of the Holy Spirit for believers.

But there is one place where Jesus spoke about the Holy Spirit, and I pray God will enable me to convey all the emotion of Jesus in that instance.

In John 7, it says that Jesus went up to Jerusalem to a feast; it was the Feast of Tabernacles. It was the biggest Jewish Festival of them all, and one of the most sacred. Tabernacles is another word for "tents", and *this feast symbolized God dwelling with His people.*

All through the Old Testament, the prophets all spoke of God's original desire and intent to dwell among His people.

So here at this Jewish festival, commemorating God's desire to dwell among His people, Jesus stands up at the very last day of the feast.

He had gone to this feast in disguise, because the Jews were lying in wait to kill him—but here on the last day of the feast, He completely blows His cover and exposes Himself to their murderous rage.

"On the last and greatest day of the feast, Jesus stood up and called out in a loud voice, "If anyone is thirsty, let him come to Me and drink. Whoever believes in Me, as the Scripture has said: 'Streams of living water will flow from within him.'" He was speaking about the Spirit, whom those who believed in Him were later to receive. For the Spirit had not yet been given, because Jesus had not yet been glorified...." (John 7:37-39).

I pray with all my might that we can truly perceive the significance of the Lord Jesus standing up, exposing Himself to the murderous rage of those who wanted to kill Him, during the Jewish feast that commemorated God's desire to dwell with His people, crying out with the invitation to come to Him to drink of the Living Waters of the Holy Spirit. *Jesus crying out with a loud voice—that is how much He desires our fellowship! He exposed Himself to the murderous hatred of those serving Satan, because He desires our fellowship that much!*

Father God, right now in the name of Jesus I pray for those who right now are agonizing over what feels like a bridge they just cannot seem to find a way to cross, into Your presence, into your lap, and into your fellowship, into your Fatherly love for them—a gap that You have already bridged by your Spirit.

There's just one thing remaining; for them to receive the Spirit of adoption, the Holy Spirit.

Father God, I ask you to do whatever it takes, just like you did with me. You pursued me, and for 39 years now I have known you intimately as my Heavenly Father, because by your Holy Spirit You minister to me and speak to me every single day, all day long, in unexpected ways, through my grief of losing my wife, the Love of my life, and You have brought me further than I would've ever imagined.

But my heart breaks for my sisters and my brothers who don't know Your presence like I have experienced. I know they read it in the Word, and they've seen it in the Word, but they just don't know how to make the connection. Help them to understand, and help them to know that just coming to You as a little child, like in Luke 11, that their Heavenly Father desires to give them the Holy Spirit, that is why He is called the Promise of the Father—The Spirit of Adoption, that joins the Father's spirit to the child's spirit. In Jesus' name, Amen.

CHAPTER 5

THE SHELTER OF THE LORD

"Has not My hand made all these things? And so they came into being,"
declares the LORD. "This is the one I will esteem: he who is humble and
contrite in spirit, who trembles at My word." (Isaiah 66:2).

O*ur attitude toward the Word of God is the barometer of our life, of
our very existence...And it is God's barometer of our relationship to
Him.* Our heart attitude toward His Word, and what we do with
it on a daily basis, determines the inflow of His mercy, His provision, His
protection, and His guidance into our lives. It is our love for Him that
equals our love for His Word, and our love for His Word equals our love for
Him—and that love remaining in us on a daily basis as the highest priority,
is what will shelter us in the days to come.

The Psalmist said, "I have hidden Your word in my heart that I might
not sin against You." (Psalm 119:11). *In other words, by guarding my heart
with His Word, I guard my relationship with Him.*

**Our attitude toward the Word of God is the barometer of our life,
of our very existence...And it is God's barometer
of our relationship to Him.**

Our heart attitude toward His Word, and what we do with it on a daily basis, determines the inflow of His mercy, His provision, His protection, and His guidance into our lives. All of those provisions and benefits of God that we need to flow to us, are determined by where we set the thermostat of our hearts concerning the Word of God.

Is our thermostat set on cold or room temperature, where we really don't set a high priority at all on receiving His Word into our being, and into our life?

Or is the thermostat set on "heat", meaning, we have a heated passion for His Word, and we say like Job, "I have not departed from the command of His lips; I have treasured the words of His mouth more than my daily bread." (Job 23:12).

"But Jesus answered, "It is written: 'Man shall not live on bread alone, but on every word that comes from the mouth of God." (Matthew 4:4).

That word that Jesus used there—"proceeds"— denotes *an ongoing present tense meaning, as in, we need to live moment by moment by the words of God.*

Remember the words of Jesus; "He went on to say, '*Pay attention to what you hear. With the measure you use, it will be measured to you, and even more will be added to you.*" (Mark 4:24).

If our attitude toward the Word of God is casual or careless, then when we Really need to hear from God, there may be a problem.

God said, "Has not My hand made all these things? And so they came into being," declares the LORD. "*This is the one I will esteem: he who is humble and contrite in spirit, who trembles at My word.*" (Isaiah 66:2)

Jesus said, "Jesus replied, "If anyone loves Me, he will keep My word. My Father will love him, and we will come to him and make our home with him." (John 14:23).

As I related earlier regarding fellowshipping with the Father, it is our love for Him that equals our love for His Word, and our love for His Word equals our love for Him—and that love remaining in us on a daily basis as the highest priority, is what will shelter us in the days to come.

Something occurred to me today, something I have never considered in over 44 years as a believer: David was a warrior. In fact, he was recognized as one of the greatest military fighters of his time—so much so that songs were written about his military successes, successes that made king Saul violently jealous.

Our warrior king David writes in Psalm 144, "Of David. Blessed be the LORD, my Rock, who trains my hands for war, my fingers for battle." (Psalm 144:1).

But the Lord showed me that David was not talking in that instance of physical warfare—he used his hands and his fingers for playing worship to the Lord on his harp; ***Worship was where David did his warfare!!!***

And if we are going to be an overcoming people in the hour of testing that is coming, we will have to be a people who war through worship and prayer!

Notice the context of David's words in Psalm 144–"Blessed be the LORD, my Rock, who trains my hands for war, my fingers for battle. He is my steadfast love and my fortress, my stronghold and my deliverer. He is my shield, in whom I take refuge, who subdues peoples under me." (Psalm 144:1,2)

The entire book of Psalms (at least most of it) is written by *a worshipping shepherd boy who became a warrior, because he was zealous for the glory of God*—that was what motivated him to go after Goliath, who was insulting the armies of God, and therefore God himself.

Throughout the Psalms we see a man who outwardly, to many, appeared mighty—but we get to see his heart, *because this warrior king had the heart of a dependent little boy toward his God.*

He poured out his heart in total dependence upon the Lord; he held back nothing—And so, the Lord held back nothing from him.

Psalm 119 is the longest scripture passage in the Bible, and it has to do with David's heart attitude toward God and His Word.

Also, Psalm 119 is almost exactly in the center of our Bible—Just as our heart attitude toward the Word of God is at the center of our lives—for better or worse. And in Proverbs 8, Wisdom speaks and says, "I love those who love me, and those who seek me early shall find me", "But he who fails to find me harms himself; all who hate me love death" (Proverbs 8:17, 36)

I don't think it could possibly be overstated that our attitude toward the Word of God, **our heart attitude toward the Word of God, is what will determine the quality of our life.**

And I have found that it doesn't matter how weak I might feel; how alone I might feel; how inadequate I might feel; how overwhelmed I might feel with my shortcomings—if I keep coming back to the Word of God, *God will make up the difference.*

Where I am weak, He will be strong; where I feel alone, He will comfort me; where I feel defeated, He will turn the situation around.

But the thing that I most want to get across is this:

Learning to make the Lord our refuge in all situations, means making His Word our refuge in all situations.

If I say I am trusting in Him, but I am not meditating on and speaking His Word over my situation, and letting His Word renew my mind in my current situation, then the trust I say I have is not built on any foundation.

I know in my heart that we are walking into a time that very few of us have ever really envisioned; and I know without a doubt that we are going to need a faith we've never known before....A trust and a dependence on God that we've never known before....and we may very well have to believe Him for things that truly look impossible, but that is the God we serve; The God of the impossible....the God who parts the seas.....Who causes the storms to cease....manna to fall from heaven....enough water in the desert to take care of the thirst of millions of Jewish people journeying through a desert.... For as long as I can remember—and I mean for at least three decades or more—I have believed to the core of my being, that the Endtime Church would see some of the most miraculous things the world has ever seen....Miracles such as those that took place in the Old Testament and the Book of Acts....

But there will be a very steep price to pay for those miracles, and it is a price that Western believers have never been willing to cough up before....It is the price of total and complete devotion...

Like the woman who poured out that expensive ointment on the feet of Jesus, and washed His feet with her hair and her tears—and that ointment she poured out in her love for Him, by washing His feet using ointment that was reserved for very expensive burials....She was completely devoting herself to Him in love, knowing that it would involve intense suffering.... Perhaps she did not know this consciously, but her actions were very prophetic and of the Spirit, so I believe on some level she understood this.

If we're honest, our "love" in the West has been primarily towards being comfortable, being secure, being well provided for, and well fed—and all of these things are quite temporal.

That is another reason why I believe God has allowed these past 26 months or so, the disruption of all of the things that outwardly we held so dear.

In His mercy, He is trying to break the vice grip of the temporal upon our hearts—Because until we truly see the temporal for what it is, there will always be relentless competition in our hearts for true devotion to Him, and to Him alone.

In a perfect love story, you are willing to give up and sacrifice—and yes, even walk away from everything that you held dear, all that you once knew, to be with that One—that One in a million true love, that you know will Never come again—and if you don't give up everything Now to be with them, you may lose that chance Forever...

I am unspeakably blessed, to be able to say I know Exactly what that feels like....I waited 39 years to meet the most amazing woman God ever put on this earth...and it happened in a way that God sovereignly orchestrated Himself...and I was willing to walk away from the only place I had ever called home; my home state of Florida, everything that I ever knew..... to move to Canada, have weird colored money in my wallet, to never have grits with my bacon and eggs again; to never have sweet iced tea with a ham sandwich, to never be three minutes away from the beach again...OK, yes, that also meant that my Christmases would never include brown grass and 80° temperatures, and palm trees decorated to "look like" Christmas trees...

And sometimes, the perfect love story means you embrace that person's suffering as your own; without batting an eye, without even the slightest moment of regret....

Roopa was very brave and honest with me, before we even met face-to-face, about her disability from polio...She expressed how she did not feel like—in her words—"marriage material".

But I had already fallen hopelessly in love with her spirit and her soul, and I told her, "Your battles will be My battles".

And after our precious daughter was born in 2004, I had 16 years to make good on my promise, as Roopa's precious body rebelled against her in ways that no human should ever have to suffer...We went through one fiery trial after another together, with hundreds of hospital stays....ambulance rides to emergency rooms almost every month....countless doctors who had no heart or soul...When I wasn't working my sales jobs, I was in the trenches battling for my wife's well-being...Finding one supposed miracle treatment after another, only to watch our hope evaporate once more... Only to watch my wife's spirit be crushed yet one more time, with nothing I could do about it...

And in the end, I had one more choice to make: Choose between juggling both sales career and taking care of my wife, or devote myself completely to taking care of her as the end approached, and trust God to take care of the rest.

After all, He had entrusted me with this unspeakably precious woman as a gift from His heart to me, and I believed if I was faithful to care for this precious gift, he would take care of all of us—and he Did, overwhelmingly.

I have learned something over the past 19 years....that **the Greatest Love we will ever experience, is the love that we willingly enter into knowing full well that it will involve suffering....it will involve, inevitably, identifying completely with someone else at our own expense...**

A Love that will mean so much to us, that we are totally willing to set aside everything that meant something to our own sense of self....

Dare we even begin to believe, that that Someone could be Jesus??? Our Heavenly Father??? The Holy Spirit, the Spirit of grace???

That that someone could be the Body of Christ??? My brothers and sisters who need me now, even when I am at my weakest...my most vulnerable, shattered self????

Do I even have anything to offer in my brokenness, which rears its head multiple times every day and night????

Do I even dare take a single step of Faith and put out a one minute podcast, promising that I will be doing more podcasts to minister to my brothers and sisters for the Lord???

What if it turns out that I am too broken, and in too much pain to keep this promise, then I will have disappointed so many people....

Yes Lord, there were those wonderful days when I ministered and taught Your Word so long ago, but I wasn't broken, and I was still in one piece...

But one thing that I saw in Roopa that is with me every single day, is how in her pain and her suffering, in her isolation, she continually blessed and ministered to people, and encouraged them and made them feel loved—Even when her own family had turned their backs on her, and there was no one visiting her in her suffering and in her pain....There was no one here knocking on our door, wanting to come in and befriend her...

I was married to an absolute saint of a woman, who gave far more out than she ever received in return, but she was never bitter....she never once engaged in a moment of self-pity that I ever saw... *she always relentlessly turned her heart toward her Heavenly Father, in total dependence upon Him.*

My precious wife suffered more than anyone I have ever known in my entire lifetime, and yet in her last few weeks she only became more peaceful, more devoted to Him...searching her heart, asking God to heal her of any unforgiveness toward anybody for anything, because she did not want to have anything between her and her Father God.

Her whole heart's desire was to have a conscience that was clean and pure before Him, and totally yielded into His hands. That is the woman that I was married to, and I still consider myself her husband—I do not apply the "W" word to myself in any way, shape, or form. I don't even think it.

To me, Roopa was the example that should be preached to every Christian believer in Western society—***Live in exactly the way that you want to meet your Heavenly Father the moment you draw your last breath.***

Yes, that sets the bar pretty high—but then, we stand to gain Eternity... *And that is all I ever saw my Wife live for....*

Roopa caused me to see Eternity more clearly than anyone I've ever known, and so it is this that I wish to pass on to all of you, my brothers and sisters—the clearest view possible of the Eternity that is stretched out before us....The only price we have to pay is wholehearted devotion to Him to the very end....

My choosing to suffer with Roopa, my choosing to embrace her sufferings as my own, did not take anything away from me—***it actually made me more whole and complete, more fulfilled, than I could've ever imagined...***

Did it hurt????

It was an "exquisite agony", I believe is the phrase that C.S. Lewis used.

It is very difficult for me to put into words in the human language what it feels like, to enter into the sufferings of the person you love more than you ever thought you could love anyone.

What I Can promise you, is that to the one who enters into the sufferings of their loved one, and who endures faithfully, and who becomes ever more compassionate, and gracious, and long-suffering towards their suffering loved one—the experience will Completely and totally Transform you Forever; you will never be the same person again—it would be Impossible.

Entering into your loved one's sufferings willingly, with a heart of relentless, militant devotion, will transform you just like gold is transformed in the furnace...And that is what I believe is just up ahead for the Church....

And perhaps that is why He has chosen me to share the things that I have, because I have been through a 16 year furnace.... I know what it is like, and I also know what the sufferings to come are going to feel like...

So it has fallen to me, and to others, to prepare the Lord sons and daughters...to ready their hearts, their minds, their souls, and their spirits, for what is coming—and to help them see clearly the Eternity that awaits us just on the other side of that suffering....the suffering that my Wife passed through, where she waits for us....

CHAPTER 6

LISTENING TO THE HOLY SPIRIT

My prayer for you today, Child of God, is "that the God of our Lord Jesus Christ, the glorious Father, may give you a spirit of wisdom and revelation in your knowledge of Him." (Ephesians 1:17).

I was sitting outside tonight for a while, just looking up at the night sky and watching the clouds slowly passing overhead.

As I was gazing into the night sky, I could feel the overwhelming sense that we are in an unspeakably significant moment in time in the Spirit.

With every fiber of my being, I am overwhelmingly persuaded that we are in that very moment of time where Jesus is even now speaking to the Church worldwide; speaking things very directly, and very authoritatively—and He is issuing the command, "He who has an ear, let him hear what the Spirit says to the churches." (Revelation 3:6).

Please, please make careful note that as Jesus is addressing these churches, it is in an Endtime context, and the ONLY overarching priority and mandate that Jesus is speaking, in addition to the specific rebukes, corrections, and expectations to each of the churches, is this One Single Directive—From Revelation 3:6, His one overriding command to all of the churches, "He who has an ear, let him hear what the Spirit says to the churches."

I truly believe that we are living in that moment of time right now, where Jesus Christ, who resides in the heavens, is speaking those words to us right now—to all believers currently present on this earth. THAT is the one overruling mandate he is calling us to pay heed to, with every fiber of our being, no matter what we have to set aside—That is job #1.

With everything that the Lord has been impressing upon me these past few years to speak and to write on various social media, the overriding theme has been hearing the Holy Spirit, and walking with the Holy Spirit. Without that reality being realized in our everyday lives, the Bible is just a book full of black letters on white paper.

Remember, Jesus said, "The Spirit gives life; the flesh profits nothing. The words I have spoken to you are spirit and they are life" (John 6:63).

He never said they are religious doctrine only, or they are Sunday school teaching only. It is only the Presence, power, and anointing of the Holy Spirit that can take the words of Jesus, and make them Life—and it is the voice of the Holy Spirit speaking to our hearts individually, on a daily basis as the Third Person of the Godhead, that keeps us walking in His life, in the Spirit.

Again, as it says in Romans, "For all who are led by the Spirit of God are sons of God." (Romans 8:14).

This is an ongoing daily lifestyle; a daily interacting with the Holy Spirit—THAT is what makes us Believers, and not just religious church goers.

Partaking of the very life and nature and moving of God every day via the Holy Spirit is the very thing God always had in mind.

Today, Western believers are so mind-oriented; everything has to pass through their brain and make perfect intellectual sense to them, or they reject it. Being led by Someone you can't see, feel, or touch makes no sense to them.

Being led by an invisible person of the Godhead, the Holy Spirit, makes absolutely no sense to 90% of American Christianity; they would much rather quote a pastor or listen to a pastor or quote some dead theologian—but be led by the invisible Holy Spirit of the living God???? No, sounds too weird and flaky.

But scripture only gives us TWO options; be led by the Spirit and be spiritually minded, OR, be carnally minded and be in the flesh—and I don't think the outcome for the second choice is all that good.

The fact is, every professing Christian in the Western hemisphere needs to just stop, take a reality check, and realize that if tomorrow you drop dead and end up in heaven, that is the realm of God and the Holy Spirit, and it is completely unlike anything your human brain has ever encountered down here—so why don't you start living like a current resident of Heaven NOW, by walking with the Holy Spirit, instead of walking around down here on earth professing to be a Christian, but living like someone who's a complete stranger to His voice????

I am phrasing things the way I am to try to break through the thinking that has kept so many in religious grave clothes forever and ever, and suffocated us spiritually to the point where all we do is try to get through each day on our own strength, our own power, our own thinking, our own emotions—and quite frankly, I did that for the first five years of my Christian life and it was exhausting, and nearly killed me.

"The thief comes only to steal and kill and destroy. *I have come that they may have life, and have it in all its fullness.*" (John 10:10). But that life is through His Holy Spirit, and through no other channel, and through no other conduit—and it's time to stop trying to find some other way to live the Christian life apart from his power.

It's time to stop running on our own human effort; it's time to stop trying to solve our own problems; heal our own hurts by our own power; it is time to receive with open hearts and open arms the promise of the Father, the gift of the Holy Spirit, who has come to breathe the very breath of God into our beings; to speak to us gently and powerfully every single day, concerning every little detail of our life—to lead us, guide us, warn us, protect us, comfort us, counsel us.... and to use us to do the same for others.

* *

OK, so it's time to take this subject out of the realm of the theoretical, and put it squarely smack dab where it belongs—into the realm of our every day boots-on-the-ground life. If living a life in the Holy Spirit is never taken out of the realm of theory, we stay stuck right where we are folks. The good news is, it doesn't have to be that way. But there's a price to pay for it.

So, let me share with you a little something that happened to me many years ago that will bring this out into the Real World.

It's a story about a young mother named Rosie, and her little baby girl who had stopped breathing.

Back in 1995, I was living in West Palm Beach, Florida, and I was very blessed to live in a neighborhood that was very conducive to taking quiet prayer walks every night.

Well, on this particular Florida evening, I was sitting on our screened in back porch, in a nice rocking chair, enjoying a very comfortable breeze.

The breeze was so relaxing, that I felt I would drift off into a nice nap anytime....

And then, I began to feel a quiet little nudge...not forceful at all, just suggestive. The soft but distinct prompting was for me to take a walk.

Now, any of you who have ever been sitting in a rocking chair or on a swing, enjoying a nice Southern breeze, know full well that you don't just walk away from that—it's too luxurious! You can't Buy that kind of relaxation!

So I continued lightly rocking, trying to soak in a little bit more of that breeze...And then the prompting came again, still distinct and clear; "Go for a walk".

I had learned that when the voice of the Lord, the gentle prompting of the Holy Spirit, was urging me to do something outside of my creature comfort, it was definitely from God—it wasn't my head roaring.

So I got up and put on my shoes, and started out walking in my usual prayer walk direction around the development. Now, the development was shaped like an elongated oval, with the main exit/entrance being at the front of that oval, opening up to the main highway. So, I rounded the bend in front of the development, and started to make my way around the curve, *when the prompting urged me to go back to my starting point.*

So I walked back across the front of the development to the other curve where I had begun, and the Holy Spirit prompted me once again to walk back the other way, so I began walking, feeling like a ping-pong ball going back-and-forth.

At this point, I realized that this was an unusual direction from the Holy Spirit, so something must be up—I just didn't know what.

I continued my back-and-forth walk, praying in tongues, and remaining quietly alert and attentive to whatever He was doing.

It was now dark, but as I continued walking and praying in tongues, there was suddenly a loud, panicked shrieking and screaming of a woman coming from one of the houses that I had walked past.

My spiritual alert level was on high, as I tried to peer through the darkness to see what was happening.

I finally saw a woman running across her yard, as though she was trying to find someone, and she was screaming at the top of her lungs, "My baby! My baby!! Someone please help my baby!!!"

By the time I got to her, she was approaching the front door of a neighbor's house, but she saw me and turned to me, and handed me her baby like she'd known me her whole life. She said her baby had stopped breathing, it was a little girl, and she looked to be about two years old.

At that moment, the front door of the house she had run to opened, and she began talking with the lady who answered the door.

I felt this sensation that I was right where I was supposed to be, like this cloak of overwhelming, quiet authority was wrapped all around me, and as the two women went into the kitchen to talk, I went into their living room and laid the little girl down on the couch and began praying over her in tongues. I rebuked the spirit of death, and commanded life to return to her body, and continued to pray in tongues over her intently.

In looking back, I remember that during the entire time I was praying over the little girl, the two women stayed in the kitchen—it was as though they were allowing me to watch over the little girl, as though it was the most natural thing to do.

The next thing I remember, there was a sound at the door as paramedics began to come in, and the moment one of them put an oxygen mask on the little girl, she immediately revived.

I then quietly left and went back home.

A few weeks later, as I was walking to the community mailboxes to check mail, I looked and saw the woman walking towards me with two other women, and when she saw me she started shouting and telling the women, "That's the man that saved my baby! That's the man of God that saved my baby!"

She introduced herself to me, her name was Rosie, and God forgive me, but to this day I cannot recall her little girls' name, but she said that she was doing perfectly fine.

I have thought about Rosie, her husband Keith, and their little girl many, many times throughout the year since then, and I pray and believe that God's hand remains on them.

That particular night will be alive in my memory forever....the night I learned that responding to the slightest prompting of the Holy Spirit could truly mean the difference between life or death for someone.

* * * * * * * * * * * * * * * * * * * *

This is what Jesus said; "The wind blows where it wishes. You hear its sound, but you do not know where it comes from or where it is going. So it is with everyone born of the Spirit." (John 3:8)

The Greek word for 'wind' in this verse is the word 'pneuma', from which we get the word 'Spirit'.

In other words, He is letting us know that, although you cannot see the Holy Spirit, He is actively moving, constantly, according to His will and desire, but it is up to us to be willing participants—much like the sail on a boat, yielding to the force of the wind blowing. *If the sail on the boat is not open and ready to receive the force of the wind, the boat will not be directed anywhere.*

Likewise, if we are closed off in our mindset and are not open to the moving of the Holy Spirit, and not allowing ourselves to be in a position to be directed by Him at any given moment, then we will remain stationary and stagnant in our walk with God.

So, will we be like the boat with the sail wide open, ready to be moved by the slightest breeze or wind of the Holy Spirit?

Or, will we keep our sails half open, or maybe even closed???

Just because the Holy Spirit is invisible, doesn't mean He's not ever-present. David said in Psalm 139:7, "Where can I go to escape Your Spirit? Where can I flee from Your presence?"

But the only way to be in a position to hear the Spirit, and respond to the Spirit, is to—as continually as possible—pray in the Spirit, and have an attentive attitude of listening to the Spirit; *whether He speaks or not is beside the point—the primary thing is to "have an ear to hear", always....*

CHAPTER 7

RECEIVING & EXPERIENCING THE BAPTISM OF THE HOLY SPIRIT

Welcome to the final chapter in section 1, and I truly hope by this point, dear child of God, I have shared enough with you from the Word of God—and experience—concerning the reality of the Holy Spirit.

I have strived to speak & share as clearly and straightforwardly as possible from the Holy Spirit, His ministry & activity in my life, in order to bring this subject out of the realm of theory and conjecture, and into our present day reality.

It is at this point that I want to clearly spell out from the Word of God how to receive the baptism of the Holy Spirit personally, in as simple a manner as possible.

I believe that the New Testament—beginning with the gospels—does indeed present this in a very simple, easy to understand way, but I also realize that there have been decades of religious misinformation and disinformation that we must work through as well.

But again, from my own experience, *the straightest path to receiving anything from God is by being humble & childlike in our faith, and in our asking & Believing.* As Jesus said, "Ask, and it will be given to you; seek, and you will find; knock, and the door will be opened to you". (Matthew 7:7).

It is our Western religious system that has made things so complicated, primarily because men in ivory towers with pulpits have insisted on their intellect being the arbitrator of what is really truth in God's Word.

But, *we have been long on theory, conjecture, and debating—and tragically short on spiritual reality.*

It's time to move forward from all of that.

So it is to the spiritually thirsty and hungry that I speak, write, and minister.

"Taste and see that the LORD is good; blessed is the man who takes refuge in Him", said the Psalmist, and *I believe it truly is that simple* (Psalm 34:8).

Now, once again dear child of God, I don't know where you are in your walk with the Lord right now, but if you have read this far, I would believe you are very committed and eager to have a deeper, more powerful walk with the Lord than you've ever known before.

So let's take some time now to let Jesus speak directly to this subject, as He is the ultimate Divine Authority on the Holy Spirit, and on the Holy Spirit's relationship to us.

This means that we have to set aside anything & everything out of the mouth of any preacher, or Bible teacher, or next-door neighbor that does not agree with the words of Jesus Himself. Once we can agree on that, the rest is very simple.

First of all, let's look at what Jesus had to say about the Holy Spirit's ministry *To us* and *Through us* in the Church, through all generations— And remember: **it is what Jesus said and taught that is foundational for Everything that we believe and walk out.**

Religion is what you get when man adds to the things that Jesus said and taught—And religion almost Always complicates everything that Jesus made simple and straightforward....we have put up with that for far too long....

One of the first things that Jesus did with His disciples, concerning receiving the Holy Spirit and His ministry to us, was to teach about it in the simplest, most concrete terms possible—And He did so by using the example of a child asking it's father for a gift.

Now, just sit back and close your eyes for a minute, and let that sink in.

According to Jesus, receiving the Holy Spirit is as simple and intimately personal as receiving a gift from your own father.

Now, I'd like to offer a very personal word here from my own life, because I realize that there are many who did not have a healthy relationship with their earthly father….like some of you, I did not have an example of a loving, giving, caring father as a part of my childhood. But as time progressed and the traumatic elements of my childhood were removed, I began to have a sense of "a God up there" who Did care about me.

But even after I was dramatically born again at age 17, I continued to feel like God was distant and difficult to connect with. I had no doubt that He loved me, because He had powerfully and supernaturally revealed Himself to me.

But there was always an undefinable "something" missing between God and myself….A missing dimension to our relationship, though I could not put a finger on what it was.

I cried out for quite a long time for God to show me what exactly was missing—and in 1983, in very direct answer to my prayers, a passage from the Book of Luke came to me, and suddenly all the lights went on.

"So if you who are evil know how to give good gifts to your children, how much more will your Father in heaven give the Holy Spirit to those who ask Him?" (Luke 11:13)

That verse truly became revelation at that point, and it was like my mind was suddenly and completely at peace, free from all of the anxiety and confusion that I had been fighting with for months….And just like a child, I realized that this was something I had never asked my Heavenly Father for—the gift of the Holy Spirit.

So just as simply and innocently I said, "God, your Word says that you will give the Holy Spirit to those who ask, so I'm asking".

As I have shared elsewhere in the book, several weeks later the Lord made a way for me to receive prayer for the baptism of the Holy Spirit, and the rest is history.

Now, for some who truly want the baptism of the Holy Spirit, I realize that there may be misconceptions or possibly even some apprehension as to what to expect.

What I want to do is point you back to Jesus, and the things that He said about the nature of your Heavenly Father and His desire to give you the Holy Spirit.

Also, remember how you came to the Lord, at your point of salvation, when you realized down to the core of your very being your desperate need of Him, and your own desperate inability to save or deliver yourself....

You knew that if you were going to be saved and delivered, it was going to All have to come from Him, and Him Alone.

And now here you are—saved, delivered, and walking with God!

How much more then, will God—who delivered up His only Son for you—how much more will He give you His Holy Spirit?

So, before you read any further, I would like to invite you to simply—right where you are—close your eyes, and open your heart wide to your Heavenly Father, and say, "Father God, I cry out to you with all my heart for the precious gift of the Holy Spirit! I need Him as much as I need your Son Jesus! I need them both equally, and just as urgently! And I want to thank You with all my heart for the precious gift of your Holy Spirit, who has been sent to lead me and guide me into all truth; the Holy Spirit from You who is the Spirit of Adoption—the Spirit of Adoption who gives me intimate relationship with you. He opens the eyes of my heart to comprehend You and know You intimately as my Heavenly Father, and also to comprehend everything that belongs to me in Jesus Christ. He anoints me and fills me with His own Divine presence, so that I am joined to You spirit to spirit, so that I may worship You in spirit and in truth—so that I may praise you and worship you in the very language of the Holy Spirit that He will give me freely."

And as you feel the presence of the Holy Spirit filling your being to the point of overflowing, let His overflowing presence within you find expression through your lips, as you speak forth everything that He is filling you with. Feel absolutely free, like a little child, to be joyful in His presence with singing and glorifying Him with all the fullness that the Holy Spirit is causing to bubble up and overflow within you.

You may feel a beautiful sense of a river wanting to gush out of you in words that you've never heard before, but it's from Him, just as Jesus said "from your belly shall flow rivers of living water"....rivers are mighty and powerful—and in this case, they are of the Holy Spirit, so let them flow through you freely....let the Holy Spirit find beautiful expression through you, as He expresses Himself through you, His own child of God, for the first time, and let the rivers keep on flowing...."

* *

"On the last and greatest day of the feast, Jesus stood up and called out in a loud voice, "If anyone is thirsty, let him come to Me and drink. Whoever believes in Me, as the Scripture has said: 'Streams of living water will flow from within him.'" He was speaking about the Spirit, whom those who believed in Him were later to receive. For the Spirit had not yet been given, because Jesus had not yet been glorified...."

(John 7:37-39)

"While Peter was still speaking these words, *the Holy Spirit fell upon all who heard his message*. All the circumcised believers who had accompanied Peter were astounded that *the gift of the Holy Spirit had been poured out even on the Gentiles. For they heard them speaking in tongues and exalting God.* Then Peter said, "Can anyone withhold the water to baptize these people? They have received the Holy Spirit just as we have!" (Acts 10:44-47)

"While Apollos was at Corinth, Paul passed through the interior and came to Ephesus. There he found some disciples and asked them, "Did you receive the Holy Spirit when you became believers?"

"No," they answered, "we have not even heard that there is a Holy Spirit."

"Into what, then, were you baptized?" Paul asked.

"The baptism of John," they replied.

Paul explained: "John's baptism was a baptism of repentance. He told the people to believe in the One coming after him, that is, in Jesus."

On hearing this, they were baptized into the name of the Lord Jesus. *And when Paul laid his hands on them, the Holy Spirit came upon them, and they spoke in tongues and prophesied.* There were about twelve men in all." (Acts 19:1-7)

PART 2:

FULLNESS OF THE HOLY SPIRIT; DEVELOPING SPIRITUAL CLARITY AND STRENGTH

The Holy Spirit's presence within you is actually a Supernatural, Heavenly depository guarantee of the Kingdom you are going to inherit—And, you are enabled to begin "tasting" of it—appropriating it experientially in your life—Right Now

CHAPTER 8

THE SUPPLY OF THE SPIRIT

Welcome to the biggest ocean that ever existed. If you set sail today, and had 1 million years worth of blank pages in your logbook, you would never, ever reach the other side.

And I will tell you this: *Until we see the Holy Spirit as limitless as that, we have not even begun our walk of faith.*

I don't say that to dampen anyone's spirits, but to help you take your first steps into spiritual freedom and liberty—because as long as we impose our limitations on the limitless Holy Spirit, we will never experience the things that we've been praying for, the things that we have been believing for—because as long as we are imposing our limitations on the Holy Spirit, our praying will be too shallow, and our believing will be too small.

I don't know to how many of you this is apparent, but there has been an all-out spiritual war waged by Satan against the Holy Spirit and against the things of the Holy Spirit for decades now!

But do you understand Why that is so????

Do you for a moment comprehend what the enemy is Really after?????

It doesn't take much to snatch candy out of the hand of a baby—but if you are going to succeed in taking millions of dollars away from your unsuspecting victim, you're going to have to employ very strategic deception to steal it, OR, you're going to have to convince your victim that their treasure is worthless, and they would be better off just forfeiting it.

And from where I stand, with a perspective spanning almost 44 years, I would have to say that the enemy has done an overwhelmingly strategic job of convincing the modern church to forfeit all of her heavenly riches in the Holy Spirit, by convincing her that those riches were for a long time ago, and are no longer needed. "Here you go, just trade all of that in for my jewels of the rapture and once saved always saved, that's what you really need"—and so the church traded spiritual courage and vitality for the lies of comfort and security for the flesh.

Boom! Endgame won.... Or so it seems.

But I believe God is awakening a remnant of believers who have somehow seen through all of this, and are not content to live in the misty lowlands of a weak and worldly spirituality any longer....

They've been weary, they've been battered, but they still have the strength to fight for the true spiritual heritage that they know rightfully belongs to them....And, they've got nothing left to lose—which makes them spiritually hungry, and Very dangerous....*Because they are Ready & Willing to do whatever it takes to become Fully Empowered by the Holy Spirit!*

They have no "Plan B"; they have no "Exit Strategy". The World has nothing else to dangle in front of them as bait or a distraction! They have been totally stripped down to the frame; they are lean, have no confidence in the flesh, and the things of this world are now nothing more than dust under their feet....they are now, Bond Servants of the Lord Most High.

They don't fear death, because they've already died to Self. They can't be bribed or bought, because they have their eyes fixed on the Crown of Righteousness....They can't be shamed by their Past, because all that's left of THAT is the place where the Blood of Jesus flowed and washed it all away....

Now, *remember how Jesus described the coming ministry of the Holy Spirit to ALL believers;*

"However, when the Spirit of truth comes, He will guide you into all truth. For He will not speak on His own, but He will speak what He hears, and He will declare to you what is to come. He will glorify Me by taking from what is Mine and disclosing it to you. Everything that belongs to the Father is Mine. That is why I said that the Spirit will take from what is Mine and disclose it to you." *("apokalupto", a disclosure).* (John 16:13-15)

"Revelations" in the Greek is 'apokalypseōn', meaning, *an unveiling, uncovering, revealing, revelation.* From apokalupto; a *disclosure.*

So, the major part of the Holy Spirit's ministry to us is by way of revelation.

The purpose of revelation from the Holy Spirit within the church is not in any way meant to "add" to scripture, as some errantly protest.

Rather, it is meant to add to our intimacy in fellowshipping with the Father, and it is meant to deepen our understanding of His nature and our union with Him. In fact, the apostolic letters of Paul all testify to this.

Real-time, ongoing revelation is also necessary from the Holy Spirit in directing our daily lives, and our walk & ministry with Him—And it is absolutely essential when it comes to ministering to the Body and edifying our fellow believers. Otherwise, why would Paul earnestly exhort believers to desire spiritual gifts, especially prophesying?

The foundational understanding is that our relationship with God is spirit to spirit, and Jesus said so Himself. It is not fellowshipping with the Lord through your mind or your emotions—at least not primarily.

Jesus laid the foundational understanding for this when He said, "God is Spirit, and His worshipers must worship Him in spirit and in truth." (John 4:24).

Again, **Jesus Himself made ongoing revelatory communication from the Holy Spirit part and parcel of our relationship with Him. As** *far as Jesus is concerned, it is meant to be a part of our daily life until He returns.*

The apostle Paul expresses this countless times in his letters to believers, in passages like these that reveal *the Holy Spirit's ongoing ministry to us;*

When we stop and consider the fact that we are still in these earthly bodies that are waiting to be transformed like the Lord's body, and that *these temporary earthly bodies are the house of the Holy Spirit who dwells within us*—that alone is a mindbending, humbling thing to think about.

As Paul said, "Now we have this treasure in jars of clay to show that this surpassingly great power is from God and not from us." (2 Corinthians 4:7).

I think perhaps most of the time we are more mindful of the earthen vessels side of that equation, as opposed to the exceedingly glorious treasure that we have within us—And part of what I would like to do, and part of what I feel my ministry to the Body of Christ is, is to bring attention (rightfully deserved attention) to that glorious treasure that is inside of us, the Holy Spirit…*The limitless Holy Spirit who has full access to All of the things of God, to all of the thoughts of God Himself, to everything that God is and has and will ever be—the Holy Spirit alone, who lives within us, has access (FULL access!) to all of that, 24 hours a day, seven days a week—and He Lives Inside Us!*

In this Endtime, we Must as individual believers have a vision of the Holy Spirit that eclipses anything and everything we have ever, ever known. It must eclipse everything we've ever, ever been told, everything we've ever, ever read—Because I guarantee you one thing: we have not seen or known the Holy Spirit for who He is yet.

Right Now, Professing believers all over the world are feeling the uprising of the Holy Spirit in their hearts in such a powerful way, and they are throwing off the religious shackles and chains that said the Holy Spirit is 'just a doctrine'!

All over the world, believers are waking up to the reality that the Baptism of the Holy Spirit is a gift from the Father in heaven, to each and every one that will ask and receive like a little child.

All over the world, believers are waking up to the magnitude of the awesome power of the Almighty Holy Spirit living within them, catching a burning glimpse of all that He is capable of doing in and through them each and every day!

No longer is there any way to confine them to any place, any building! The Holy Spirit, the Spirit of the Living God, is fully mobilizing believers by the hundreds of thousands all over the world, turning them loose like a flood of spiritual liberators and spiritual life givers!

Years ago the Lord gave me such a powerful prophetic word regarding those whom the enemy was working overtime to derail and wipe out:

"Survivors Will Be the Endtime Revivers!!!"

Hundreds of thousands of believers out there where Jesus used to be, doing the works of Jesus, bringing spiritual life and liberty to the rest of the world that is darkened and in shackles and spiritual chains, waiting to be released from spiritual captivity and bondage; waiting for the church of Jesus Christ empowered by the Holy Spirit to be released like a Spiritual Divine Flood, Overcoming all the works of the enemy!

So, how do we make that transition???

As with all things, we Begin in the Spirit.

We begin to move from where we are right Now, to where we Need to be IN THE SPIRIT.

How do we BEGIN?

Praying in Tongues/Praying in the Spirit moves you into the unseen realm.

In Mark 11:23, Jesus says, "Truly I tell you that if anyone says to this mountain, 'Be lifted up and thrown into the sea,' *and has no doubt in his heart but believes that it will happen, it will be done for him*".

But isn't believing where our problem has always been????

That's because the problem is, we keep reading that verse, and *we make the mistake of assuming that believing begins with our Mind*—but True believing is born of Faith, and Faith is born of the Spirit. If you wait till your MIND can believe all things are possible, you will be waiting a very, very long time.

Remember what Jesus said; "The Spirit gives life; the flesh profits nothing. The words I have spoken to you are spirit and they are life." *(John 6:63).*

Your mind is the problem. *Your mind will Never be the answer;* **your mind will never ever believe 'enough'.**

The faith that is born of true believing, is born of the Spirit.

Now, when we think of the limitless supply of the Holy Spirit, the next thought that comes to our mind is, "How does He give to us out of His limitless supply? **How does He get His supply to us?"**

Again, the primary way, according to the New Testament, that the Holy Spirit ministers to us out of His abundance, is by means of revelation to our spirits.

This is Exactly why the apostle Paul prayed for All believers Everywhere, in All times, when he prayed This (and You need to pray these words over yourself & your family every single day);

"I have not stopped giving thanks for you, remembering you in my prayers, that the God of our Lord Jesus Christ, the glorious Father, *may give you a spirit of wisdom and revelation in your knowledge of Him.* I ask that *the eyes of your heart may be enlightened, so that you may* **know** the hope of His calling, the riches of His glorious inheritance in the saints..." (Ephesians 1:16-18)

As I quoted a few moments ago, Jesus specifically said of the Holy Spirit's ministry to us, *"He will glorify Me by taking from what is Mine and disclosing it to you." (John 16:14)* Again, just as we mentioned a few pages ago, "apokalupto", a revelation, a disclosure.

The beginning of the Holy Spirit-led and directed Church is clearly seen in the Book of Acts, and even though Western believers have made the fatal mistake of assuming that the leadership and empowerment of the Holy Spirit somewhere a way back there stopped or ceased or diminished, there is nothing in scripture that states that.

In fact, when one bothers to take an even cursory look at the Book of Acts and the New Testament letters, it is fully apparent that the Church is emphatically built to be operated by the ongoing leadership, direction, and empowerment of the Third Person of the Eternal Godhead.

The one thing that you Don't see in the Book of Acts, is the proliferation of church buildings and the "nomination of pastors".

The fact is that, yes, there are some nice church buildings out there with some wonderful people in them—but if you could truly see in the spirit what our fixation with buildings and pastors and pews and church times has done to us, You would tremble; your knees would shake, and you would probably feel like fainting….Once you were able to see the magnitude of the spiritual power, life, and vitality in the Holy Spirit that has been Lost, because we shrunk the Holy One of God, the Mighty Holy Spirit, down into a snack size portion that we could fit into our choreographed services—The same Spirit that rose Jesus from the dead! The same Spirit that hovered over our entire planet at creation! Yes, we put THAT same Holy Spirit into a little church building and said "now y'all come, ya hear?"

And we had No idea just how vile that sounds in the spirit realm; just how horrifically demeaning and diminishing it is to the very nature, power, and magnitude of all that the Holy Spirit is.

We tossed aside any chance of glimpsing a vision of all that He is, wants to be, and wants to do—in favor of our convenience, our comfort, because after all, who's got the charisma and courage and strength to live this seven days a week (we could maybe spare Sunday and Wednesday night God)!

And we would all probably have a heart attack right now on the spot if we saw all at once what that has done to us; what we've lost; what we've allowed ourselves to be robbed of in the face of all the evil that is swirling over this planet. We forsook the Rivers of Living Water, so we can get a few God bless-me sprinkles on Sunday. I'm telling you, if we don't get a blazing, out of control fire in our spirits, we will never reclaim what we've lost—and that is what we need to see.

I woke up the other morning from a dream, where I saw so many people praying in tongues—it was like an ocean of people praying in the Spirit, it was just so awesome a sight.

But the entire dream was about the people of God moving into the Spirit, *and feeling completely at home in that environment.*

That is the vision the Holy Spirit has for His people, and we need to catch onto that, and we need to move into it and yield every part of ourselves to Him, so He can move us into that place in the spirit.

But for us to move into that place in the spirit, where the supply of the Holy Spirit is 24/7, we have got to make some very clear-cut choices, regardless of how hard they may be—Because God never changes, He is still the God that said, "You shall have no other gods before me" (Exodus 20:3).

And that is what is reverberating in my spirit and in my heart tonight. I'm nine pages into this message, and this is the fire that started burning and it won't quit—The Holy Spirit is a jealous God, and yes, as children of God we are free to partake of everything in His kingdom, everything that Jesus purchased for us with his blood.

But because the supply of the Spirit was purchased by the blood of Jesus, and made possible by the blood of Jesus, it is a very holy thing—and we here in Western Christendom have been far too casual about the things of the Holy Spirit, for far too long, and I feel him saying tonight, Enough is enough! Either you're all in or you're not, but if you're halfway in, do not play games with Me, and do not expect Me to meet you halfway.

As you look throughout the Word of God from Genesis to Revelation, the one thing the one thing that God expects and requires from each and everyone that names His name is faithfulness—*Not perfection, but faithfulness.*

If you've got $.10 worth of ability, then be faithful with that $.10 worth, and you will receive the same reward as the one who's got $1 million worth of ability—it's not the amount, it's the quality.

So if you've been baptized in the Holy Spirit and you can pray in tongues, then you be faithful with praying in the spirit every single day, and when He has seen your faithfulness, He will add to that—but He's looking for faithfulness first. Faithfulness can't be bought, it can't be faked; it is what it is.

We can talk about the magnificence and the glory of the supply of the Holy Spirit, **but it is our inner heart condition as vessels of the Holy Spirit that determines just how much of that supply we can actually receive—** and that, in turn, determines just how effectively we can be used by Him as ministers of the spirit to others.

2nd Timothy 2:20-22 says;

"A large house contains not only vessels of gold and silver, but also of wood and clay. Some indeed are for honorable use, but others are for common use. So if anyone cleanses himself of what is unfit, he will be a vessel for honor: sanctified, useful to the Master, and prepared for every good work. Flee from youthful passions and pursue righteousness, faith, love, and peace, together with those who call on the Lord out of a pure heart...."

Now, here we come to a literal *gold mine of revelation,* a passage that sums up everything we would ever need to know about the supply of the Holy Spirit!

If this was the Only piece of the Bible we had in our hand in a Chinese prison, this would sum everything up that we need to know about the supply of the Holy Spirit (That was just to give you a little perspective—the apostle Paul wrote most of these amazing, revelation-filled letters from prison cells. You see, to him, **being in a prison cell did not limit or hinder the supply of the Spirit**—and *that* is a Huge revelation that we need to have made very, very real to our hearts, especially in this day and time of spiritual darkness).

"As it is written: "Rather, as it is written: "No eye has seen, no ear has heard, no heart has imagined, what God has prepared for those who love Him." **But God has revealed it to us by the Spirit. The Spirit searches all things, even the deep things of God.** For who among men knows the thoughts of man except his own spirit within him? **So too, no one knows the thoughts of God except the Spirit of God. We have not received the spirit of the world, but the Spirit who is from God, that we may understand what God has freely given us. And this is what we speak, not in words taught us by human wisdom, but in words taught by the Spirit, expressing spiritual truths in spiritual words**" (1st Corinthians 2:9-13).

You and I are in intimate Fellowship with a God Who desires to Reveal even His deepest thoughts, especially as those thoughts pertain to our relationship to Him.

For those of us who are getting weary, and maybe at times wondering if the battle is all worth it, now we know without a doubt that the things our faith is based on—the unseen realities that we have pledged our lives to—are indeed far more valuable than we've ever imagined before....And guess what???? Far more unbelievers are closer to being believers than they ever were before!

That is precisely why Jesus said, "When these things begin to happen, stand up and lift up your heads, because your redemption is drawing near" (Luke 21:28)

In other words, the unseen realities that we have been clinging to are closer now than they ever were before!!

So now is the time—if there ever was a time—to become more immersed in the Holy Spirit, more full of the Holy Spirit, more functional in the spirit, than ever before in our lives!!!!

And all of the experiences that the Lord has given me over the past 40 some odd years; all of the spiritual lessons that He has taught me over the past 40 some odd years; everything that He has deposited in me over four decades, were for this time right now—to give out to all of you, to share with all of you, to deposit in all of your lives, to make you stronger, more battle ready, more functional in the Holy Spirit—so that you may in turn do the same for others!

I'm hearing from brothers and sisters who have been having spiritual battles like they've never had before—some encountering spiritual conflict that they've never had in their entire life…. battles with anxiety, oppression, and they need real-life Holy Spirit answers. So this is not a time for theory and conjecture; this is the time for Holy Spirit reality that is bigger, stronger, more powerful than anything of the enemy you or your loved ones are facing.

This is why I keep coming back to this topic, because it is God's number one priority for the Body of Christ right now!

Walking in the reality of the Holy Spirit to the nth degree is Heavens' mandate for this hour!

Why?

Because nothing else will do! Nothing else will work!

God does not have a substitute for Holy Spirit power.

He does not have a substitute for the anointing of the Holy Spirit on your life, and flowing through your life!

No substitute exists!

And it is my calling that burns in me day and night, and has for at least the past 20 some odd years—to help prepare the Body of Christ in every way possible, to facilitate the working of the Holy Spirit in the Body of Christ in every way possible, to emphasize it and re-emphasize it; to share from every experience I've ever had, combined with the Word of God, and after I say it one-way, come back and say it a different way, so that everybody gets the point.

All things pertaining to life in the Spirit, all things pertaining to walking in the Spirit, have got to be front and center of our lives, right here and right now.

We literally need to become obsessed with the Holy Spirit functioning in our daily life—the Word of God declares, "The mind of the flesh is death, *but the mind of the Spirit is life and peace,*" (Romans 8:6), so there's no way that could become a bad obsession. "The world is passing away, along with its desires; *but whoever does the will of God remains forever.*"(1 John 2:17), so it sounds like a pretty good obsession to me.

And we must become more and more diligent about stoking the fire in our fellow brothers and sisters around us, and when you're willing to do that, God will make sure that whoever needs it will cross your path, trust me on that. God brought a brother in Arkansas across my path, and here I am in Canada, and God saw to it that we met at the same intersection on Facebook, and now we're both getting truly blessed.

My primary calling in the Lord is to get believers fully functional in the Spirit. *My Calling is to help prepare You for Yours!*

But, in helping my brothers and sisters become fully functional in the Spirit, we must always focus on what is demonstratable in the Spirit. The time for theory and conjecture is long past. As Paul the apostle said, "My message and my preaching were not with persuasive words of wisdom, but with a demonstration of the Spirit's power"(1 Corinthians 2:4).

If it cannot be demonstrated, then it remains in the realm of theory and conjecture—*and **there is no spiritual power in theory and conjecture.** The supply of the Spirit is not in the realm of theory and conjecture. The supply* *of the Spirit is meant to be manifested, and manifested abundantly where you and I both live and breathe.*

In order to help facilitate us becoming much more hands-on with this subject of the supply of the Holy Spirit, I felt led to share an experiment that I did several months ago.

I thought I would just simply document two or three days of what I feel, sense, and observe, as I go about my daily business, but doing it while praying in the Spirit.

I have never known anyone who did this before, and it's the first time I've ever done it.

I've had the notion to do it before, but I just never followed through.

Actually, the last Summer that my darling Roopa was with us, I had the idea of just putting out a little challenge to everyone on my podcast to try documenting—for one week—their observations and experiences while praying in the spirit throughout their regular workday, and just going through daily life—Primarily just to become more conscious of making the time to pray in the spirit, because I know that most of us who have the Holy Spirit pray in tongues in our own prayer time, but not necessarily throughout the day while we're doing our daily life stuff, which is really where we should be doing it the most.

I mean, it has always made sense to me that if you want to be led by the Spirit on a daily basis, then you need to be praying in the spirit to be led by Him.

So, this was my humble attempt to put down on paper something that I've never done before, and I hope my notes from this effort will be a blessing and an encouragement to you, to spend much, much more time praying in the spirit, building your own spirit man up, to the point where your receptivity and sensitivity to the Holy Spirit grows exponentially in the next few weeks and months—because friends, we are living in a time where that is the most valuable commodity we will have; our ability to walk in the Spirit, be led by Him, and be directed by Him, even in the most minuscule ways.

I believe this exercise will help us to realize just how wonderful a benefit praying in the spirit is, and how indispensable it can be to walking in the fruit of the Spirit, being open to the operation of the gifts of the Holy Spirit, as well as producing an abiding sense of the Lord's presence with us and in us, regardless of the circumstances. At least, that is my hope and my prayer.

So, here are my notes and observations from—

"An Experiment in Walking in the Spirit: Day 1"

"The thing that is most noticeable, as I am praying in the spirit while driving around, running errands, etc., is that I have a very real sense of living from another dimension of myself.

I mean, I'm physically driving my car, and mentally I'm aware of my surroundings, but my emotions and my soul realm are not engaged (at least, not on the surface), and my thoughts are quiet and subdued (in other words, I don't have a lot of mental chit chatter going on right now).

I feel calm and steadily focused in a way that is completely different from my mental and thinking or emotional processes.

It really is like I am living from another part of myself that is every bit as real as my mind or emotions, but yet different—*it's not subject to the same fluctuations as my mind or emotions.…*it is almost separate from everything I see around me.…it's higher than everything I see about around me; it's above everything else that I see around me. *It's like I'm connected to a place that is above everything that I see around me*—a place it is more real than the buildings, the cars, and everything that I'm driving past or driving around."

{*End of Day One*}

"An Experiment in Walking in the Spirit: Day 2"

Thoughts & observations regarding praying in tongues throughout the day.

"Day 2—Just drove Asha to school, and it is lightly snowing again....nothing but white everywhere on the ground, in contrast with the tall evergreens standing guard around her school.

There's a completely unmistakeable stillness in the air, even with the slight breeze blowing little snowflakes everywhere.

I've been sitting here in the van praying in the spirit probably for the last half hour or so, with a very real sense that there's an invisible veil just out there in front of me somewhere, a veil that's inviting me to press in and come through...but inwardly, I know that won't be easy. Because pressing through the veil almost never is....

＊ ＊ ＊ ＊ ＊ ＊ ＊ ＊ ＊ ＊ ＊ ＊ ＊ ＊ ＊ ＊ ＊ ＊ ＊

"Now, after praying quietly and reverently in tongues for the last 10 or 12 minutes, I feel like I'm just on the other side of that veil, in a very quiet, worshipful place....but I know that that is just the starting point, because once you have pressed through the veil, there remains communion with the Holy Spirit...

Every day, we must pass through this....This veil of being more conscious of the world and our physical surroundings, and our earthly thoughts....

You know you are on the other side of that veil, once those things no longer occupy your thinking.....once you are aware of simply being in His presence, even in the quietest of ways....

Again, it's so easy to read the verse that says "to be spiritually minded is life & peace", *but to actually come into that place where that scripture is a reality in your existence, at any given moment—that is something else entirely— and this is where I come back to, the thing I will keep on repeating endlessly: we cannot live in the realm of theory and conjecture. We cannot live in the realm where we simply 'know' a scripture in our head.*

It is lifeless to us until we LIVE it; the Word of God is alive and powerful, is it not????

And so as long as we are content to remain in the letter of the Word, we will experience no Life, and no spiritual changes will ever come to us—*it is only as we set ourselves to determine to enter into scriptural, spiritual reality in a very Experiential way, that the Word becomes life and health to all our flesh—because Jesus said (and I'll keep on repeating this as well), "The Spirit gives life; the flesh profits nothing. The words I have spoken to you are spirit and they are life." (John 6:63).*

The scripture says, "The LORD confides in those who fear Him, and reveals His covenant to them." (Psalm 25:14).

And yes, while everyone who has received the baptism of the Holy Spirit has access to the full supply of the Holy Spirit, **there are not many who will ever take the time needed to press through the veil of worldly distractions, and press through the veil of even legitimate things, such as business and family life, to seek Him, and Him alone.**

If we want to be anointed as those who have been set apart, then we must be willing to pay the price to Live as those who have been set apart.

He cannot anoint the carnal, the distracted, the worldly, the half-committed, the half-hearted. But He is abundantly willing to give all of Himself to those who have given all of themselves to Him.

This brings us right back to a passage we looked at in previous chapters, Luke 8:18; "*Pay attention, therefore, to how you listen.* Whoever has will be given more, but whoever does not have, even what he thinks he has will be taken away from him."

Are you listening intently for the voice of the Spirit? Have you shut out all other voices, all other distractions? Or are you listening for the Holy Spirit's voice with one ear, while paying attention to other voices with the other ear? Because if so, chances are you're not going to hear very much with either ear.

{*End of Day Two*}

CHAPTER 9

SPIRITUAL CLARITY—
SEEING WITH KINGDOM EYES

God the Father and God the Son sent only One Divine Representative to this Earth to guide the people of God, and that is the Holy Spirit—without His ongoing, direct Leadership, Guidance, Wisdom, Power, and input, you are relying only on your own mind, your own thoughts, your own perception.

We must become completely and totally spiritually ready and equipped for what is coming, and stop looking through natural eyes at the natural world, but begin to see through spiritual eyes, toward the spiritual realities that surround us.

One thing is for absolutely certain—There has been an absolutely horrific lack of sound, easy to understand teaching on the Holy Spirit in the last several years.

With this world quickly moving forward into the end of the Endtimes, there is not a more important Bible subject for us to get deep into the soil of our hearts and our spirits.

The Western professing church has abysmally failed to treat spiritual things with the degree of seriousness needed—And I believe we have limited time to catch up to where we should be.

I am truly endeavoring to be as pinpoint accurate biblically and spiritually as I can possibly be, while focusing on the New Testament topics that impact our daily spiritual life and walk.

I am being very careful to take my every cue from the Lord, as He spoke and ministered to the apostle Paul, who established more churches and discipled more believers than probably any man who ever lived.

If you read the New Testament with a set of spiritually militant eyes, you will see that *every single thing that Jesus, the disciples, and the apostles did, was completely and totally spiritually strategic, warfare-minded, and kingdom-establishing focused.*

I know that was a mouthful, so take the time to read it again a couple of times real slowly and let it sink in, because I guarantee you, at some point you will come to understand that that is precisely *the three-pronged focus of everything said and done in the New Testament.*

So much of the language of Jesus and the apostles was militant and warfare-minded in nature, with the focus of representing and moving in the authority of God's kingdom.

Western churchianity has done a real hatchet job on our spiritual understanding, and there is so very much we have to unlearn and then relearn, in such a short amount of time.

Forget everything you think you know—And then, take everything that you *Think* you know, and run it through the funnel of nothing but scripture and the Holy Spirit, and see what comes out at the end.

Because beloved, we are heading into the spiritual fight of our lives, and if there is a single religious thought in our heads that takes away from the power of the Word of God and the power of the Holy Spirit in our every day life, it needs to be immediately incinerated.

And you have my assurance that nothing I say, nothing I have to offer in the way of spiritual counsel, is colored by a love of this world whatsoever.

Since the 1990s, I have been watching the spiritual horizon and seeing this time we are now finding ourselves in. I always thought that the church would come to it's spiritual senses, and begin to train and disciple believers accordingly—but I was tragically very wrong.

So as your brother, I vow that I will do everything in my power—God helping and enabling me—to share every single thing that I believe will be needed in our spiritual walk in this Endtime....And I promise you, I will leave no stone unturned. I am a man on a mission. If there is something that my heart tells me is for your spiritual benefit, I will focus on it like a laser. All I could ever ask in return, is that our focus stay 100% on the Word of God, and on the inspiration, the leading, the guidance, and the instruction of the Holy Spirit...Because when it comes right down to it, the Holy Spirit and the Word of God are all we have.

The Believers' Number One source of All true spiritual wisdom is the Word of God and the Holy Spirit combined.

The professing church of the West has almost completely divorced the Holy Spirit from the very Word that He inspired—And I am afraid that the majority of professing believers do not comprehend the profoundly perilous position this has placed them in.

We've lived with a religious system completely void of power for so very long, that we simply don't know anything else.

People get upset at their governments for the astronomical deficits, being trillions of dollars in debt, but what the Western church hasn't been the least bit upset about, is the fact that it has been running a *Spiritual Deficit* forever! But as long as they could open the church doors and get people on the pews, they really haven't cared about that very much—That is because *they do not understand the high price tag that's coming for operating in a spiritual deficit, in a fallen sinful world, where only the power of God will accomplish anything.*

We're seeing the forces and the powers of evil swirling like hurri-canes all over the planet, growing in power and in ferocity, *and now we're waking up to the fact that we don't have the spiritual power within our-selves to match that! That's because we were content with living with a form of godliness, while completely being void of the power of God....*

And now the bill is coming due, and we are running out of time fast to make a course correction...*Not a slight adjustment, but a complete change of spiritual course that must be made if we are going to make it!*

We must have a complete and total spiritual overhaul of how we Think—a complete and total assessment of the Beliefs that we have clung to that have kept us in this half dead/half alive spiritual state for so long, and we have got to have the courage to prostrate ourselves spirit, soul, and body before the living God, and say, "Holy Spirit, come inside me, come within me, and remake me from the inside out according to Your power and Your wishes and Your authority, because I've been bought with a price and I am not my own, and I no longer hold any claims over myself!"

That is the point of desperation, surrender, and consecration we have Got to come to, whatever it takes, because nothing else will work.

We have lived for so long as though we just live on a physical planet, surrounded by physical people and physical jobs, and entertainment and worldly distractions—we have failed to understand that as professing chil-dren of God, You are part of a Spiritual Kingdom, and this fallen world is a fallen spiritual kingdom, and if your spiritual eyes could be opened so that all you see in front of you were the things in the spirit realm (the fallen angels, the demons moving through and motivating people, God's holy angels in the heavenlies), suddenly none of this material stuff would mean anything to you, *because you would be confronted with nothing but the spiritual realities that exist around us every single day*—we just don't pay any attention!

What I am trying to do with every fiber of my being, to the full-est extent that I can, is let the Holy Spirit speak through me and minister through me, to get my brothers and sisters completely and totally spiritually ready and equipped for what is coming—*to help you stop looking through natural eyes at the natural world, but begin to see through spiritual eyes the spiritual realities that surround us—the spiritual realities that are coming at us like a freight train; the spiritual realities that we will be forced to deal with at some point, whether we are prepared or not.*

That is what weighs on me every single day, and has for the last 30 some odd years. One thing, brothers and sisters, that we have got to begin doing now—Today—is reading your New Testament **though spiritual eyes**, and you will see just how much everything that was said or written, was said and written **with the power of God in mind**.

What I so desperately want to paint a picture of, that I believe will **re-calibrate our spiritual thinking,** is to pay very close attention to how the apostle Paul spoke to the churches—the language that he used (*and I mean the spiritual language that he used*).

The New Testament church did not know what it was to be a disciple, to be a believer, apart from the operation and power of the Holy Spirit on a daily basis.

What we call Western Christianity, they would have regarded as just dead temple worship—which is basically what we resurrected, thinking it was a good idea. But it was just as dead in Jesus' day as it is now!!

Once we can come to that point where we truly understand and comprehend that it is by the power of the living God we are meant to walk in and live in every single day, and that power is how we walk out "the Christian life", then phrases like "the baptism of the Holy Spirit" no longer confuse us, or threaten somebody who may have a religious bias—it simply becomes a matter of spiritual fact.

What the New Testament reiterates over and over and over throughout the Gospels and through every apostolic letter, is that it is the power of the Holy Spirit continually working in us that makes us the Church, that brings us to maturity in Jesus Christ, and that Empowers us to be spiritually effective ministers of the gospel of Jesus Christ, each and every one of us....

It is also the continual working of the power of the Holy Spirit that enables us to minister to one another, to edify one another, and to build one another up spiritually.

God Almighty never expected a single one of us to walk out a single day as a believer without the full, complete, and total empowerment of the Holy Spirit.

The New Testament that our persecuted apostles wrote to persecuted believers—all of whom were facing very real life or death possibilities, while living in environments that were completely hostile to Christianity—environments that were completely and totally hostile to them.

That New Testament that we have been reading forever with our Western mindset, our "land of the free home of the brave" mentality, *speaks of realities that we have continually overlooked, **because we have not been desperate enough....we have not been uncomfortable enough**,* to dig with our bare hands until we unearth the buried treasure right in front of us... The buried treasure in verses that we have read 100 times, but missed the otherworldly treasures freely given to us...

Let's look at a few passages, while paying special attention to the Greek wording, and what that means to you and me...

Acts 1:8 – "But you will receive **power** when the Holy Spirit comes upon you, and you will be My witnesses in Jerusalem, and in all Judea and Samaria, and to the ends of the earth."/ "Power"; dunamai; force; specially, miraculous power. / "Witnesses"; μάρτυρες (martyres) A witness (judicially) or figuratively (genitive case); by analogy, a 'martyr'.

Acts 2:4 – "And they were all filled with the Holy Spirit and began to speak in other tongues as the Spirit enabled them."

Acts 6:8 – "Now Stephen, who was full of grace and **power**, was performing great wonders and signs among the people." / dunamai; force;

specially, miraculous power/ δυνάμεως (dynameōs) The Greek word we get "Dynamo" from.

Romans 15:19 – "by the **power** of signs and wonders, and by the **power** of the Spirit of God. So from Jerusalem all the way around to Illyricum, I have fully proclaimed the gospel of Christ." / dunamai; force; specially, miraculous power/ δυνάμει (dynamei)

Romans 15:13 – "Now may the God of hope fill you with all joy and peace as you believe in Him, so that you may overflow with hope *by the* **power** *of the Holy Spirit."* / dunamai; force; specially, miraculous power/ δυνάμει (dynamei)

1 Corinthians 2:4 – "My message and my preaching were not with per-suasive words of wisdom, *but with a demonstration of the Spirit's* **power**" / dunamai; force; specially, miraculous power/ δυνάμει (dynamei)

1 Corinthians 4:20 – "For the kingdom of God is not a matter of talk, but of POWER." / dunamai; force; specially, miraculous power/ δυνάμει (dynamei)

The majority of so-called "preaching" in the West is just empty, pow-erless chatter....Completely Void of the Life-Giving, Captive Liberating, Bondage-Destroying, Demon-Smashing, Body-Healing, Mind & Soul-Restoring Power of God! *I pray in Jesus' mighty Name, dear Child of God, that YOU will become an Anointed Weapon of God in the hands of the Holy Spirit!!!*

I pray He will absolutely EXPLODE FORTH from your innermost being like a star going Super Nova, blasting all the strongholds of the enemy, absolutely SHATTERING EVERY CAGE of addiction, bondage, torment, depression, oppression, sickness & infirmity, Setting Captives Free into Glorious Heavenly Liberty in the Holy Spirit!!!!! In Jesus' Mighty Name!!!!

Philippians 4:13 – "I can do all things *through Christ who gives me* **strength**." / ἐνδυναμοῦντί (endynamounti)/ To fill with power, strengthen, make strong. From en and dunamoo; to empower. *The Life of Jesus Christ, administered to us by the indwelling Holy Spirit, is our spiritual dynamo!*

Ephesians 6:10 – "Finally, be strong in the Lord and in His mighty ***power***." / "be strong in the Lord"—*"To fill with power, strengthen, make strong. From en and dunamoo; to empower."* (same as Phil. 4:13) "in the power of His might"— ἰσχύος *(ischyos) 'power'* + κράτει *(kratei) 'Dominion'*; ***So, be strong in the Power that is derived from His Dominion!!!!*** Remember, we are Seated WITH Him in Heavenly Places, FAR ABOVE ALL principalities and powers (Ephesians 1:20,21; 2:6).

Ephesians 1:19— "and the surpassing greatness of His ***power*** to us who believe. These are in accordance with the working of His mighty strength" / ἰσχύος (ischyos) 'power' + κράτει (kratei) 'Dominion'/ "the working of His mighty strength", Greek, "kratous"=***The exercising of His Dominion Power on our behalf!!!***

Ephesians 3:7 – "I became a servant of this gospel by the gift of God's grace, given me through the working of His power."/ dunamai; force; specially, miraculous power/ δυνάμει (dynamei)

Once again, the Dominating Spiritual theme of the New Testament is absolutely, unequivocally, undeniably a matter of Living a God-Empowered Life as a Temple of the Holy Spirit, and Not a religious life "powered" by "Trying to be a good Christian", "Trying to please God", and "Trying to", and More "Trying to", until you completely exhaust yourself & fall flat on your face.

For the Spirit-baptized Child of God, you are now able to Boldly declare, it is God ("Is"; "presently, ongoing") Who works in ME ("Works"; ἐνεργῶν (energōn) "active Divine energy") to will and to act on behalf of His good purpose!

Ephesians 3:20 – "Now to Him who is able to do immeasurably more than all we ask or imagine, according to His power that is at work within us"/

dunamai; force; specially, miraculous power/ δυνάμει (dynamei)/ "at work within us"; ἐνεργουμένην (energoumenēn); to energize actively.

Colossians 1:29 – "To this end I also labor, striving with all His energy working powerfully within me." / ἐνεργουμένην (energoumenēn); dunamai; force; specially, miraculous power/ δυνάμει (dynamei) "Laboring by being energized by His divine power".

So, right there we have 13 to 16 verses from the New Testament that we have read forever in the King James—but when we take a very close look at the Greek language, a whole new world is opened up to us.

The King James language—poetic as it may be—has concealed the true spiritual power of these passages! We have read those passages probably hundreds of times never realizing what we're missing—And that's only 14 verses out of the New Testament!

So before I go any further, let me wholeheartedly exhort you, dear reader, to take the time to look up every verse in the New Testament wherever you see the words "power", "authority", and look closely at all of the verses that have to do with God working in us.

What you will always see, as bright as the noonday sun, is the reality that we are meant to live by a power that is beyond this earth….that is beyond human ability, and that is part of the Kingdom that we will inherit.

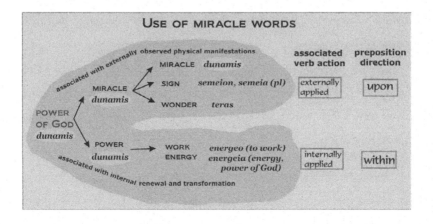

CHAPTER 10

TEMPLES OF THE HOLY SPIRIT VS. STRONGHOLDS OF THE RELIGIOUS SPIRIT

The Lord gave me a prophetic word on September 11, 1993.

It was a word that He spoke to my spirit personally and very directly;

"I have broken the yokes of men and tradition off of you. I have removed the burden from your shoulder, and set you free to walk in My Spirit. Just as I have broken the yoke off of you, so you will do for others—you will clearly see and discern the yokes of men and speak against them and destroy them, and lead many into liberty".

And I would have to say in looking back over my life, that the religious spirit is the one demonic stronghold I have had the most direct confrontation and battles with, almost all of them being within the religious church structure.

But in all honesty, the greatest source of the heaviness I feel, is the unspeakable awareness I carry, that the Holy Spirit's voice is being heard by so very, very few....

And without any exaggeration whatsoever, I feel the Holy Spirit's agony because of the religious multitudes who don't want to hear His voice, who don't think it's "necessary"....I feel His heartache over those who are choosing their own doom....The casualties are going to be catastrophic.

This is a spiritual burden that I feel and carry every single day and night....It is an awareness that never shuts off, and I feel overwhelmed so much of the time, because I'm only one man—what can I change?

And an online confrontation last night only intensified all of this for me.

Someone responded to a post I made a couple of weeks back, and he was clearly not someone acquainted with the Holy Spirit—in fact, he made it quite clear that he was not of that persuasion.

My response was to share the link to my podcast, letting him know that all of his questions could be answered through those.

Long story short, he messaged me privately and said he had some honest questions, but he also was very clear concerning his present religious mindset.

I went to bed with a very heavy heart last night, endlessly pondering this young man's words, and the religious spirits quite obviously coloring his beliefs.

Today when I woke up, the heaviness was still there...It was like a very intense burden that I simply didn't know where to set it down.

Now, just to clarify, this was not a simple matter of "feeling discouraged" or down—it was a burden in the spirit that I simply did not know how to resolve.

I know that those of you whom the Lord has used in intercession will understand this.

Many times, when encountering a situation of a heavy spiritual nature, it is simply something you will have to carry within yourself until the Holy Spirit brings a solution or an answer to light. Sometimes, you're just to simply intercede and pray in the spirit till the burden lifts, and you know the Holy Spirit has taken care of it.

As I have spent time this week walking and praying in our home and interceding, the Holy Spirit shook me to my core with this thought—The Westernized religious system outwardly calling itself the church, is potentially our greatest mission field.

There are multitudes of professing believers, engaged in all the religious machinery, waiting to be set free from the shackles of religious bondage and religious blindness—And they need our intercession; they need our Spirit-empowered ministry to them, even though for the most part they don't know that—And I make that statement based on over 43 years of personal, first-hand experience.

The Scripture says, "Now the Lord is the Spirit, *and where the Spirit of the Lord is, there is freedom*" (2 Corinthians 3:17), and I can honestly say without exception, *I have never met a religious professing believer without the Holy Spirit, who had real spiritual freedom and liberty in their life.*

In fact, what led me to being open to the baptism of the Holy Spirit was encountering believers who walked in and demonstrated tremendous liberty and joy in the Spirit.

I encountered them as customers on a job where I worked at in 1982, and just the radiance in their faces told me they had something I desperately needed, but didn't have.

It was the religious, joyless, ritualistic professing Christians at a huge church in Jacksonville who tried to dissuade me from making such a decision.

Most of that came from the pastor and his wife. They actually tried to warn me frantically on many occasions to "avoid those people because they're dangerous", and my thought was, *"I'd rather avoid You people because you just make me more depressed"*.

In fact, it was the spirit of religious bondage and deadness that filled the huge first Baptist mausoleum in downtown Jacksonville that made my

own spiritual condition worse, and I only felt relief when I stayed away from it.

I decided in November 1982 to make a clean break from the dead religious system that was only serving to worsen my own spiritual battles.

In my heart, I felt that I would only find spiritual freedom if I broke away from that system, and gave God the time to work things out in my own circumstances—Which He did, by bringing the Spirit-filled customers into my workplace a couple of months later.

I think there's a real lesson for us to learn here:

Religious spirits only serve to exacerbate the spiritual battles professing believers are already going through—and after 39 years as a Spirit-filled believer (with five years before that being a believer without the Holy Spirit), I can speak to both sides, abundantly so—and I can tell you from very personal experience, that the only antidote to religious spirits, is a spirit of humility. The only way out of bondage to religious spirits, is to humble oneself completely and totally—beginning with humbling your mind—to God Almighty himself. And that is the most formidable battle to be won when setting someone free from this bondage—Because it is impossible to set someone free who does not believe they are in bondage to begin with.

In over 39 years experience in dealing up close and personal with religious spirits, it's very interesting for me to note that in all of the years where I have encountered hundreds of individuals who are against the baptism of the Holy Spirit, the gifts of the Holy Spirit, etc., *it is very revealing to note that all of these individuals responded in almost exactly the same way in every instance.*

That is because the religious spirit is very set in how it operates—It fights to justify and defend its dogma, because dogma is it's LIFE; Dogma is all that matters to it.

That is precisely why, even though Jesus did such good in healing people in the synagogue and casting demons out of people in the synagogue and setting them free, the Pharisees responded only with murder and anger in their hearts.

They did not care that people were being set free and ministered to—what they were enraged about was that their dogma was being challenged and offended. They did not care about anyone's quality of life improving; their dogma was all that mattered—it was their end-all and be-all.

That is what makes the religious spirit so evil and so difficult to break as a stronghold. Someone with a religious spirit has a very determined wild dog inside them that will bite the hand that reaches out to save them.

They will fight to maintain their set, carved-in-stone mindset. It does not matter what the real facts are; it doesn't matter if you parade 100 people in front of them who have been healed and delivered and set free.....it doesn't register with them at all. That is precisely why Jesus said to them, you cross the ocean to make one convert, and then make them twice the son of hell that you are.

The Tactics of religious spirits as revealed in the Gospels and the New Testament are (and in no particular order):

- Religious spirits seek to draw you into an argument of their own design—Their intent in doing so is to further justify themselves; to justify their rebellion and their lovelessness (Matthew 22:15-39; Luke 16:15);

- They esteem the things of men higher than the things of God (Luke 16:15);

- They esteem the praise of man more than the praise of God (John 12:43, John 5:44);

- They value outward religious appearance and conformity more than inward Spiritual reality (Luke 11:39, Luke 18:9);

- They insist that their rules regulations and traditions be obeyed as though they were from God himself;

- They equate adherence to and obedience to their rules, as being equivalent to obedience to God himself;

- They detest any spirituality that requires a true humbling of their minds—Their intellect is their god, and their warped grasp of scripture is the badge they wear;

- They detest spiritual liberty, because they so highly prize religious control and conformity;

- In Galatians 3:1-3, the apostle Paul equates the religious spirit with witchcraft, it's goal being to pull believers out of operating in the Spirit, and into operating in the strength of their own flesh;

- The reason the religious spirit is so evil and hateful, is because it esteems everything that the sacrifice of Jesus was meant to destroy—Jesus paid the price for our sins so that we could have a new heart of flesh, under the control and direction of the Holy Spirit.

By satanic contrast, the religious spirit wants control over you based on outward conformity to rules and regulations and demands, that it makes equal to God himself.

The religious spirit, at its most devious and vile, promises "a form of godliness", while allowing Self to remain in control and on the throne of your heart, refusing to be submitted to God and His Spirit.

THAT makes the religious spirit the most hateful, evil, wicked spirit of ALL of them. Just look at the gospels, folks! Which demonic spirit was it that tried to kill Jesus, slander him, and rallied for His crucifixion???? THAT is the nature of the religious spirit, and you must keep that in mind every single time you are dealing with it in operation within someone else!

You are dealing with a very deceptive, manipulative satanic stronghold, that will resist any and every attempt to get it to humble itself to the Word of God—it will fight to remain in control of the person in whom it operates.

If there's a positive side to this at all, *it is Spiritual Warfare 101 with a textbook example of how a demonic stronghold operates*; all of its qualities, and what it will take to dislodge it. In this case, nothing but intercession, laser-sharp spiritual discernment, and above all else, staying in the Spirit while you are dealing with the person under the religious spirits influence, and having prayer back up so that the scales may be removed from this person's eyes, and they may "recover themselves out of the snare of the devil by whom they've been taken captive at his will". A textbook example of deliverance from this spirit would be Saul of Tarsus, knocked off of his horse by the appearance of Jesus Christ—Because that is what it took to deliver him!

Do not let someone under that spirit cause you to waste hours and hours debating with them, *because that's what the religious spirit feeds on, and it will wear you out.*

If you treat it first and foremost as a demonic spirit, then you won't give it the time of day; you will try to help that person understand this is what they are dealing with.

One key scripture to keep in mind when dealing with this spirit:

"But He gives us more grace. This is why it says: "God opposes the proud, but gives grace to the humble." (James 4:6). *The Devil's not going to flee from anyone who is operating in pride as he does—without humility, you cannot expect any deliverance)*

"Therefore, get rid of all moral filth and every expression of evil, and humbly accept the word planted in you, which can save your souls." (James 1:21). This is a key scripture to meditate on, understanding that **it is in the soul realm that this stronghold is lodged.** Understand that *religious pride is the most spiritually destructive weapon the enemy uses against the people of God.*

"The weapons of our warfare are not the weapons of the world. Instead, they have divine power to demolish strongholds. We tear down arguments and every presumption set up against the knowledge of God;

and we take captive every thought to make it obedient to Christ. " (2 Corinthians 10:4,5)

"Is not My word like fire," declares the LORD, "and like a hammer that smashes a rock?" (Jeremiah 23:29)

"In truthful speech and in the power of God; with the weapons of righteousness in the right hand and in the left" (2 Corinthians 6:7)

"He changes the times and seasons; He removes kings and establishes them. He gives wisdom to the wise and knowledge to the discerning." (Daniel 2.21)

One other vital thing to keep in mind when dealing with the religious spirit is that Jesus equates it to murder.

Remember how Cain killed Abel over his OFFERING???

So many times those with the strongly entrenched religious spirit actually manifest hatred for anyone who does not agree with them, or anyone who tries to put forth a different point of view.

That is the spirit of murder, which is attached to the religious spirit— ***especially when it is heavily entrenched and has already established control over others, such as in a church hierarchy or something similar.***

This is why it is so important for us to spend much time praying in the spirit, worshipping, and meditating on the Word, because unless your spirit man is strongly built up and fortified, don't even waste your time on this demon—you will not have what it takes.

Jesus had to be anointed by the Holy Spirit before He ever confronted these spirits head on, and that alone should be hugely indicative of the demonic power of these spirits.

Nowhere in scripture does it indicate that Jesus ever went head-to-head with the demonized religious leaders of His day, until after the Holy Spirit had descended upon Him at the river Jordan.

Our example for this would be, of course, Jesus Himself, in every situation where the Pharisees and the other demonized religious leaders tried to entrap Him with questions and situations devised specifically to attack His ministry.

Another New Testament example which correlates with our walk in the Holy Spirit would be Steven, when speaking to the religious rulers—it says he was filled with the Holy Spirit and boldness (Acts 7:55).

I don't think there's an example of confronting the spirit in the flesh or in the natural, and at this point we should all understand the reason why that is so.

"But God chose the foolish things of the world to shame the wise; God chose the weak things of the world to shame the strong. God chose the lowly things of this world and the despised things—and the things that are not—to nullify the things that are, so that no one may boast before him."

(1 Corinthians 1:27-29)

1st Corinthians 12 & 14 show that *the gifts & operations of the Holy Spirit are intertwined with the very existence of the Church*......as long as the Church exists here on earth, the gifts & functions of the Holy Spirit are an expected part of the life of the Church.....and *THIS is the Primary target of satan and his hierarchy of religious spirits; the ongoing Government of the Holy Spirit within His Church. And really, there are only TWO sources of governmental direction for the Church; the ongoing influence, direction and guidance of the Holy Spirit, or that of human self-will, which gives way to the religious spirit.*

The religious spirit is Satan's counterfeit for the government of the Holy Spirit—there is absolutely NO "middle ground", no "neutral zone", no "gray area"; you are either under the guidance of the Holy Spirit, or the influence of Self.

That is precisely why passages such as Romans 12 are of such primary & central importance to the life of every believer—

"Therefore I urge you, brothers, on account of God's mercy, to offer your bodies as living sacrifices, holy and pleasing to God, which is your spiritual service of worship. Do not be conformed to this world, but be transformed by the renewing of your mind. Then you will be able to test and approve what is the good, pleasing, and perfect will of God." (Romans 12:1,2).

There are two classes of believers according to God's Word: those who have the Spirit, and those who are without the Spirit.

This is a Primary & Basic reality addressed by the Apostles Themselves, so therefore, it is NOT something we are free to disregard or minimize. We have covered this very thing in previous chapters, but I will touch on it again quickly, because it is a pivotal issue that cannot be ignored.

In Acts chapter 8, Peter and John go to Samaria where the gospel has been preached with signs and wonders following by Philip (which, by the way, fits the New Testament pattern laid down by Jesus Himself in Mark 16:17), so right away we see that *Jesus' stated pattern for Spirit-empowered ministry is foundational to the Church.*

Also foundational to the Church was continuing obedience to the words of Jesus Christ, Head of His church, when He said, "And behold, I am sending the promise of My Father upon you. But remain in the city until you have been clothed with power from on high." (Luke 24:49).

That was Precisely the mission that Peter and John were on when they went to Samaria, and laid hands on the new believers to receive the baptism of the Holy Spirit—something that was so dramatically displayed, that Simon the sorcerer wanted to buy that power with money (Acts 8:18,19).

The manifestation of the baptism of the Holy Spirit on the Samaritan believers was not something that happened quietly in a corner somewhere.

And in spite of what religious mindsets dare to think in minimizing this, I will shout it from the rooftops, that this was Apostolically Enforced, and we do not have the right to move the boundary markers that Jesus and the apostles laid down for the church in all generations, in all geographical locations and times.

The apostle Paul also reinforces this when he comes upon some new believers in Acts chapter 19 (Acts 19:1-6). *And in every instance where the believers receive the baptism of the Holy Spirit, it states that they prophesied and spoke in tongues—that was the clear proof given from Heaven that these believers have now officially become temples of the Holy Spirit, the third Person of the Eternal Godhead*—And may God soundly convict and rebuke those who speak against the Holy Spirit—in the words of Jesus, "Whoever speaks a word against the Son of Man will be forgiven, *but whoever speaks against the Holy Spirit will not be forgiven, either in this age or in the one to come.*" (Matthew 12:32).

I pray that God will strike the Western church with a holy fear so strong and so deep, that no one will be able to shake it off or sleep for months! We have disdained the things of God; we have spoken irreverently, mockingly, and spitefully against the holiest things of the living God, and we haven't lost any sleep over it—all while judgement is rumbling at our doorstep...And at this point, I do not believe that judgement will be averted at all.

Time is of the essence to get aboard the ark of the Holy Spirit in total abject humility of heart and submission. *The Western church is completely void of true godly fear, which to me is a very terrifying place to be.*

I don't fear totalitarian, antichrist governments; *I fear a Western church void of the fear of God!*

Trying to explain the things of the Spirit to a man without the Spirit, is like trying to describe the ocean to a man who has always lived in the desert. Perhaps he has read books about the ocean, maybe even seen pictures of the ocean, but he's never swam in it, never felt it's salt spray or heard its waves...He might even think it a foolish thing to try and make the effort to even get to the ocean...

But what he doesn't see, is that there's only so far you can go in the desert....in the ocean, you can go Anywhere....And with far more ease than you can travel in a desert....

The apostle Paul made this distinction when he said, "The natural man does not accept the things that come from the Spirit of God. For they are foolishness to him, and he cannot understand them, because they are spiritually discerned." (1st Cor. 2:14)

Now, notice that Paul did NOT say, "The person without **Christ**". He said very clearly, "The person *without the Spirit*".

When attempting to speak to someone who is without the Spirit, concerning the things of the Spirit, you need to try to till the soil a little bit before you start sowing the Word...you Know you're going to encounter rocky ground and shallow ground, so try to prep the soil by removing some of the rocks and digging a couple of furrows...

Since we already know from the Word itself that the natural mind does not receive the things of the Spirit (1 Corinthians 2:14), that indicates rocky, hard, obstinate ground that needs to be dealt with Before sowing the Word.

If possible—and usually I would do this only when such a person has asked me to comment on the subject—Brief that individual right up front, explaining to them that first of all, nothing that you are about to say or share is intended to deliberately offend them.

However, their mind is going to naturally be offended as an internal reaction to the words of the Spirit.

Let them know that the Word of God already states that *as long as someone is in their natural, human thinking, they are going to be offended by the things of the Spirit; they are going to see the things of the Spirit as foolishness.*

A perfect example of this is when Jesus began teaching and saying, "So Jesus said to them, "Truly, truly, I tell you, unless you eat the flesh and drink the blood of the Son of Man, you have no life in you." (John 6:53). Naturally, those who were listening all heard it with their natural human mind; **they did not have the capacity to interpret Jesus's words spiritually, and so they were hugely offended.**

Now, watch how the Holy Spirit dealt with *the offence of the natural mind* in another situation.

In John chapter 1, one of Jesus' disciples, Philip, excitedly approaches his brother Nathaniel, saying, "Come and see, we have found the Messiah, Jesus of Nazareth." Immediately, Nathaniel's prejudiced mindset is revealed, because he said, "Can anything Good come from Nazareth?"

Let's look at the full story.

"The next day Jesus decided to set out for Galilee. Finding Philip, He told him, "Follow Me." Now Philip was from Bethsaida, the same town as Andrew and Peter.

"Philip found Nathanael and told him, "We have found the One Moses wrote about in the Law, the One the prophets foretold—Jesus of Nazareth, the son of Joseph."

"Can anything good come from Nazareth?" Nathanael asked.

"Come and see," said Philip.

When Jesus saw Nathanael approaching, He said of him, "Here is a true Israelite, in whom there is no deceit."

"How do You know me?" Nathanael asked.

Jesus replied, "Before Philip called you, I saw you under the fig tree."

"Rabbi," Nathanael answered, "You are the Son of God! You are the King of Israel!"

Jesus said to him, "Do you believe just because I told you I saw you under the fig tree? You will see greater things than these." Then He declared,

"Truly, truly, I tell you, you will all see heaven open and the angels of God ascending and descending on the Son of Man." (John 1:43-51)

Now watch this:

The Holy Spirit disarmed the stronghold in Nathaniel's natural mind by giving Jesus a vision and a word of knowledge regarding Nathaniel, which he speaks to Nathaniel upon their meeting.

The Holy Spirit reveals His intimate, personal knowledge of who Nathaniel is as a person, which dissolves the mental stronghold of prejudice, and opens his heart to an intimate relationship with Jesus through the Holy Spirit.

THAT is operating in the Spirit, and not in the natural!

That is why we must not deal with strongholds in others in the flesh, or in our own reasoning—because then we're just "fighting fire with fire" (or, in this case, flesh with flesh). *Only as we walk in, talk in, and minister in and respond in the power and influence of the Holy Spirit, do strongholds become powerless and dislodged.* **As a result, the stronghold in Nathaniel's mind of racial origin was replaced by a spiritual revelation of who Jesus is—a revelation that is personal to Nathaniel.**

This is Holy Spirit 101, class.

Just because someone calls themselves a 'Christian', does not mean that they will Not be offended by the things of the Spirit. If they have not been baptized in the Holy Spirit, the chances of them being offended by the Word of God are pretty good.

Most believers who have not been baptized in the Spirit are very conditioned to think in religious terms, because that is how their mind works—the things of God have to be compartmentalized somehow, and without the Spirit, they have to resort to religious thinking, which is not the same at all as Spiritual thinking.

In fact, religious thinking is a horrible substitute for spiritual thinking.

Religious thinking likes to masquerade as spiritual thinking, and it likes to Believe that it's spiritual thinking, which just makes things worse. It makes things worse for the person with the religious thinking, because they already think they're seeing correctly—and then you come along with your spiritual thinking, and they think You're the one that's nuts.

That is the power of the religious stronghold, because it creates such a powerful blindness in those who are bound by it.

"Are you so foolish? After starting in the Spirit, are you now finishing in the flesh?" (Galatians 3:3)

The apostle Paul dealt with the same stronghold, just in different clothes—Which makes perfect sense, **because this religious stronghold has to adapt itself to the culture that it is operating in, in order to insulate itself from being detected and challenged.**

Remember, anything that opposes or resists the knowledge of God is a spiritual stronghold, demonic in nature, and empowered by corresponding principalities and powers that work to make sure that their strongholds are as embedded as possible in human culture and human natural thinking, so that they are never dealt with directly as demonic strongholds.

But Paul the apostle said, "The weapons of our warfare are not the weapons of the world. Instead, they have divine power to demolish strongholds." (2 Corinthians 10:4).

So, when attempting to speak with someone about the things of the Spirit—someone who is already inoculated against the things of the Spirit—you're dealing with the person, *AND, you're dealing with the spirits trying to keep that person bound and blind.*

If you go into it as though you are just having a one on one conversation with another flesh & blood person, you are fighting a losing battle.

You Must remember that you are walking onto the enemies territory, regardless of whether or not that person calls themselves a Christian—in their minds, they are still blinded to the power and life of the Holy Spirit of God.

I am speaking 1000% from personal, direct experience.

I spent my first five years as a believer without the Holy Spirit, and it was horrible—and yet, when confronted with the precious baptism of the Holy Spirit, all of my claws and bristles came out, because I thought that I was being attacked with a demonic teaching.

Thankfully the brother trying to help me was profoundly humble and completely undefensive, which is why when God finally broke my religious pride and humbled me, I went back to this brother asking him for prayer.

But God had to shatter the demonic strongholds in my mind and in my life, and bring me to a place of childlike humility.

So I am living proof that the religious strongholds can be broken in someone's mind, and they can be awakened to their desperate need of the Holy Spirit—but until they come to the place where they feel their true, honest, desperate need, they will not budge.

Another thing to keep firmly in mind, is that when you are dealing with the strongholds keeping this person from the knowledge of the Holy Spirit, you are dealing with spirits that want to keep them blind to the Holy Spirit, *because they don't want them delivered either.*

In so many cases where spiritual strongholds have someone highly resistant to and defensive toward the things of the Holy Spirit, those same strongholds are trying to maintain their beachhead in that person's personality, because they've been there for a very long time—spirits that have been with that individual since before they got saved, and they don't want to come out—And they certainly don't want the Holy Spirit as a roommate!!!

Again, I am speaking 1000% from personal experience; because it was only After I was baptized in the Holy Spirit that I myself was able to get deliverance from spirits of fear, anxiety, etc.

This is where we come full circle to the understanding of what God's Word declares: "For though we live in the flesh, we do not wage war according to the flesh" (2 Corinthians 10:3); "He has rescued us from the dominion of darkness and brought us into the kingdom of His beloved Son" (Colossians 1:13). We are in a spiritual realm, not fighting flesh and blood on any level whatsoever.

What we have to understand is that for those who resist the things of the Holy Spirit, *the spirits keeping them bound are using their own mind against them, by using their mind to resist the Holy Spirit; to argue against Him; to reason against Him, because they want to keep that person bound no matter what it takes!*

If we can arm ourselves with the spiritual understanding, that behind those religious strongholds that are designed to keep us from advancing against them, a spiritual battle is raging inside of that individual we are approaching—spiritual battles that they've never been able to get the victory over, and they know it! If we can put our finger on That, then they might begin to see their real enemy is not US, but the entities behind the spiritual battles they have been facing.

For me, I already Knew I was fighting spiritual entities that I had no power over. God had finally brought me to a place where I understood very clearly that the nature of my battles were demons, not myself, and that on my own, I had no power to overcome them.

However, that was apparently not enough for me to receive the baptism of the Holy Spirit, because I also had religious strongholds in my mind that had to be overcome.

*It was not until the Holy Spirit put His finger on my **religious pride** that any real change came—And that is the thing about the Holy Spirit;* Jesus said, "But if I drive out demons *by the finger of God,* then the kingdom of God has come upon you." (Luke 11:20), and in another passage referring to the same exact event, Jesus says, "But if I drive out demons by the Spirit of God, then the kingdom of God has come upon you." (Matthew 12:28).

So the Spirit of God is "the finger of God"; the Holy Spirit goes straight to the very heart and source of every situation, every spiritual condition.

This is the Perfect place to segue into our focus on Believers as the Temple of the Holy Spirit.

By taking a very detailed look at the enemy's counterfeit (the religious spirit) and how it works against God's purposes & against God's people, we have gained a much clearer spiritual perspective on what it means to walk in the Spirit, the extremely vital importance of understanding the spiritual realm, and the spiritual forces that oppose us.

What is one distinctive feature of the child of God?

Walking in the fear of the Lord—an ongoing attitude of reverence and submission to the Spirit. "Do not let your heart envy sinners, but always continue in the fear of the LORD." (Proverbs 23:17).

By stark contrast, someone operating by a religious stronghold is self-willed, presumptious.

When you contrast the two, it becomes very easy to see what the qualities of a Spirit-led child of God are, versus those who are not led by the Spirit, and those who oppose the Spirit.

Furthermore, I believe this topic to be profoundly relevant, and even pivotal, to the very moment in time we find ourselves living in.

Many years ago, I was listening to Derek Prince, and he made a very prophetic declaration regarding the Endtimes.

He said that there was going to come a polarization between two opposing spiritual forces—the forces of God in the true church, and the forces of Satan—And from where I stand right now, I would say he was speaking precisely by the Spirit.

And for all my readers, I honestly do not believe that there is a more vital subject for each of you to spend time studying intensely and meditating on: the subject of walking in the Spirit, and what it truly means for you personally to be a temple of the Holy Spirit.

I believe the spiritual survival of many is going to depend on having an intimate heart understanding of this.

Now, I want to spend just a little more time focusing on walking in the fear of the Lord, as an ongoing attitude of reverence and submission to the Holy Spirit. This was Foundational in the life of believers in the Book of Acts, and I believe it MUST become Foundational once again—and for the vast segment of the Religious professing Western "church", I don't believe we will see that happen, short of nationwide catastrophes driving them to their knees.

Here are some Scriptures that I myself have been meditating on:

"The LORD is exalted, for He dwells on high; He has filled Zion with justice and righteousness. He will be the sure foundation for your times, *a storehouse of salvation, wisdom, and knowledge*. The fear of the LORD is Zion's treasure." (Isaiah 33:5,6)

Do we long to see the Lord's righteous judgement on our behalf? Do we want to experience the security that comes from God being our very Foundation for Life & Eternity? Do we long to experience His Storehouse of Abundant Salvation, Wisdom, and Spiritual knowledge that will strengthen & sustain us? *Then the thing we must treasure Most is the Fear of the Lord, because That is the Key to His Storehouse.*

"He who fears the LORD is secure in confidence, and his children shall have a place of refuge." (Proverbs 14:26)

"The Spirit of the LORD will rest on Him—the Spirit of wisdom and understanding, the Spirit of counsel and strength, the Spirit of knowledge and fear of the LORD." (Isaiah 11:2)

I think this verse abundantly speaks for itself, as to the Benefits of walking in the Fear of the Lord—being Baptized in the Holy Spirit is to receive the fullness of the Spirit of the Lord, who imparts to us in our inner man the spirit of wisdom and understanding, the spirit of counsel and might, the spirit of knowledge and of the fear of the LORD.

No longer are we limited to walking in our own finite human reasoning, limited to only the knowledge we can gain through our 5 senses, but we are now able to receive HIS counsel, HIS wisdom, HIS understanding. We are able to receive HIS spiritual might & power in spiritual warfare & battle.

Psalm 27:1; "Of David. The LORD is my light and my salvation—whom shall I fear? The LORD is the stronghold of my life—whom shall I dread?"

Psalm 28:8; "The LORD is the strength of His people, a stronghold of salvation for His anointed."

Psalm 140:7; "O GOD the Lord, the strength of my salvation, You shield my head in the day of battle."

Proverbs 19:23; "The fear of the LORD leads to life, that one may rest content, without visitation from harm."

Psalm 34:10; "Young lions go lacking and hungry, but those who seek the LORD lack no good thing."

I don't believe Western churchianity will ever admit that, for the most part, *it's insistence on being able to grasp everything concerning the Word of God & the Spirit of God with their finite human mind* **is a direct result of the Fall, and Satan's offer to make us wise apart from God**—*Because after well over 30 some odd years of battling with religious spirits in the minds of professing Christians in the West, I am convinced that the nature of this battle is completely spiritual, and finds its source in that one event.*

Adam and Eve were seduced by the offer of attaining God-like wisdom apart from God Himself, and that has been part of our fallen nature ever since: but we've never come to the place, that I've ever heard of, where we've acknowledged and admitted it.

There has never been an instance where someone who is born again, suddenly has a completely spiritual, renewed mind; **renewing the mind is a process**. And apart from the direct activity of the Holy Spirit, renewing one's mind is going to be a really challenging prospect.

Without the baptism and the indwelling of the Holy Spirit, you are left leaning on your own intellect to process and grasp of the Word of God—and since your mind is not fully renewed yet, you are using your unrenewed, fallen mind to try to grasp spiritual truth, and your fallen, unrenewed mind is the ground upon which religious spirits build their strongholds. That's why someone who is a professing Christian is still far from Thinking like a new creation.

A Final Word Regarding Religious Spirits

I feel compelled to add just a little bit more in the way of context to this chapter regarding encountering religious spirits, because I have had so many sincere, God-seeking believers reach out to me over the last few years seeking spiritual counsel and help in this area.

The common battle that these precious brothers and sisters face, in pursuing a truly Spirit-led, New Testament-based relationship with the Lord, is legalistic, religious persecution and shaming from those in the institutional system. It is such a brutal, relentless spiritual assault that many of them end up caving into the spiritual bullying, and they simply acquiesce and slink back into the deadness of the religious tomb they just left.

So, I am including a little more revelation on the subject that goes right to the heart of the spiritual battle—a battle that is against your mind and emotions, which is exactly where the enemy sends his sharpest arrows.

Now, I am arming you with spiritual information that will equip you to protect yourself from the enemies **slander, manipulation, and intimidation.**

Religious spirits not only intimidate, accuse, undermine and belittle—they also insinuate, just as Satan did through Peter, when he appeared to speak sympathetically to Jesus regarding His going to suffer and die in Jerusalem. "Peter took Him aside and began to rebuke Him. 'Far be it from You, Lord!', he said. 'This shall never happen to You!' But Jesus turned and said to Peter, 'Get behind Me, Satan! You are a stumbling block to Me. For you do not have in mind the things of God, but the things of men.' (Matthew 16:22,23).

They come alongside you as a friend, because they know a direct assault would be too obvious—but if they appear to actually be sympathetic to you, then you will lower your defenses, lower your guard, and their sweet, kind words of insinuation will slip through your armor, and cause you to doubt your own purpose.

Now, THAT is the religious spirit in "stealth mode". Satan did not use the religious leaders against Jesus in this instance; he did not use some crowd of haters; **he moved in through someone who was closest to Jesus.**

Notice Jesus didn't rebuke Peter, because He knew he wasn't dealing with flesh and blood human beings—He was dealing with Satan.

Likewise, those in bondage to the religious system do not perceive what powers and spirits they are being used by, and when we speak against or confront those powers, those who do not perceive the system for what it is believe we are accusers, when we are actually exposing the satanic system for what it is, and working to set people free.

Understand THIS: Satan has invested much into the system, and he does not want it being dismantled by anyone, and he will do everything in his power to stop those who are working to dismantle it and expose it—Because he does not want his captives going free.

However, I am an ambassador of the Holy Spirit, as are hundreds of thousands of others, and *we are working in the Spirit to bring others into spiritual liberty.*

If you look at the overall ministry of Paul, it was a ministry of bringing sons and daughters into spiritual liberty, and teaching them how to WALK in spiritual liberty, and how to MAINTAIN spiritual liberty—the letter to the Galatians is an excellent example of that battle.

This is why Satan fights so hard to keep his counterfeit religious system intact; because it is a system of religious bondage and captivity, and what was the Holy Spirit anointing Jesus to do???? To set the captives free, and to destroy the works of the evil one.

So if anyone attempts to insinuate that you are working against *individuals*, they simply do not perceive the principalities and powers behind the scenes operating the system, and they do not understand the battle at stake.

We live in a time where so many in the religious system have been conditioned to believe that only "soft words" are from God, that only speaking soft things is what believers do—well, that would rule out most all of the New Testament in that case, because Jesus's words against the religious system are not kind, were not soft, and the apostle Paul and Peter's words against the religious system were likewise very direct, blunt, and to the point. Likewise the apostle Jude and the apostle John— these men of God saw the religious system and the spirit operating it, and THAT is what they were dealing with head on....And we are in a moment of time right now where dealing with it in any other way will not do one bit of good. We are living in a time right now where principalities and powers must be exposed for what they are, and their works must be exposed for what they are as well. The eternal destiny of many is at stake, and that is what must be our motivation....

CHAPTER 11

TEMPLES OF THE HOLY SPIRIT, PART 2: DEVELOPING & WALKING IN A SPIRITUAL SELF IMAGE

In Part 1 of Temples of the Holy Spirit, we addressed Public Enemy Number One, the Religious spirit. Just to reiterate, this stronghold is the primary enemy of the true body of Christ.

I firmly believe, due to the vastness of its operation and the long history of its opposition to the kingdom of God here on earth, I am fully persuaded that it is not just a system of strongholds, but it is indeed a global principality, with powers of darkness operating underneath it worldwide.

This is the primary spiritual enemy of the global Body of Christ, and it is as ruthless as it is relentless—And if you are determined to grow as a Spirit-filled believer, you will have to be on guard against it and be in continual opposition to it.

So, before I move on to the more positive side of being Temples of the Holy Spirit, I feel it's very important to touch on a couple of additional things.

*Understanding **how** the religious spirit operates is only one side of the coin.*

The other side is understanding how to minister to those who have been affected by that spirit or harmed by it. Having a clear spiritual understanding of how religious spirits operate is to protect ourselves, but we must also be in a position to minister to those who have been under its influence.

One sign that a person is afflicted by or under the power of a religious spirit is condemnation—a feeling of never being able to measure up to God's standards, of never being deserving enough of His love; unable to have a true and abiding sense of God's nearness, always trying to figure out how to qualify for God's love and acceptance.

One way this can come about is by being in close proximity to religious leaders who constantly make you feel like you have to perform in order to earn God's love, or you have to meet certain ongoing religious criteria in order to be accepted by Him.

This can even take place when the head of a household imposes undue religious demands upon family members, thus having the same effect.

A spirit that works quite often in conjunction with condemnation is legalism, especially in a religious setting or home environment.

Romans 8:15-Functioning under a religious spirit can also lead one to being in a spirit of fear and bondage. "For you did not receive a spirit of slavery *that returns you to fear*, but you received the Spirit of sonship, by whom we cry, "Abba! Father!""

So from this we can clearly see again, the division & distinction God makes between the operation of the Holy Spirit, and the operation of the Religious spirit—One brings you into freedom and Sonship, the other one brings you into bondage and slavery.

Thank God, He Always makes the clear distinction between what sets us free and keeps us free, and that which would seek to enslave us!

The religious system of the West is largely a system of bondage to the doctrines of men and slavery to religious rituals, in direct opposition to the Holy Spirit by whom we would walk in freedom.

He wants us to walk free as sons and daughters, not religious slaves.

And guess what? The good news is, we individually have the God-given power to choose!

And with all of the above mentioned, once again we can clearly see that **the casualty of a religious spirit is always personal spiritual liberty, or a lack of feeling truly spiritually free.**

The keyword for every Christian to keep in the very front of their thinking and believing every single minute of every single day is the word "liberty".

The other word for "liberty" would be "freedom".

So, two scriptures I would like you to keep in mind on a daily basis, if you are having any struggles in this area:

"It is for freedom that Christ has set us free. Stand firm, then, and do not be encumbered once more by a yoke of slavery." (Galatians 5:1).

So, your freedom in Christ through the Spirit, according to this verse, is something that you have to be vigilant to protect and maintain, and not be brought into bondage by any contrary spirits or mindsets.

The professing Western church is completely overrun by spirits of religious bondage. I wouldn't be surprised if those spirits number into the millions.

Spirits of bondage to particular denominations; bondage to a specific day of worship; Bondage to dozens and dozens of doctrinal "isms"; Bondage to the clergy/laity system, and too many more to discuss here.

So I feel it is perfectly safe to say without any exaggeration whatsoever that if you are a Christian living in North America, the Number One thing you must fiercely guard against is anyone being used by the enemy to come against your liberty and freedom in Jesus Christ. Galatians 2:4 refers to those who would seek to undermine your liberty as false brethren—and trust me, those are in huge numbers these days.

OK, I promised you two verses, and I've only touched on one, so here is verse number two, and please, beloved, meditate heavily on this one. Let it become your very favorite scripture, it will serve you well; "Now the Lord is the Spirit, and *where the Spirit of the Lord is, there is freedom.*" (2 Corinthians 3:17)

Now, I'm going to quote the passage where we find that verse, because that passage beautifully and powerfully illustrates *Why your spiritual liberty is so valuable*—and is such a threat to the kingdom of darkness, and it is why Satan makes your spiritual liberty his number one target—Never forget that, and never become complacent.

Here is that verse in its powerful, life-changing context:

"...But whenever anyone turns to the Lord, the veil is taken away. Now the Lord is the Spirit, and where the Spirit of the Lord is, there is freedom. And we, who with unveiled faces all reflect the glory of the Lord, *are being transformed into His image with intensifying glory, which comes from the Lord, who is the Spirit.* (2 Corinthians 3:16-18)

As we walk in the spiritual liberty that comes from the Spirit of God, we are transformed into the likeness of the Lord Jesus Himself!

Now do you understand why religious spirits hate spiritual liberty as vehemently and as relentlessly as they do???? Satan does not want you becoming transformed into the image of the One that he killed, and Who was raised from the dead again to defeat him!!!

Your spiritual transformation into the likeness of Christ is a testimony once again to his eternal defeat! As you shine with the light of the Lord, you are a blinding reminder to his downfall!

So remember, you are not obligated to subjugate yourself to any man on this earth!

I wasn't going to go into this subject except only briefly, but I had a dream from the Lord this morning that was a clear sign I'll need to deal with it a bit further.

I'll try to keep it brief.

In my dream, I was in a large church.

Now, I want to let my listeners know that I have not been part of the institutional church system since 1993, and in all of the dreams that I have had since then, where I was in a church building of any kind, it was the Lords way of showing me in the spirit what is operating in the church system, and letting me see it for what it is and how to confront it and deal with it. Those dreams are the Lords way of pulling back the veil or the curtain, so to speak, to show me the spirits operating behind the people.

In the dream last night, there was a young man who suddenly came into the huge main sanctuary, demanding that everyone gather together in front of him, because he was now put in charge of them in some capacity.

He was extremely young, and to me, his demeanor was one of extreme self-importance, like he had just been made Lord over all these people. He was clearly exuding a spirit of religious intimidation, as though his authority—however newly found—was not to be questioned.

I immediately walked up to him, demanding to know what his exact position was, and who he had been given this authority from, and he just stuttered and stammered and looked extremely uncomfortable, *as though he was not anticipating being confronted*. I told him I wasn't someone who was going to bow down to him, and walked out.

You have to be so completely discerning when it comes to those who would attempt to impose their agendas upon you in a religious/spiritual context.

I really love what Paul said to the believers at Philippi, and here is another verse for you to get deep into the soil of your heart:

*"And this is my prayer: that your love may abound more and more **in knowledge and depth of insight**"* (Philippians 1:9)

The Greek word for "knowledge" there is from "epiginosko", meaning, *a recognition that comes via full discernment*, and the very same word is used in another apostolic prayer by Paul in Colossians 1:9, where he says, "For this reason, since the day we heard about you, we have not stopped praying for you and *asking God to fill you with **the knowledge of His will in all spiritual wisdom and understanding**"*.

So, when you take these 2 verses together, *walking in the love of God and **walking in keen spiritual discernment at the same time** are not mutually exclusive; in fact, **the one protects the other.*** Did you notice that BOTH verses are "1:9"? Interestingly enough, Ephesians "1:9" speaks very similar language, about God "making known to us the mystery of His will"! ("And He has made known to us the mystery of His will according to His good pleasure, which He purposed in Christ"; Ephesians 1:9)

So many believers seem to be almost afraid of walking in discernment and speaking against the things that are contrary to the Holy Spirit, because they don't want to appear as unloving.

But keep in mind that *a false sense of tolerance leads to permissiveness, and permissiveness leads to lawlessness, and lawlessness breeds a lot of other demonic garbage.*

It's like the parents that never put their foot down and set boundaries for their child, and so the child just becomes more and more and more rebellious, to the point where no one can ever bring correction, and now the parents have a monster on their hands.

It is genuine love that sets boundaries, and makes distinctions between what is good and what is bad, what is proper and what is not.

God is the same way; "This is spiritual liberty, and this just leads to legalism and bondage".

He divided the light from the dark in Genesis, and God always divides between what is good and what is evil, because what is evil doesn't always LOOK evil—that is why we always need to be keen and discerning in our spirits (Hebrews 5:14; "But solid food is for the mature, who by constant use have trained their senses to distinguish good from evil.").

And it is right here at this point, that I want to give all of my readers something that will help anchor you spiritually, so that none of the preceding will ever have a chance to build a stronghold in your life.

In the early days after I was baptized in the Holy Spirit, the one theme that was embedded in my spiritual mentality was my identity in Christ Jesus, empowered by the Holy Spirit.

To put it another way: everything that I was led to focus on in terms of teaching and Bible study, etc., was with a two-pronged focus on **what my identity was in Christ Jesus, and how that identity was empowered by the Holy Spirit.**

That must be foundational in each of our lives—and even for those of us who feel like we have a good handle on it, *we should revisit our foundations with all of the tools at our disposal, to reassess that foundation and make sure it is spiritually "up to code".*

My family and I bought our current home in April 2008, and the area we live in is subject to a lot of shifting in the ground due to weather extremes, etc., and so without even realizing it, our home began to lean to one side by 3 inches—And that of course took place over the last 12 years or so.

It wasn't until I discovered some things that were amiss, like doors sticking when they didn't used to, etc. that I called upon a housing expert who came out with his laser devices and everything else, and was able to determine that our house was off level because of settling in the foundation.

So, we could be enjoying the spiritual home we're living in all these years and everything feels as it should be—But if we were to do a reevaluation, we might find one or two things that are slightly off—And if we don't allow the Lord to shine His Word and His Spirit on those places where we're slightly off, in five or 10 years we could find that we are way off course.

So, the best place to begin a spiritual assessment is focusing on our identity in Christ Jesus, and our relationship to the Holy Spirit. That is our foundation. If you are not solid in who you are in Christ Jesus and what that means, and if you are not solid in your ability to walk in the Holy Spirit and hear from Him and have ongoing intimate communication with Him, then how are you going to proceed further & build?

The very first thing that I hope and pray with all of my being, is that every one of my readers not only understands, but relates to intimately and personally is one fact: *that our relationship to God is supernatural. Your relationship to God did not come about by human means, or a human decision, and your relationship with God will not be maintained by human means, And it most certainly will not be threatened by human means.*

Now, for those who might not, for whatever reason, clearly understand what I just said, let me state it another way, by giving you the short version of my own personal testimony.

I was raised Presbyterian, my whole family was in the Presbyterian Church for as long as I could remember, but to me, Jesus was just another historical figure, like George Washington or Abraham Lincoln.

However, that completely changed when I had a "road to Damascus" experience as a 17 year old camping in the forests of Germany in 1978.

I was actually trying to sleep in a van one night, because it was brutally cold and had been raining, and my tent had gotten soaked in the rain.

Someone had left a Bible in the van, and there was an inner prompting to pick up the Bible and read it.

Now, I was freezing cold and I had put on every piece of clothing that I had brought on my camping trip—every single pair of socks, underwear, pants, shirts—everything. I wasn't feeling like reading ANYTHING.

I opened to the front of the Bible, where there was an introduction to the gospel message, and my head was full of mental assent, because I had been through all the Presbyterian catechism classes and so on, so I had a pretty good head knowledge of the Bible—but that was it. I came to a paragraph about the sacrifice of Jesus on the cross, and the heading to the paragraph was just 4 words; "He died for you".

I nodded in agreement, yes, I remember that from catechism class, and turned the page—And then the inner prompting came back again, stronger this time, and said, "Read it again".

So I turned the page back, and the minute my eyes fell on those four words "he died for you", Suddenly everything else on the page completely blurred out, and the words "He Died For You" Became blood red and filled up the entire page!

At the very same moment, it was like a color movie began playing in my head, complete with sound, and I saw Roman soldiers hammering nails into Jesus on a large wooden cross that was laying in the mud, as the rain poured down on them. I could even hear the soldiers' sandals sloshing in the mud!

Then, at that same moment, a loud voice boomed in my chest, and declared as loud as thunder, "You are as guilty as they are!"

I suddenly broke down weeping and sobbing uncontrollably; I could barely even breathe because of what I had just seen and heard!

All I could say over and over again, as I wept and cried like my soul was breaking was, "God, I am so sorry, please forgive me! God I'm so sorry, please forgive me, please change me!"

The next morning when I woke up, I was firstly very glad to still be alive, because of the freezing overnight temperatures—and secondly, I felt like I was not the same person as I had been the night before. I could not have put it into words for anyone, but I knew I was a completely different human being.

I even sat down and wrote letters to my family and friends back home, saying look something's happened to me, and I'm not going be the same person when I come home, so I just want to let you know now what to expect". No one told me to do that, it was just a very strong inner prompting that I had, to let the people in my life know I had changed completely and totally.

I later happened to find a man who was a Christian, and so I thought he'll be able to explain this to me. After I described to him what it happened, he simply said, oh, you were born again".

My response was, "What does that mean?" I literally had no idea what being born again was; all I knew was that the God of the universe had come to me in that van, and showed me what the death and sacrifice of his son really meant, and that it was supernatural; it was something that transcended time and space, and that it was very personal to me!

The God of the universe had let me know that His Son had been brutally killed for me, for my sins, and for my sake, even though I had no idea what sin even was.

Now, please understand that at no point in time whatsoever did I ever equate what had happened to me, with the Presbyterian Church—in fact, to me, the church world and this event were completely and totally separate from each other, and in no way truly connected in reality.

The God that met me in that van was the ocean and sky, and the church was a little stone pebble at the bottom of that ocean—completely insignificant and lifeless.

In all my life, I have been profoundly grateful and indebted to the Lord that He met me in the way that He did, because it was a dividing line without beginning or end—a dividing line between who God is, everything that He is, and the religious systems that men have made with their desperate little hands...Little hands that have feverishly worked to build religious little kingdoms that they control, that they own, that they preside over; little religious kingdoms that will be blown to dust when our Lord sets His feet again on the Mount of Olives, and brings down every high and proud and lofty thing.

No, the God of the universe that came down to me in that van and revealed His Son to me, and the Holy Spirit who met me in that van and reproved me of sin and of righteousness, will never be contained in an abomination built with the hands of men....And that God of the universe came down to me in that van to show me, down to the core of my being, that He is God and I am not—but I AM one whom he bought and paid for by the blood of that precious Son that He allowed to be brutally hammered to a cross....And THAT must be the foundation—the singular foundation for each and every one of us: a supernatural, inward revelation of the Son of God that was sacrificed for you and me—a revelation that is so powerful, so alive, so earth-shaking that we know we can never be bought or owned by anyone but God Himself, and no one but God Himself has any rights to us. That, and that alone, must be your foundation and mine.

If you're building on something else, your building is something that is going to come down. The Only foundation that you can build on is a living, breathing, unassailable revelation on the inside of you that Jesus is your Lord; that Jesus shed every drop of His blood for you, and that His sacrifice is the only thing that will ever make you what God can accept into His Kingdom.

And the good news is, Jesus is everything that you will Need as entrance into His Kingdom—but that same Jesus must be formed in you, and in me.

The good news is, He has sent His Holy Spirit, and if we will humble ourselves, humble our minds, humble our thoughts, humble our percep-tions, and say "Father God, I want the gift of the Holy Spirit", then *He will*

live in you wall-to-wall, top to bottom, and he will be IN you, working 24
hours a day, to build the image of Jesus Christ on the inside of you.

Even after my powerful, humbling encounter with the Lord in
Germany, it would be five years later before I would receive the baptism of
the Holy Spirit—and those years in between, unfortunately, were hijacked
by the religious system which slowly took away my intimate encounter with
the Lord, and turned it into something ritualistic and rigid and formal....
Taking me right back into the religious bondage of my Presbyterian days.

However, unbeknownst to me, I was now inhabiting the religious
world AND the spirit realm, because the enemy knew full well what had
happened to me on that night in Germany—and I was targeted with
extreme prejudice.

By 1981, I was being tormented by spirits of anxiety, depression,
and uncontrollable, irrational fear. It got so bad that when I was at work,
I would take repeated bathroom breaks just so I could sit in the stall and
read my little pocket New Testament, where I would read in the Psalms to
calm my mind down and try to find some relief.

And that was the way I lived for about four years. In early 1983, after
I had received gracious help from the Lord in showing me that my problems were not me, not myself, but rooted in demonic oppression and torment, I received the baptism of the Holy Spirit, and now something new
and miraculous happened.

Remember the God that met me in Germany in 1978? Well, now this
mighty, holy God of the universe was suddenly living inside me—and He
wasn't this big, huge, austere, holy God somewhere "out there"; He was so
personal, and even fatherly and loving and kind, and He was living inside
me now by the Holy Spirit, and no longer did I feel that I was talking to
a God "Somewhere up there", but He was now right here with me and in
me. The horrific anxiety and overpowering fear were now gone, and I was
walking to work every day with limitless Joy, singing in tongues at the top
of my lungs all the way to work every day.

I was a son of God walking in spiritual liberty.

And there we have the New Testament foundation for walking in the Spirit and walking in your spiritual identity as a child of God.

That is the foundation we build on—The entire tone and tenor of everything that is written and said in the New Testament is a reflection of that fact. Spirit-filled apostles writing to Spirit-filled believers, **building upon the foundation of the revelation of Jesus Christ in their hearts; a Revelation fuelled and empowered by the indwelling of the Holy Spirit of the living God.** God Himself does not know of or acknowledge anything else that will try to call itself the church; He doesn't Now, and He never will.

And that brings me to one more foundational aspect to you and I being the New Testament church, as God envisioned it.

Remember earlier when I shared the scripture with you from 2nd Corinthians?

Let's revisit that again—"Whenever anyone turns to the Lord, the veil is taken away. "Now the Lord is the Spirit, and where the Spirit of the Lord is there is freedom; and we who with unveiled faces all reflect the glory of the Lord, are being transformed into His image with intensifying glory, which comes from the Lord who is the Spirit..." (2 Corinthians 3:16-18). The veil mentioned is the darkened understanding that covers our hearts before the Lord reveals Himself to us.

Notice, the Spirit is mentioned three times in that one short passage.

It is by the operation of the Spirit, and the Spirit alone, that the veil of darkness is removed from our hearts, and it is by that same Spirit that we are transformed into the likeness and image of Jesus Christ.

Not only that, but you will notice in verse 17 it specifically states that "the Lord is the Spirit."

Do you begin to understand now, the giant problem inherent in the Western religious system? The Western religious system that, for the most part, denies and neutralizes the life and power of the Holy Spirit?

If we are not transformed into the likeness of Jesus apart from the operation the ongoing operation of the Holy Spirit, then what happens to those who deny the Holy Spirit and block Him from operating within His own church???? Satanic Checkmate! People who have only a religious appearance of godliness, but no corresponding spiritual reality.

Jesus said, "I am the vine and you are the branches. The one who remains in Me, and I in him, will bear much fruit. For apart from Me you can do nothing." (John 15:5).

"So Jesus replied, "Truly, truly, I tell you, the Son can do nothing by Himself, unless He sees the Father doing it. For whatever the Father does, the Son also does." (John 5:19)

Now remember, Jesus did not begin doing the works of His Father until after the Holy Spirit came upon Him at the river Jordan—He did not do a single miracle (or, a single work) of His Father until after that very event.

And then Jesus said, the works that He did, we will do also; "Truly, truly, I tell you, whoever believes in Me will also do the works that I am doing. He will do even greater things than these, because I am going to the Father" (John 14:12).

So, as we are pursuing the topic of developing and walking in a spiritual self-image, we have to embrace this one foundational reality: that we who want to be transformed into the image of Jesus Christ, must also embrace that part of That is doing the works that He said we are called to do—if we are to be transformed into His image, then we must be transformed into Him living His life through us.

That includes Jesus by the Spirit **continuing to do through us** what He did when He was physically here. "For both the One who sanctifies and those who are sanctified are of the same family. So Jesus is not ashamed to call them brothers." (Hebrews 2:11)

We are all sons of the same Father, so why would we not do the same works that the First Son did????? (Hebrews 2:10; "In bringing many sons to glory, it was fitting for God, for whom and through whom all things exist, to make the author of their salvation perfect through suffering")

*So, foundational to our walking in a true spiritual self-image, is understanding that we are already—according to God's own Word—identified as brothers of Jesus, having the same Father—**does it make any spiritual sense whatsoever that we should be living a different kind of life than the one Jesus lived?*** "So Jesus replied, "Truly, truly, I tell you, the Son can do nothing by Himself, unless He sees the Father doing it. For whatever the Father does, the Son also does." *(John 5:19)*

*This is where we must take the Holy Ghost bulldozer to every religious concept that has been force-fed into our brain and turn it into rubble, and **rebuild true spiritual foundation in our understanding—By the renewing of our minds according to the Word of God, completely and utterly void of any religious fillers whatsoever.***

Our consumer society is so obsessed with a diet for their physical body that is gluten-free, dairy-free...***But what about a spiritual diet that is religion-free????***

*What about a spiritual diet that is free from all of the religious, man-made additives that actually serve to only **contaminate or weaken your spiritual system—reducing your spiritual vitality, reducing the level of your spiritual liberty and oneness with the Lord???***

Why aren't we as fiercely conscientious when it comes to what is going into our spirits???

The apostle Peter said, "Like newborn babies, crave pure spiritual milk, so that by it you may grow up in your salvation" (1 Peter 2:2).

The apostle James said, "Therefore, get rid of all moral filth and every expression of evil, and humbly accept the word planted in you, which can save your souls." (James 1:21).

The apostle Paul made the distinction between having to give milk to the Hebrew believers, after saying that they were at a place where they should've been on the meat. "Although by this time you ought to be teachers, you need someone to reteach you the basic principles of God's word. You need milk, not solid food! For everyone who lives on milk is still an infant, inexperienced in the message of righteousness. But solid food is for the mature, who by constant use have trained their senses to distinguish good from evil." (Hebrews 5:12-14).

All of this to say that our spiritual identity in Christ Jesus—our spiritual self image, as developing & growing sons and daughters of God—is at the mercy of our spiritual diet—and only We can control the kind of spiritual food that we are eating or taking in.

"But Jesus answered, "It is written: 'Man shall not live on bread alone, but on every word that comes from the mouth of God." (Matthew 4:4). In the Greek, we are given the word "ἐκπορευομένῳ" (ekporeuomenō), meaning, *"ongoing, present tense" (in other words, not a one-time thing spoken).*

So, your spiritual life is derived from your ongoing relationship to the Holy Spirit who is transforming you into the image of God's dear Son, and NONE of that takes place without the baptism of the Holy Spirit & the indwelling of the Holy Spirit, and the ongoing filling of the Holy Spirit.

One thing that was so foundational in my Christian life in 1983—after I was baptized in the Holy Spirit—*was a growing and developing awareness that God Himself was living inside me through the Holy Spirit.*

Now, if you can hold that one thought in your mind, you will never be able to read the New Testament in the same way ever again.

"For it is God who works in you to will and to act on behalf of His good purpose." (Philippians 2:13)

"Being confident of this, that He who began a good work in you will carry it on to completion until the day of Christ Jesus." (Philippians 1:6)

CHAPTER 12

WALKING IN FAITH & SPIRIT

Because Faith relates to the Eternal, and therefore the Unseen, then Faith becomes an indispensable part of our walk.

The role of Active faith is to the believer, what military training & armament is to the soldier on the battlefield.

Without actively engaging the spiritual force of Faith on a daily basis, we are left vulnerable and under-equipped for spiritual confrontations and conflict.

True Faith is a direct result of His presence inside you, coupled with your daily, moment-by-moment awareness of & cooperation With His Indwelling Presence.

A theme that runs throughout the Bible is that of discerning the times, making the appropriate & necessary spiritual adjustments, and taking a course of action according to the guidance of the Holy Spirit. This has been a Primary focus of Vigilance for the Endtimes podcast.

Most of the religious system in the West has conditioned the minds of professing Christians to treat faith as nothing more than an inanimate object, a rather benign, innocuous concept—instead of recognizing Faith as a vital part of our spiritual armor that we need on a daily basis.

Paul the apostle said, concerning our spiritual armor, *"In addition to all this, take up the shield of faith, with which you can extinguish all the flaming arrows of the evil one."* (Ephesians 6:16)

This chapter takes a very hard look at what it actually means to walk in faith, and to exercise the measure of faith that Scripture says we have been given.

Our religious institutions have spent almost no time at all teaching on the subject, and what teaching they have done is more like discussing the lovely pieces of armor in Ephesians, and having nice little discussions on each piece *without ever providing any real spiritual training on how to wear that armor and utilize it in daily life.*

It's like having a mannequin dressed in military gear, but that mannequin remains in a nice shopping mall, nowhere near a field of conflict.

The faith that we will be discussing is that of the heroes of faith in Hebrews 11, a faith that is designed by the Holy Spirit for the Real world; real battles, and real victories. It is for those who would be counted among the Overcomers in these last days...

Faith is always expressed as something Active, even though the promises one may be standing for may not be received in this lifetime. It is quite possible to stand in faith believing, never throwing down your shield of faith, but continuing to hold it up even till the day you die. And then, there is faith operating in the Now.

Our hope and confidence do not come from knowing When and How our deliverance will come; our hope and confidence comes from knowing that our Deliverer will deliver!

The Bible says resist the devil and he will flee from you, *but the devil doesn't show up looking like the devil—**the devil shows up looking like a problem that you can't solve; A mountain that you can't go over or*** *around; a sea that you cannot part or cross; A stone that you can't roll away; A battle that you cannot win; a need that you see no provision for.*

But the presence of battles does not mean the absence of God's faithfulness, and His ability to come through for us. Jesus affirms this in Luke 18, and the context is of God moving on behalf of His people to deliver and avenge them—But then Jesus asks a question, a question that goes straight to the heart of what we are discussing;

"Will not God bring about justice for His elect who cry out to Him day and night? Will He continue to defer their help? I tell you, He will promptly carry out justice on their behalf. *Nevertheless, when the Son of Man comes, will He find faith on earth?"* (Luke 18:7,8)

That is probably the most sobering question in all of the Bible.

Now, contrast Jesus' question here with what He says elsewhere, regarding the specific time occurring just before His return.

In Luke 21:26, Jesus says, "Men will faint from fear and anxiety over what is coming upon the earth, *for the powers of the heavens will be shaken."*

So, take these two verses—Luke 21:26, and Luke 18:8—And place them right next to each other, and we see a picture of the Endtimes being so severe that not only will people in the world faint from fear and anxiety, but even the people of God will find it a challenge to hold on to their faith.

That is part of what God has commissioned me to do for my brothers and sisters, by creating these podcasts and this discipleship manual as a means to reach out and be an encourager and a strengthener of your faith.

I have been personally of the conviction for the last 25 years or so, that those who overcome in the Endtimes will not be found inside our religious institutions.

They will be found in caves and solitary places, having left the religious noise to be with Him...And that is truly the soil in which Endtime faith will grow; By willingly choosing to be separated unto Him, and Him alone—because in the very end, it will be Him and Him alone before whom each of us will stand.

By willingly being separated unto Him Now, we give Him full opportunity to purify our faith, purge us of any impurities, and strengthen us personally to stand through all that is coming, and to be found standing & Watching for Him when he returns.

For most of my life—for as long as I can remember—I have seen this world in only one way; as an outward facade, behind which exists an enormous backdrop of spiritual reality.

Most of humanity lives, breathes and behaves as though the outward facade IS reality, Never ever seeing the backdrop of Eternity just behind all that is visible. And yet for most of my life, I have seen it just the opposite way. I have simply Never been able to see it any differently. That makes it very difficult to find anyone to really relate to for very long—Especially within the Western religious world, where most people seem very happy living with a mix of what they call Christianity, and the world.

But the thing about faith, is that **Faith is Forever rooted in the Eternal**—and those who have one foot in the things of God, and the other foot in the world, will never—absolutely Never—know what it means to walk in and maintain true, biblical faith; *And those who have lived in this way for decades, will find as the things of this world are shaken more and more, faith will become an even more difficult thing for them to realize.*

In this hour, true faith—as the Bible portrays it—will only become real, and actual, and effective, in those who allow themselves to be separated more and more unto God, and more and more focused on Him and Him alone.

To the degree that we allow a mixture of the world into our lives, to that degree we render our faith inoperative and ineffective.

Those that we refer to as Heroes of the Faith in Hebrews 11, all made the same choice that's available every single day to you and me—*They chose to look at the things which are unseen, not at the things which are seen...They chose to set their affections on things above, not on the things of this earth...*

They chose to continue walking toward the City whose builder and maker is God, while walking away from every earthly city....

Noah chose to be obedient and build an ark....

Abraham chose to raise a knife and sacrifice his only promised son...

What actions of Ours will broadcast to the heavens Our faith???

What are we prepared to Build in obedience to His voice????

What are we prepared to Sacrifice in obedience to His voice????

And it won't matter how close we get to the finish line if, just before reaching the finish line, we do what Lot's wife did, and just take a final glance back....

You can make it almost all the way to the end...the finish line is only a few feet away—and yet, just like checking the blindspot in your mirror while you're driving, just a momentary turn of the head—And you've chosen to look back at the things of this world....

You've chosen to take your eyes off of that Heavenly City that awaits us, and in that moment of time, the true loyalties of your heart have been betrayed...But it doesn't have to be that way.....

In this time of everything being shaken that can be shaken, in this time of so many of us being isolated and very limited, perhaps, in terms of availability of fellowship and activities....

This is the time of God's sovereign sifting process...

Invisible, and unrecognized to most everyone on the planet—but as Jesus said, 'He who has an ear, let him hear what the Spirit says to the churches." (Rev. 3:6).

Faith sees the unseen hand of God moving;

Faith sees the unseen day of visitation...

Faith sees the invisible wind of the Holy Spirit blowing and moving in a new and pronounced direction....

And THEN, faith Responds, with the actions, the consecration, the surrender, that Heaven is looking for!

And that moment is when your heart shouts, "I am crucified to this world, and this world is crucified unto me!"

That is when your heart cries out like Stephen as he was being stoned, saying "Look," he said, "I see heaven open and the Son of Man standing at the right hand of God." (Acts 7:56)

And believe me, when I declare with every fiber of my being, that the unseen will Have to become as real to us as it was to our brother Stephen!!!

Any faith less than that, will simply not be enough.

I'm not talking about giving anyone "5 keys to building miracle working faith".

I'm talking about embracing a lifestyle that enables you to cultivate a solid foundation of faith in your spirit, and that takes an every single day commitment and focus.

I'm talking about spending more time looking at the unseen realities in God's Word, than in front of the TV and football games, and gardening and cooking shows, and shopping....

"For where your treasure is, there your heart will be also." (Matthew 6:21).

To have greater Faith, we just need to assess our lives and do a check up—"Where is most of my treasure right now? In things that I can See, or in things that I Can't?"

And if the pluses are all in the wrong column, it's time to change it up, while there's time. And all of the free time that God blesses us with like while we're showering or washing dishes, pray in tongues or listen to a teaching video, or some worship music that will bless your spirit.

Sow to the Spirit by feeding your spirit; by nurturing your spirit, by feeding the Word of God in one way or another to your spirit; by fellowshipping with the Holy Spirit, by praying in the Spirit.

Jude the apostle said "But you, beloved, by building yourselves up in your most holy faith and praying in the Holy Spirit" (Jude 1:20). So start with that one.

And if you haven't been baptized in the Holy Spirit, that is your next focus—make it predominant. And at this point, I hope we're beyond denominational arguments and resistance—a drowning man does not argue over the color of the life preserver being thrown to him.

And someone who truly understands their profound spiritual needs in this hour, will have the trusting heart of a child, and come to God in all His fullness with that trusting child-like attitude that says, "Father God, give me everything you've got, so I can make it faithfully through this hour, and to the end."

Paul the apostle said to the believers, *"For I long to see you so that I may impart to you some spiritual gift to strengthen you" (Romans 1:11).*

*Beloved, let us get one thing settled here right now, before we move one more inch forward—**ALL the provision that we are going to need is Spiritual, and its source is in God, and God alone.***

Do not allow the reasonings of men rob you of the full spiritual provision that God has provided through Jesus, paid for by his blood, and abundantly supplied through his Holy Spirit!

Because as I live & breathe, I can guarantee you—you are going to need absolutely every ounce of what the Holy Spirit is here to provide us, to make it through what is coming!

You're going need a lot more than a little rubber religious raft to get through the perfect storm that is on its way!

You are going to need all of the might of God, all of the insight and wisdom and guidance of the Holy Spirit, and all of the faith, to make it.

If the apostle Jude exhorted his persecuted brethren to pray in the Holy Spirit to build themselves up in the face of persecution, do you think you're going to do any better without Him???

Just like Jesus spoke to the churches at Sardis and Laodicea, when He diagnosed their true spiritual condition, so the Holy Spirit is speaking to us because He wants to give us the true spiritual remedies that will result in true spiritual life, true spiritual sight, and true spiritual health.

This chapter has been concerning building our faith, **but it is also important that we understand Faith depends on US understanding our true spiritual condition.**

We need to allow the Holy Spirit to put His finger on those areas that He wants to change, heal, transform, and strengthen—just as He spoke through Jesus to these two churches.

To continue on as they were, would have meant disaster. Jesus assessed their true spiritual condition, and gave them His remedies (Revelation 3:2,18)

We who are in these last days, Must allow the Holy Spirit to do the same for us.

That is why the baptism of the Holy Spirit is all-important; because without Him living inside you, directing you, guiding you, speaking to you, and correcting you, your True, actual spiritual condition remains largely unknown...

What's More, is that *True Faith is a direct result of His presence inside you, coupled with your daily, moment-by-moment awareness of & cooperation With His Indwelling Presence.*

How inwardly sensitive do we have to be?

Well, imagine you are the apostle Paul, and you have just begun your ministry to the Gentiles, preaching by the power of the Holy Spirit, miracles attending your every move—and as you're heading to a certain region, the Holy Spirit suddenly rises up within you and says No.

By the way, that really happened—it's in the Book of Acts 16:6.

What does that tell us first of all?

That the gospel is the Holy Spirit's business.

From the moment He was sent, the Church is HIS operation, not man's.

It's activities belong under HIS authority and guidance, not man's.

But man has been running the show so long, that we no longer understand who is really in charge here.

And I guarantee you, that those who have usurped His authority and His position will be like chaff in the wind with what is coming. And it is up to each one of us to begin living NOW, taking our directions from the Holy Spirit, period—Whatever it takes.

In Acts 8:29, the Holy Spirit said to Philip, "Go over to that chariot and stay by it." Philip obeyed the Holy Spirit, and ended up bringing a very high ranking Ethiopian official to salvation.

Much like the testimony I gave in a previous episode, of a young woman named Rosie whose baby girl stopped breathing late one night—and because I was obedient to the Holy Spirit to go take a prayer walk, when I had been comfortably relaxing in a rocking chair on my back porch, the Holy Spirit moving through me spared the baby girl's life.

Faith is the byproduct of daily sensitivity and obedience to the
Holy Spirit, and much time spent planting the Word of God into
our spirits.

As I have shared previously, I spent the first 5 years as a believer without the Baptism and power of the Holy Spirit in my life, and I would Never want to go back to that.

John 7:37-39 says, "On the last and greatest day of the feast, Jesus stood up and called out in a loud voice, "If anyone is thirsty, let him come to Me and drink. Whoever believes in Me, as the Scripture has said: 'Streams of living water will flow from within him. He was speaking about the Spirit, whom those who believed in Him were later to receive. For the Spirit had not yet been given, because Jesus had not yet been glorified."

Again, I can attest from very personal experience, that I never received the Holy Spirit until being in a spiritual desert made me so thirsty that I finally humbled myself, and did exactly what Jesus said in Luke 11:13; I asked our Heavenly Father for His Gift of the Holy Spirit, and the last 38 years have been a Testimony to His Power and His Sovereign Leadership.

To all my Readers, if you have been enduring unbearable spiritual dryness, a feeling of spiritual barrenness, I point you to Jesus and His words that I have just shared with you, from John & Luke. Take these Promises from the very lips of Jesus and go before your Heavenly Father as I did 38 years ago. Reach out to me if you would like prayer for this, and in the words of Paul, "And now I commit you to God and to the word of His grace, which can build you up and give you an inheritance among all who are sanctified." (Acts 20:32)

CHAPTER 13

OVERCOMING HINDRANCES TO FELLOWSHIPPING WITH THE FATHER, PART 2—HAVING CONFIDENCE TOWARD THE FATHER

have noticed over the last two or three years that there is a prevalence of this very subtle form of "theology" that seems to express itself in getting believers to become fixated on their lack of worthiness, their shortcomings in the spirit...It seems to manifest in getting believers to amplify, in their own minds, their supposed spiritual incompleteness.

I perceive it as a spiritual problem with two halves.

The first half I am well acquainted with from personal experience, and it stems completely from trying to walk out the Christian life apart from the empowerment of the Holy Spirit.

The other half of this problem I believe to be a strategy of the enemy, and it is a strategy that he seems to use very successfully against those who have a very pronounced tendency to think very intensely and deeply about things— which on one hand is a good quality, but it also can become a curse when we become so inwardly focused that all we are focused on is ourself, and not the Holy Spirit, and not on what the Word already says about us.

In men, but especially in women, who may have deep father wounds, there is a very pervasive sense of being unworthy; of not having God's approval because you didn't have your father's approval or acceptance, and so the enemy convinces you that it must be because there's something wrong with you, therefore you unconsciously bring these feelings into your relationship with God, and they become invisible obstacles to intimacy with your Heavenly Father.

You end up living with a never ending cycle of trying to measure up to all of your Heavenly Father's standards and all of His "demanding righteous requirements", and you never ever seem to quite measure up enough—whatever "enough" is.

When you are constantly fighting that emotional/spiritual battle, you lose sight of the fact that you are saved by grace through faith—And that is how you live your Christian life every day; by faith through grace.

God's grace is extended toward you every single day, not just to get you saved one time. He doesn't extend His grace to you so you can be born again, and then withdraw it and demand that you measure up for the rest of your Christian life.

However, You must perceive that reality, in order to freely receive it for yourself, just as He is extending it to you freely every single day.

And I think for believers in this present time, that accepting ourselves as He has accepted us in the Beloved, is the Number One issue affecting our walk in the Spirit.

If we do not truly see ourselves as freely accepted by our Heavenly Father, then that sense of unworthiness and of not measuring up affects every other aspect of our relationship with Him.

It hinders us from receiving the baptism of the Holy Spirit, because we are only acutely aware of our shortcomings, and so we feel we aren't worthy of it or deserving of it.

And if we Do have the baptism of the Holy Spirit, then it keeps us feeling inadequate and unworthy to hear His voice, or operate and minister in the gifts, or receive specific loving instruction and counsel and guidance from Him.

In short, we always walk with a pervasive attitude of unworthiness that blocks us from fellowship with Him, and receiving from Him. The main weapon against the enemy's insinuations that we are unworthy, is to completely saturate our minds with the Word of God—specifically as it pertains to our legal, blood-bought position in Christ Jesus.

This means you must first and foremost understand this is a spiritual battle, and a passive attitude is only going to prolong your suffering.

You have an enemy who does not want you to see yourself as God the Father sees you; he does not want you to see your worth through the blood of Jesus, and through the gift of the Holy Spirit that the Father has poured out for your benefit and to bring you into deeper fellowship with Himself.

You must realize that the longer you allow the enemy to keep your focus on YOU, the longer you delay your own freedom.

You have already been freely accepted in the Beloved.

You have Jesus as your High Priest, interceding for you constantly at the right hand of the Father in heaven. You have the everlasting invitation to come boldly before the throne of grace every moment of every day.

The gift of the Holy Spirit has been freely and abundantly supplied to you, and all you need to do is receive Him. The spiritual reality that belongs to you is that everything that belongs to Jesus has been freely given to you, and you are free to experience as much of it as you wish.

As I stated in chapter 4, *there is probably not a more important topic than developing true, heart to heart fellowship with our Heavenly Father through the Spirit.*

In picking up where we left off, I also want to restate from Ephesians 2:18 a foundational promise that will bring healing and confidence to those who may be struggling in this area.

Ephesians 2:18 declares, "For through Him we both have access to the Father by one Spirit."

Ephesians 3:12 says, "In Him and through faith in Him we may enter God's presence with boldness and confidence."

I would have to say that one spiritual character trait that is noticeably absent among believers, especially in their prayer life, is that of confidence—And yet right here in Ephesians 3:12, it says that we are granted boldness of access with confidence. As I was writing this, I glanced over to the t.v. which is on a Christian devotional channel, and this is the Scripture that appeared on the screen; "And this is the confidence that we have before Him: If we ask anything according to His will, He hears us." (1 John 5:14). How's that for confirmation?

After being a believer for 44 years now, I believe that I can safely say the Christian life can be summed up in one word: Confidence.

I'm not speaking of a confidence that is simply born of human emotion. Proverbs says, "The wicked flee when no one pursues, but the righteous are as bold as a lion." (Proverbs 28:1).

David said, "Though an army encamps around me, my heart will not fear; though a war breaks out against me, I will keep my trust." (Psalm 27:3).

It's easy to have confidence in the Lord when everything is going well, but when you are living in a day and time when everything that can be shaken IS being shaken, to be able to have immovable confidence in the Lord in That time, is to dwell in the shelter of the Most High.

So, Lord willing, I'm going spend some time addressing this very subject, and breaking it down into the simplest possible ways, *so that those who are wrestling with these types of questions can begin to gain a solid, unshakeable confidence that the Holy Spirit can be fully trusted and fully relied upon to lead them and speak to them in everyday situations and circumstances, all the time.*

Let's take a moment to look at a passage from the Old Testament that gives us a beautifully worded illustration of the creative and restorative work God has done, to restore us to full and complete fellowship with Himself.

"I will also sprinkle clean water on you, and you will be clean. I will cleanse you from all your impurities and all your idols. I will give you a new heart and put a new spirit within you; I will remove your heart of stone and give you a heart of flesh. And I will put My Spirit within you and cause you to walk in My statutes and to carefully observe My ordinances." (Ezekiel 36:25-27)

Now remember, it is God who made us—spirit, soul, and body. That should remove a lot of the mystery and uncertainty from this equation for everybody. Why?

Because God built us for fellowship with himself—God is a spirit, and He made man spirit, soul, and body. That means you are already built and equipped to fellowship with God on a spirit to spirit basis.

God has even taken it one step further, by saying He will put HIS Spirit within us. Now, there is absolutely no gap between you and your Creator. If you have received the baptism of the Holy Spirit, He Himself has indwelt you.

THAT is the starting point for fellowshipping and communicating with the Lord spirit to spirit.

Notice that God's full and comprehensive provision for us is designed to restore us to full, complete and unbroken fellowship with Himself.

The prophet Jeremiah, speaking the word of the Lord, adds even more intimate detail to God's ultimate intention:

"I will give them my heart to know me, that I am the Lord. They will be my people, and I will be their God, for they will return to me with all their heart" (Jeremiah 24:7)

When related to in this context, the gifts of the Holy Spirit, praying in tongues and in the spirit are now seen as an obvious outworking of God's expressed desire to have an intimate, ongoing relationship with His people that is spirit to spirit-based.

In fact, when we truly comprehend the awesome nature of God's intention to have eternal fellowship with us as His people, then all the provisions of the Holy Spirit—including His gifts—are a logical extension and outworking of that. As Jesus said, God is spirit, and those who worship Him must worship Him in and through the Spirit.

I understand that everybody's on a different level— some people have some pre-existing religious programming that needs to be washed away; some people have pre-existing things that hinder them being able to open up enough to the Lord in a trusting, comfortable manner.

Still others come from a more Logically-minded background, and have a tendency to need to understand everything mentally before they can accept it—even if they've gotten the baptism of the Holy Spirit, their mind still wants to be in the driver's seat.

But if you received the baptism of the Holy Spirit, that is the starting point for Everybody, regardless of any pre-existing issues that you feel might be hindering you.

*I'll state it in a different way that might register with you more powerfully and more reassuringly—**If you can pray in tongues, then you can begin to build greater and greater receptivity to the Holy Spirit.***

*For those who have been largely intellectual, **praying in tongues is the starting point for teaching your mind that intellect is not what leads you; it is the Holy Spirit who leads you.***

For those who may have emotional difficulty relating to your Heavenly Father as a father, and so therefore you feel unsure and possibly even reticent or uncomfortable opening yourself up to a deeper level of trust, just remember that Jesus said *the Holy Spirit is your Comforter— and as you step out in faith, independent of any feelings of insecurity, you will begin to feel a sense of His comfort, His peace, and His assurance beginning to heal those emotional areas that have experienced broken trust, and other sources of insecurity.*

I can speak to that area directly myself, because of my own childhood, and I can testify that the baptism of the Holy Spirit, speaking in tongues, and singing in the spirit, set me free from years of insecurity and abandonment that nearly drowned me.

So, no matter what has been trying to hinder your growing fellowship with your Heavenly Father, I hope that I have been able to show you just how completely He has made total provision for you to personally experience His ongoing, intimate involvement in every area of your life.

If any of what I've addressed in this chapter describes what you are going through, I encourage you to write out the scriptures that I am posting below—put them on your refrigerator, put them on your bedroom mirror, bathroom mirror, and in your car where you will see it constantly, and bathe your mind in the scriptures. This list of scriptures is by no means comprehensive, but it will be powerful enough to get you started renewing your mind, washing you clean from all sense of unworthiness, and giving you a more established assurance of your complete acceptance in Him.

Read these scriptures out loud to yourself, but personalize them and speak them over yourself, because it is God's Word concerning His relationship to you, and your value to Him—your Eternal value.

Ephesians 1:5,7; "He predestined us for adoption as His sons through Jesus Christ, according to the good pleasure of His will.... In Him we have redemption through His blood, the forgiveness of our trespasses, according to the riches of His grace."

Colossians 1:13; "He has rescued us from the dominion of darkness and brought us into the kingdom of His beloved Son"

Romans 3:22; "And this righteousness from God comes through faith in Jesus Christ to all who believe. There is no distinction"

Romans 8:1,2; "Therefore, there is now no condemnation for those who are in Christ Jesus. For in Christ Jesus the law of the Spirit of life set you free from the law of sin and death"

Romans 5:1; "Therefore, since we have been justified through faith, we have peace with God through our Lord Jesus Christ"

Isaiah 61:10; " I will rejoice greatly in the LORD, my soul will exult in my God; for He has clothed me with garments of salvation and wrapped me in a robe of righteousness, as a bridegroom wears a priestly headdress, as a bride adorns herself with her jewels."

Psalm 35:9; "Then my soul will rejoice in the LORD and exult in His salvation."

Isaiah 12:2; "Surely God is my salvation; I will trust and not be afraid. For the LORD GOD is my strength and my song, and He also has become my salvation."

1 Corinthians 2:12; "We have not received the spirit of the world, but the Spirit who is from God, that we may understand what God has freely given us"

CHAPTER 14

EXERCISE THE SPIRIT, RENEW THE MIND, SUBDUE THE FLESH: PART 1

Probably one of the main hindrances to spiritual growth that is common to most believers, is the failure to distinguish between spirit, soul, and body.

One thing that will greatly help facilitate our spiritual growth, development, and maturity, is observing 1 Thessalonians 5:23.

The apostle Paul says, "Now may the God of peace Himself sanctify you completely, and may your entire spirit, soul, and body be kept blameless at the coming of our Lord Jesus Christ."

Right here, Paul gives us the Starting Point for understanding the most basic—and yet the most powerful—principle of spiritual growth; *God's Word and God's Spirit deal with us on three levels, not just one or two.*

What I am going to show you is that the Word of God deals with these three parts of us in very different ways. In this one verse, we are told in crystal clear terms that there are three parts of our being that God wants to sanctify and preserve blameless to the day of His coming.

Believers can become so frustrated in their desire for spiritual growth, finding that they keep going around the same mountain over and over again, fighting the same battles and losing them over and over again, without ever understanding why they are seemingly making so little progress.

For example, most believers, when struggling with different issues in their life, seem to always end up believing that they're having a problem with the flesh.

That is the number one enemy that most believers seem to point to, when trying to come to grips with failings and shortcomings in their walk with the Lord. Very seldom have I heard them say that the culprit is, "*I haven't renewed my mind enough to the Word*", or, "*I am battling demonic spirits*"— although those two are very real and legitimate problems as well.

The starting point for our walking in freedom and liberty in the Spirit, is to understand that God has made full provision to perfect us and mature us on the three levels that Paul has mentioned (spirit, soul, and body).

Stated very succinctly, here are God's 3 remedies:

1. Exercise the spirit,

2. Renew the mind,

3. and Subdue the flesh

There are different scriptural approaches to each of these disciplines, but *there is One singular spiritual approach that applies to All of them— equally and simultaneously,* in fact! But I will circle back to that one later.

First, we will address the three areas mentioned above, and God's provision for each one.

Here is an example that I think will put all of this in the proper focus.

Let's say you're having a problem in your thought life, perhaps it's with negative or critical thinking.

And let's say you've been attacking that problem through fasting and prayer, but nothing seems to work. You've been very stringent with your fasting regimen, you've been praying fervently, and yet the negative thinking patterns seem to persist, possibly even get worse.

But, when you take the amount of time spent fasting and praying, has that been equal to the amount of time you have spent in the Word of God, renewing your mind and changing your thoughts?

If the answer is "No", then we understand what the proper solution is.

You need to spend more time allowing the Word of God to renew your thinking and your understanding. Proverbs 8 and Psalm 119 should be your mind's new address.

We will start where the Apostle Paul started. His order was *spirit, soul,* and *body,* so we will follow that Scriptural order.

1). Exercise your spirit—(Eph. 6:18; 1 Cor. 14:15–*Exercising your spirit is a Choice, an act of your will*)

Keywords—"Edify" (1st Cor. 14:4); "Build" (Jude 1:20)

Paul said, "I thank God that I speak in tongues more than all of you", **so I would fully trust Paul's assessment in regards to the inestimable spiritual benefit of praying in the spirit** (1 Corinthians 14:18).

He also said, "*The one who speaks in a tongue edifies himself,* but the one who prophesies edifies the church." (1 Corinthians 14:4).

He also understood that the Holy Spirit within him was the source of all spiritual power (Ephesians 3:16, Colossians 1:29).

Take these three things together, and we understand WHY Paul spoke in tongues more than everyone else—because that was how he stayed spiritually empowered to do his ministry, and to endure all of the hardships and tribulations that were put upon him.

It was also how he ministered in revelation, divine authority, and discipline with regards to the churches.

Taking all of that into consideration, I do not have any doubt whatsoever that all of Paul's spiritual admonitions to be strong in the Lord and in the power of his might, etc., were taken as **apostolic admonitions and directives to militantly pray in the Spirit and to tap into the strength of the Holy Spirit.**

*Exercising our faith falls under the exercising of our spirits— **Exercising our faith causes us to depend on the power, revelation, and leading of the Holy Spirit, which in turn strengthens our spirit man, and brings us increasingly into greater spiritual maturity.**

Paul said, "Now it is clear that no one is justified before God by the law, because, "*The righteous will live by faith.*" (Galatians 3:11).

Our faith comes from God Himself, and because our faith comes from God, it comes with His kingdom authority, because we have been translated into the kingdom of His dear Son.

So our faith—as it operates here on earth—is not a faith of human origin or human design; it is from the very throne of God Himself, and it has His authority behind it, and in it, and operating through it. "Again Jesus said to them, "Peace be with you. *As the Father has sent Me, so also I am sending you.*" (John 20:21).

Our faith is combined and empowered with the Kingdom authority of God Himself. Once we understand that, faith is no longer a struggle.

Now, I'm not saying that the results will come instantaneously, because we still have to Exercise & Build that faith. "The apostles said to the Lord, "Increase our faith!"(Luke 17:5), and He told them to exercise what they already had been given.

Once spiritual reality becomes as real to us as physical realities, then we're going to see something.

When we walk out of our front door in the morning to go to work, and face the morning as conscious of the spiritual dimension as we are conscious of the car in our driveway, then we will know we're on the right track.

Here is a little example of what I'm talking about.

I remember babysitting for a friend back in 1990 at a church in West Palm Beach Florida. I always rode with my New Testament on the console of my car, and I remember like it was yesterday—we were driving over a bridge going from the beach, and this little boy, out of nowhere, pointed at my little New Testament and said, "Kills bad spirits!" He wasn't even four years old, and he had more spiritual sense than most of the adult professing Christian population!!!

That is precisely the mindset and the state of heart we have to walk in 24 hours a day, seven days a week—if demons tremble at the name of Jesus and His Word, then shouldn't WE treat it every bit as much like the Power of God in our hands?

In my younger days, I used to drive with a little pewter sword on my keychain, to remind me every time I looked at it that the word of God is the sword of the spirit, and it is alive and powerful.

If we do not look at the Word of God even subconsciously as a living thing, it's not doing us any good at all—it's a paperweight sitting on a desk or a table.

And whatever we have to do to obtain, keep, and maintain that mindset, is what we have to do—because we've never lived in a time like this before, that demands such a state of heart and mind and spirit.

Spiritually, our value system has been all backwards—and that is where God will begin training us. We are conditioned by the world we live in to make our judgements based on physical appearances, and what our five senses tell us.

Our mind and emotions assess what our five senses inform us of, and we make our decisions based on that.

By contrast, how often do we make a decision based on what our spirit tells us, or based on what the Holy Spirit is impressing upon us???

Part of exercising our spirit is training ourselves to make the Holy Spirit our First point of reference in decision making, and every day choices—And we must do so in a very militant and strategic way.

"Trust in the LORD with All your heart, and lean Not on your own understanding; in all your ways acknowledge Him, and He will make your paths straight." (Proverbs 3:5,6)

Next to being receptive to and led by the Spirit, The Number One goal for every Spirit-filled, Spirit-led believer, is that of *soul maturity—Where the soul does not dictate how you feel, how you think, how you react, how you behave—it is your spirit and your sanctified will that dictate those things. Again, Militant and Strategic.*

My wife Roopa, to me, is the perfect example of someone whose soul was completely subject to her spirit, and to the Word & the will of God.

From the moment I first met her, she possessed a very peaceful, serene, and loving spirit—but what was incomprehensibly amazing to me, is that she only became More like that during the 16 years of her horrific, ever-worsening health crisis.

I have known people who were far less sick, in far less traumatic pain, who were unbearably horrific for their family to be around...And believe me, I would not fault anyone in that condition for being hard to live with. But my darling Roopa never was. In fact, over time, she only became more and more focused on others than on herself—which, to me, is nothing short of miraculous and angelic.

So, if someone in my wife's condition—being a prisoner in her own body for 16 years, struggling constantly with pain, anxiety attacks, fear, loneliness from being disowned by her own family and forsaken by the professing church—if someone like my Roopa could maintain the peaceful, loving soul that she did, then I am without excuse, 100%.

I was married to someone who showed me that it is entirely possible to be led by a spirit of love, forgiveness, and contentment in the Lord, in spite of everything horrific trial thrown at you, and she is the example that I lived with for over 19 years—a living, breathing example of an unshakeable, unbeatable Christlike spirit that I can hold up to you, my brothers and sisters, as a shining light, and say, "It IS possible to live this way!" *Your circumstances, health, and relationships do not have to dictate the condition of your soul and what emanates from it.* Trust me, I remind myself almost on a daily basis of everything that my wife endured, so I can keep myself in check.

In fact, I lay in bed one morning simply meditating on the kind of heart and soul and spirit that Roopa had, and everything that she taught me. Jesus said regarding the coming tribulations, "By your patient endurance, you will gain your souls." (Luke 21:19).

This is precisely why Paul made such statements as, "God, *whom I serve with my spirit* in preaching the gospel of His Son, is my witness how constantly I remember you" (Romans 1:9).

He did not allow his body or his soul to determine how he served the Lord, regardless of the circumstances.

If we're honest, most of us allow our soul realm to at least be a contributing factor to most of our decisions, based on how we feel; did we get enough sleep; did we get enough to eat; are we in a good enough mood, etc.

I learned while my darling wife was at home on end of life care, that my lack of sleep or any other factors were completely irrelevant. I needed to maintain a consistent level of gentleness, love and kindness, no matter what time of the night she needed to wake me up. And, I needed to do so cheerfully and reassuringly, because she felt guilty enough as it was, having to wake me up in the first place.

Walking by faith demands a mature soul, because we must walk by faith, not by sight, and the soul does not always get what it wants, when it wants it, when you are walking by faith.

That is why Paul said, "I am not saying this out of need, for **I have learned to be content regardless of my circumstances.** I know how to live humbly, and I know how to abound. I am accustomed to any and every situation—to being filled and being hungry, to having plenty and having need" (Philippians 4:11,12).

And with what is coming on the earth right now, we are going to have to have a very strong hold on our soul realm.

But in all of these things, we must continually be mindful of one thing; "For it is God who works in you to will and to act on behalf of His good purpose." (Philippians 2:13).

Never, at any time, must the focus be on only us and only on our ability.

Rather, **our focus must be on how we can cooperate with the Holy Spirit and the Word of God working in us.**

"I have hidden Your Word in my heart that I might not sin against You" (Psalm 119:11) + yielding to the Spirit.

"Be anxious for nothing, but in everything, by prayer and petition, with thanksgiving, present your requests to God. And the peace of God, which surpasses all understanding, will guard your hearts and your minds in Christ Jesus." (Philippians 4:6-7)

Something that we've got to learn and get settled in our hearts is what the Word of God says concerning the flesh, and concerning the human tendency to trust in man rather than God. *The ramifications of what that does are so severe, that God says in Jeremiah 17:5, "This is what the LORD says: "Cursed is the man who trusts in mankind, who makes the flesh his strength and turns his heart from the LORD."*

Remember now, the Word also says, "There is a way that seems right to a man, but its end is the way of death." (Proverbs 14:12).

So, while men may not see anything wrong with how they do things, **they also normally don't take eternal consequences into consideration.**

Here in the West, we have spent so much time looking to the natural, focused on the physical, caught up in the temporal, **that we have muted our spirits to a degree that we have yet to comprehend.**

I do not say that by way of condemnation, by any means. I say that as a humble but deeply felt conviction from the Holy Spirit, for All of our sakes.

These past 26 months of turmoil and breakdown in our society were meant to be used of the Lord to drive us back to Himself—but quite honestly, how much has it achieved that purpose?

I myself have endured the same 26 months of turmoil as everyone else, but I have also been stripped of so much that I held dear...It has broken me, brought me to my knees, and down upon my face like nothing else ever has in my entire life...So, I have nowhere left to look but Heavenward...

I have no substitutes, distractions, or entertainments that would hold my attention for five seconds, because the Gift that I had from God meant more to me than everything else combined...So maybe when your soul is stripped bare and raw and bleeding, it's easy to look to the one place where healing can come from...But in my brokenness, I have been called to share what I see with you, that you may see it as well...

CHAPTER 15

EXERCISE THE SPIRIT, RENEW THE MIND, SUBDUE THE FLESH; PART 2

I n our continuing focus on Exercise the Spirit, Renew the Mind, Subdue the Flesh, one Common Thread in the New Testament deserves our closest attention.

I'm referring to the ongoing relationship of the Holy Spirit, as an integral, completely indispensable part of every believers' daily walk.

I will give you *3 Key scriptures* that directly relate the power & activity of the Holy Spirit to each of the 3 areas we began dealing with in our previous chapter.

- *First, in regards to Subduing the flesh*, Romans 8:13 tells us, "For if you live according to the flesh, you will die; but if *by the Spirit* you put to death the deeds of the body, you will live." Along the same line, Romans 8:6 says, "The mind of the flesh is death, but *the mind of the Spirit is life and peace*".

- *In regards to Renewing the mind*, Ephesians 4:23 says, "to be renewed in the spirit of your minds", which is a horrible mistranslation, because your mind does not have a spirit.

The accurate rendering from the Greek would be, *'Allow the Spirit to renovate your thinking'* ("renew" comes from Greek word 'neos', which means 'to renovate', and "mind" comes from the Greek word 'ginosko', which is 'intellect', base of reasoning).

Romans 12:2 also speaks directly to this; "Do not be conformed to this world, but *be transformed by the renewing of your mind*. Then you will be able to test and approve what is the good, pleasing, and perfect will of God."

- *In regards to Exercising the spirit*, we will explore *practicing walking in the Spirit*, with an emphasis on believers who are already aware of their gifting, to begin to step out in faith more and exercise it.

I will share testimonies of my own past experiences in doing so, with a view toward encouraging you, dear reader, to begin stepping out in faith and letting the Holy Spirit minister through you to others.

In reality, walking in this realm should be commonplace for every single one of us, and that is the full intention of the Holy Spirit.

Scripture says that "every man has been given the measure of faith" ("For by the grace given me I say to every one of you: Do not think of yourself more highly than you ought, but think of yourself with sober judgment, **according to the measure of faith God has given you**"; Romans 12:3), and it's up to each of us to ensure that we do not allow it to lie dormant.

The measure of faith God has given to each one of us is meant to be exercised, so that we may;

1. *Become fruitful members in the vine, and,*

2. *Bring life and edification to others, because bearing fruit in this way glorifies God.*

Jesus compared receiving the Holy Spirit to something as simple as drinking—and giving out the Holy Spirit and His life, to something as simple as allowing rivers of living water to flow out from us.

It doesn't sound like something we have to stress and strain for, does it?

It is very simple: we humble ourselves as little children and receive Him, and then as humble children, we trust Him to hold our hand and lead the way.

Hebrews 6:4-5 makes it very clear that we are stewards of supernatural, heavenly provisions and spiritual equipment, and I believe that should be the primary understanding by which we function in the gifts of the Holy Spirit—an understanding which is rooted in the awesome wonder of us being in partnership with God.

Now, the context of that passage is one of stark warning, but *it's emphasis of spiritual stewardship is of prime importance*, and I encourage everyone to take the time to dig below the surface, to fully apprehend the full realization of what the Spirit-baptized believer has been entrusted with.

I'll quote the entire passage here, but I will then highlight one by one the powerfully descriptive phrases which will serve to equip us with a foundational understanding of the Spirit-filled believers God-given provision.

Here are the 2 verses we are looking at, and once again, I'd like to direct your focus towards *the phrases that reflect our Heavenly stewardship*:

"It is impossible for those who have once **been enlightened**, who have **tasted the heavenly gift**, who **have shared in the Holy Spirit**, who have **tasted the goodness of the word of God** and **the powers of the coming age**…" (Hebrews 6:4-5, Berean Study Bible)

- **Been enlightened**, from the Greek word, "phōtisthentas", "to be illuminated by light"; same phrase used in Hebrews 10:32; **"Remember the early days that you were in the light**. In those days, you endured a great conflict in the face of suffering."

Also, 2 Corinthians 4:6 , which says it so perfectly; "For God, who said, 'Let light shine out of darkness,' *made His light shine in our hearts to give us the light of the knowledge of the glory of God in the face of Jesus Christ".*

- Who have **tasted the heavenly gift**; *"tasted"*, from the Greek word "geusamenous", *"to personally and truly experience in reality"*. Also used in 1 Peter 2:3; "now that you have tasted that the Lord is good".

- *"Heavenly"* should be self-explanatory.

- *"Gift";* The Greek word for *"gift"* (*'dórea'*) as used here and many other places in the New Testament, is used in a rather all-inclusive sense—as in, a gift with many parts. Here are some examples:

- John 4:10; "Jesus answered, "If you knew **the gift of God** and who is asking you for a drink, you would have asked Him, and He would have given you living water."

- Acts 2:38; "Peter replied, "Repent and be baptized, every one of you, in the name of Jesus Christ for the forgiveness of your sins, and you will receive **the gift of the Holy Spirit**."

- Ephesians 3:7; "I became a servant of this gospel by **the gift of God's grace**, given me through the working of His power."

- Ephesians 4:7; "Now to each one of us grace has been given according to the measure of **the gift of Christ**."

- 2 Corinthians 9:15; "Thanks be to God for His indescribable gift!"

- Romans 5:17; "For if, by the trespass of the one man, death reigned through that one man, how much more will those who receive an abundance of grace and of **the gift of righteousness** reign in life through the one man, Jesus Christ!"

- Acts 10:45; "All the circumcised believers who had accompanied Peter were astounded that *the gift of the Holy Spirit* had been poured out even on the Gentiles."

- Acts 11:17; "So if *God gave them the same gift He gave us who believed* in the Lord Jesus Christ, who was I to hinder *the work of God?*"

- Who *"have shared" in the Holy Spirit*; the Greek word being "genēthentas", "a sharer, a participant", with those who likewise have received the gift of the Holy Spirit.

- Who have *tasted the goodness of the word of God;* the Greek word for "Word" here is *"rhēma"*, meaning "an utterance, a spoken word". This is attested to beautifully & powerfully in several places:

- Acts 5:20; "Go, stand in the temple courts and tell the people the full message of this new life."

- Romans 10:8; "But what does it say? "The word is near you; it is in your mouth and in your heart," that is, the word of faith we are proclaiming"

- Romans 10:17; "Consequently, faith comes by hearing, and hearing by the word of Christ."

- 1 Peter 1:25; "but the word of the Lord stands forever." And this is the word that was proclaimed to you."

- *The powers of the coming age…"* the powers (δυνάμεις; dynameis; dunamai; miraculous power) of the coming age (Millennial Reign).

The Greek word "dynameis" here is used throughout the Gospels when describing the miraculous works done by Jesus by the power of the Holy Spirit ("Jesus returned to Galilee in the power of the Spirit, and the news about Him spread throughout the surrounding region", Luke 4:14), *and when Jesus declared the very same power of the Holy Spirit would be upon Us* ("But you will receive power when the Holy Spirit comes upon you, and you will be My witnesses in Jerusalem, and in all Judea and Samaria, and to the ends of the earth"; Acts 1:8).

- *The coming age; "aiōni" ("Age") "erchomenō" ("is coming"),* as seen in Mark 10:29,30; "Truly I tell you," Jesus replied, "no one who has left home or brothers or sisters or mother or father or children or fields for My sake and for the gospel will fail to receive a hundredfold in the present age— houses and brothers and sisters and mothers and children and fields, along with persecutions— and *in the age to come*, eternal life."

At the culmination of everything, the Grand Finale will be God making His dwelling place with man ("And I heard a loud voice from the throne saying: "Behold, the dwelling place of God is with man, and He will dwell with them. They will be His people, and God Himself will be with them as their God"; Revelation 21:3)

But until that time, we are temples of the Holy Spirit, and stewards of His indwelling presence, and His continuation of the ministry of Jesus on earth.

I believe that for every Spirit-filled believer, the starting point for exercising our spirits begins with the very focused, primary instruction of the apostle Paul; Covet spiritual gifts, and seek to edify your brethren ("Earnestly pursue love and eagerly desire spiritual gifts, especially the gift of prophecy…What then shall we say, brothers? When you come together, everyone has a psalm or a teaching, a revelation, a tongue, or an interpretation. All of these must be done to build up the church"; 1 Corinthians 14:1,26).

The fact that there have been those who have abused spiritual gifts, does not in any way, shape or form, erase or nullify or negate the instructions and detailed training of the apostle Paul on spiritual gifts.

So yes, we acknowledge the big giant white elephant in the room of abuses, *and then we Refocus on what spiritual gifts were Meant to be used for in the first place, and keep moving forward with reverence, sensitivity, and balance, in the Holy Spirit.*

The first place of spiritual safety is in acknowledging that the gifts are HIS, not Ours.

They are not ours to put on show with, to build a ministry with, to wear like a badge of super spirituality. They are spiritual endowments belonging to the Holy Spirit, which He Loans to us on a moment by moment basis, to meet the need of a brother or sister, and then it goes back to Him. The only thing WE get to keep, is our consecration and our level of sensitivity to Him.

As long as we keep and maintain that heart focus, we will do just fine.

That is called walking in the fear of the Lord, and the Word of God says that the fear of the Lord is "pure".

"The fear of the LORD is pure, enduring forever; the judgments of the LORD are true, being altogether righteous. (Psalm 19:9).

So how do we stay spiritually pure and clean?

By walking in the fear of the Lord.

Romans 12:5-7—"So in Christ we who are many are one body, and each member belongs to one another. We have different gifts according to the grace given us. If one's gift is prophecy, *let him use it in proportion to his faith*; if it is serving, let him serve; if it is teaching, let him teach..."

So, let's look at the phrase, **"in proportion to his faith"**.

Remember, *Jesus always took note of the level of people's faith* ('little faith', 'great faith', etc.), *and our faith grows as we Use it.*

BUT, *we step out in faith,* **powered by the Holy Spirit's Grace**. We will Always Be Learning, **so we must remember to always extend Grace to ourselves as we take each step of Faith,** yielding ourselves to the Holy Spirit.

Many times, we only have enough Revelation for each step of faith, and as we take the next step in Trust and Faith, the Holy Spirit gives more revelation.

Now, notice in Romans 12:6, as Paul begins to discuss exercising our gifts, *the first gift he mentions is prophecy, or prophesying*:

"We have different gifts according to the grace given us. If one's gift is prophecy, let him use it in proportion to his faith".

There is clear reason for Paul making that the first gift that he mentions.

Remember the priority that the apostle Paul emphasized in 1 Corinthians 14?

That of using the gifts to edify the Body.

Then Paul makes the statement, "For you can all prophesy in turn so that everyone may be instructed and encouraged", 1 Corinthians 14:31.

Now, from personal experience, I have to agree with Paul's perspective and his spiritual ordering of things; the gift of prophesying is actually one of the easiest gifts of the Holy Spirit for believers to exercise.

It is also one that has the most spiritual potential for edifying and comforting other believers.

It would be difficult to explain to those who have never experienced it, but I will do my best to give some examples.

If you look carefully, of all the gifts that the apostle Paul covers in 1st Corinthians 12 through 14, prophesying is the one he has spent the most time elaborating on, due to its potential benefit to the body of Christ at large.

I'll stop right here and be quick to point out that virtually none of what the Western professing church calls prophecy is actually what Paul's talking about.

We have seen almost none of the New Testament gift of prophesying.

What we HAVE seen is a bunch of spiritual con artists and flakes saying they have the gift of the prophetic or the gift of prophecy, when really all they have is the gift of deception and conning people.

But when it comes to dealing with Bible subjects—*especially that of the gifts of the Holy Spirit—the place of safety and empowerment is when we keep those subjects within the context of their scriptural framework.*

And the context of spiritual gifts in the New Testament is when they are exercised within the framework of the Body; the fellowship of believers, whether it's at home groups, or at fellowship meetings, prayer meetings, things of that nature.

The edification of the Body, the upbuilding of the Body, for its growth and maturity into the image of Jesus Christ, is the ONLY reason for the gifts of the Holy Spirit—no other reason for them is ever given by the apostle Paul.

The gifts of the Holy Spirit are for our mutual spiritual strengthening and encouragement, in a fallen world of opposing spiritual forces, so that we might remain strong & faithful in Him.

Paul states this very clearly in Romans 1:11 and 1 Corinthians 1:7,8;

"For I long to see you so that I may impart to you some spiritual gift to strengthen you" (Romans 1:11);

"Therefore you do not lack any spiritual gift as you eagerly await the revelation of our Lord Jesus Christ. He will sustain you to the end, so that you will be blameless on the day of our Lord Jesus Christ." (1 Corinthians 1:7,8)

So once again, the primary purpose of the Holy Spirit's gifts are to keep us growing in the faith, maturing & growing in grace, growing in spiritual strength and faithfulness and endurance, all the way up to His Return.

There is nothing in the New Testament that validates using the Holy Spirit's gifts to build a public ministry or a platform ministry, PERIOD.

Now, I have had some wonderful people listening to the podcasts and fellowshipping with me on Facebook, who I know the Lord has used in intercession. A couple of dear sisters described in pretty good detail how the Lord has used them in intercession, and it blesses me to see believers yielding to the Holy Spirit for a ministry such as that—it takes a lot of love for the Lord to allow him to use us that way—It is a completely selfless ministry.

And I will say this from experience: those who are used of the Lord in intercession, usually at some point find themselves also being used of the Holy Spirit to prophesy, to give words of wisdom and words of knowledge to others, for their encouragement and their comfort.

Personally, I believe that is the Holy Spirit's way of rewarding intercessors for their selflessness— because when you are interceding for people, you do not always see the fruits of your prayers manifested—in fact, you might never see those fruits manifested.

But when the same Holy Spirit gives you a word of knowledge, or a word of wisdom, or a word of prophecy for someone, and you minister that word to them, that is an impacting spiritual gift that you can see the fruit of right away, especially when it breaks off depression or discouragement from that person, because they are receiving a word from the Lord that is speaking right to their situation and healing their emotions, etc.

I remember many years ago feeling prompted to call a friend that I hadn't spoken to for years, and as we were spending time catching up and talking on the phone, I felt an undefinable 'something' in them.

I found myself thinking, this is not the same person that I used to know—they seem hard on the inside and rigid, not warm and full of life like they once were. And then seemingly out of nowhere, it was like a breeze started gently blowing in my spirit, and I suddenly felt words coming to me for this friend.

So I stepped out in faith—somewhat hesitantly at first, but as the words came, I felt a boldness, like I was breaking a stronghold.

I said to my friend, "I feel that you have been hard on others for a while, but you've been even harder on yourself—and the reason that you have been hard on yourself and others, is because you stopped extending grace to yourself". And in that very moment, before I was barely finished speaking, my friend began to weep and weep, like something had just broken. Something that had been there for a very, very long time, something that she really wanted to be free from, but just didn't know how to get free, was now Healed. She didn't know how to find her way back into living from Grace and receiving the Fathers Grace. *But the change in her spirit and in her heart was immediate; I could feel her sense of total freedom and liberty over the phone.*

A few years later, as I was driving through the state where she and her husband lived, I stopped by for a visit, and she was still all lit up and full of light in the Lord. *1 Corinthians 14:3; "But he who prophesies speaks to men for their edification, encouragement, and comfort."*

I remember during times of prayer, I would be walking and praying in tongues, and intercession would just hit me—I remember it was most prevalent back in the 1980s and '90's.

I would spend time in prayer and Bible study on Friday nights before I would go to small group meetings, and I would always spend time interceding for the meeting before I went.

One Friday night while I was praying, I started having sharp, severe chest pains, and I had been fine the whole day.

God showed me that the chest pains were a word of knowledge for somebody who was going to be at the Friday night meeting. I had never had that happen before, so I treated it very reverently, and during the course of the small group meeting, I very reluctantly stepped out in faith and described what I had been feeling earlier that night, and that I felt it was a word of knowledge for somebody who was there. I asked, "Is anyone here suffering from severe chest pains?"

A lady who was present looked very emotionally impacted, and she said that she had been having such severe chest pains due to stress and anxiety from a job situation, that she thought she was going to have to go into the hospital.

We gathered around and prayed for her as a group, and she was instantly healed and delivered, and never had any issues afterwards.

PART 3:

FUNCTIONING IN THE HOLY SPIRIT; BECOMING DEMONSTRATORS OF THE GOSPEL OF THE KINGDOM

Growing in spiritual functionality, or, Growing in Spirit-led functionality, means that you are growing and developing functionality in abilities and giftings that are derived directly from the Holy Spirit Himself. That is the entire intention, vision, and purpose of this discipleship manual —to enable you to become proficient in the things of the Spirit.

CHAPTER 16

SUBDUE THE FLESH, RENEW THE MIND, EXERCISE THE SPIRIT, PART 3; WEANING THE SOUL FROM THE TEMPORAL TO THE ETERNAL

Without a doubt, the biggest factor in a believers walk in the spirit is going to be renewing the mind, and controlling our soulish desire to run our own life and guide our own daily affairs.

The first priority for every believer is to live to do the will of God on a daily basis, and that means that our will must be second to His.

What is Most important to understand, is that we learn to do His will one day at a time, and one step at a time—it is all a series of choices in daily situations that come up in life, choosing His will over our will, and over our desires.

The test most always will be between, do we choose a certain course of action to please ourselves, or do we put the Lord and others ahead of ourselves?

Are we more focused on serving and pleasing ourselves, or serving and pleasing the Lord and those He has put in our life?

This is the beautiful place where the fruits of the Spirit come into play; if we yield to the Holy Spirit and choose His will in certain situations, then the fruit of the Spirit will be there to give us His long-suffering, His patience with Joy, etc., to enable us to do the will of the Father in that particular situation.

Here we see the scripture fleshed out for us—"For it is God who works in you to will and to act on behalf of His good purpose." (Philippians 2:13)

In a given moment, you inwardly choose to do His will instead of your own, and THEN the Holy Spirit gives you His grace in the form of peace, patience, joy, long-suffering, etc., enabling you to carry out the will of God in that moment.

The beauty of it is that you never have to depend on "feeling like" doing the will of God—you just have to make the deliberate choice; then, the feelings will follow once your obedience is complete, after the Holy Spirit has supplied you His Grace to fulfill your commitment to obedience.

Remember, we are walking this life out by the supply of the power of the Holy Spirit, not our own strength.

This is how your soul learns to cooperate with the Holy Spirit, and this is how you mature into the likeness of His Son.

In Hebrews it says that *"Jesus learned obedience"* ("Although He was a Son, He learned obedience from what He suffered", Hebrews 5:8); He wasn't born with it.

Your soul has now gained a victory and learned what it feels like to choose the will of God, and you have now grown again in that area.

One major spiritual reality that so few Western professing believers understand is that of being separated unto the Lord—And to be Led and Taught by the Holy Spirit, Demands and Requires an inward separated-ness unto Him.

This is where you will develop an inward sensitivity to His promptings and leadings—but please understand, there is no shortcut, there is no substitute. You simply must be willing to do what it takes to Shut Out other voices to Hear His...and hearing HIS voice, is the only one with Eternal benefits.

We live in a culture that is constant busyness, constantly having our attention focused on some form of amusement or entertainment, or some other distraction.

Solitude is definitely not an integral part of our lives—And as a result, neither is the inward working of the Holy Spirit.

Our current religious system is a mirror image of the culture we are immersed in. Our religious culture is manufactured worship, manufactured religious reality, and sermons and messages that don't require too much deep thinking, but that manage to hold and captivate our attention for no more than an hour— because we have something else to do later. The one thing Western professing believers will Never do, is admit that our religious system is of the exact same spirit our Western culture is; *the two are controlled by exactly the same spirits.*

And the Word of God clearly states that there are only two spiritual forces humanity can be controlled by: the spirit of the world, the spirit of the age; or, the Spirit of God.

Once you come to the place where you can accept the fact that in the spirit realm there is no neutrality, that there is no gray area, then you will clearly understand the choices you have to make.

In Ephesians, it states that the spirit of this age is "the spirit that works in the children of disobedience" ("in which you used to walk when you conformed to the ways of this world and of the ruler of the power of the air, the spirit who is now at work in the sons of disobedience"; Ephesians 2:2).

So if the spirit of this age is what is influencing you the most, then you are living as a child of disobedience; whereas in Romans 8, it clearly states that those who are led by the Spirit of God are the sons of God.

If only we would embrace the clarity of the Word of God, it would simplify the sum total of our lives more than anything else ever will.

The Holy Spirit always gets straight to the heart of the matter, and from Genesis to Revelation, the choices we are given to live by are so clear cut and simple—but *it is the spirit of the world that complicates and obfuscates*, so that we don't know whether we're going or coming, and we aren't quite sure how to clarify our priorities.

But from the beginning, God has always made His will so simple—choose blessing or choose cursing; choose life or choose death; choose the spirit or choose the flesh.

In all of my years as a believer, I can confidently say that *the one prevailing cause that keeps professing believers from growing and maturing to any significant degree, is the unwillingness to be separated unto God.*

Now, I do not believe that it's a Conscious unwillingness, so much as it is a result of our being conditioned by our culture to need to constantly be doing something, talking to someone, or listening to something.

*Our culture simply is anti-solitude...*And I can assure you from the Word of God and personal experience, you will never ever experience significant spiritual development in the Lord, unless you enthusiastically embrace solitude in large amounts.

All of the most spiritually formative periods in my life have been where my circumstances— whether by my choice, or by the Lords doing, or a combination of both— kept me mostly isolated from the busyness, hustle and bustle all around me.

For the most part, I never have felt solitude was anything but a dear and welcome friend, here to help me grow closer to the Lord—and I can assure you, that this is the spiritual environment where the soul will mature in the Lord the most, *and the soulish things that have been holding us back will be crucified in that place as well.*

> *I think it would serve us well to remember, that this life is where we are given the time and opportunity to become the sons and daughters of God that we will be for all Eternity—so it behooves us to spend the time we have here as wisely as possible, because you are investing this time in your Eternity.*

And the time that you squander on pursuing hobbies, vacations, trips here and there, and 1000 other distractions, is time that you can never get back to reinvest on developing your spiritual life with the Lord—and that, by the way, is all you'll take with you when you draw your last breath.

Now, since our topic for this chapter is weaning the soul from the temporal to the eternal, I find this particular scripture very enlightening;

"*Where there is no vision, the people cast off restraint*; but blessed is he who keeps the Law." (Proverbs 29:18).

This illustrates a much needed perspective—*To truly wean the soul from the temporal to the eternal, and to truly have our affection set on the things above, we need a panoramic vision of God's full purpose for His people.*

To put it another way, what provides the believer the strongest source of spiritual endurance; the strongest source of overcoming faith; the most consecrated and committed spirit, is to have a clear-cut vision of what God's ultimate purpose is for His people.

And the good news is, that God Has provided a clear, majestic vision that is meant to hold our attention, and capture our deepest devotion—And that Majestic vision is that of His Eternal Kingdom, beginning with the Millennial Reign.

There are so many New Testament passages that directly reference our ruling and reigning with Jesus as a motivation to endure to the end, and to keep earthly tribulations in their proper perspective.

The problem is, none of those references have been emphasized with that in mind—they are taken, rather, as separate little pieces of encouragement that do not point to *a singular source of Prophetic encouragement; one which the Old Testament prophets elaborated on at length.*

So, it is my intention to look at the scriptural framework for the Millennial Reign, and how it serves such a multifaceted purpose in equipping the Saints today. Such an undertaking will obviously encompass more than just this one chapter, but it's my hope that you will be inspired to continue exploring this theme.

The Millennial Reign serves as a Prophetic Focal Point that accomplishes several Key spiritual benefits:

1. It is meant to give us profound clarity of vision for our future with the Lord,

2. Which in turn inspires our relentless endurance in this life;

3. The development of our spiritual character;

4. Motivation for faithfulness and fruitfulness in serving the Lord in the here and now;

5. Determination to practice and gain spiritual competence in utilizing our spiritual gifts for the edification of the Body;

6. Embracing the truth that God expects us to grow in maturity as servant leaders here, for future responsibilities in His Eternal Kingdom, starting with the Millennial Reign.

The Millennial Reign will be the singular, most pivotal event in human history, and yet almost no one is teaching on this.

Not long ago, I had a dream where I was talking to other believers about what we will be doing during the Millennial Reign, and it was the most amazing dream I've ever had about this subject. I was talking to a man—a believer I presume—about how we will be using the Bible as God's textbook to teach all the nations about God's laws and God's ways. *I also realized that the measure of faith we develop here, will be the measure of faith we have to operate in there—it will not just automatically change.*

I believe that is why Jesus asked the seemingly cryptic question, when the Son of Man returns, will He find faith on the earth? ("I tell you, He will promptly carry out justice on their behalf. Nevertheless, when the Son of Man comes, will He find faith on earth?"; Luke 18:8)

Now, why would He ask such a question, given the context will be Him returning at the end of the horrific tribulation????

Jesus asked that question almost as if He was dismissing the horrific time of trouble the earth would be going through at that point in time; His main focus was obviously on finding faith when He returns.

There are so many passages that have been speaking to us about these things, we just never see those passages of scripture in the light of this context—but now they are becoming all too real to me, like scriptures such as Romans 8:18 ("I consider that our present sufferings are not comparable to the glory that will be revealed in us") or, 2 Thessalonians 1:10 ("on the day He comes to be glorified in His saints and regarded with wonder by all who have believed, including you who have believed our testimony").

Many of the Old Testament prophets spoke of a time when the Lord Jesus would be King over all the earth and the nations would be taught by Him, and obviously by us.

His command to go and make disciples of all nations will truly be realized at that time, a time where there will be absolutely no Satanic or demonic interference among the people of the earth—*and yet we will still have one thing to contend with; **man's fallen, rebellious will**.* Just because

Jesus will be here does not mean they will willingly submit or yield their earthly rule over their kingdoms, and submit to the King of Kings' authority.

So, not only must we be in fellowship with the Lord now, and in His Word now for our personal growth and spiritual development; *we must also begin to look at His Word as our training manual for reigning when He returns, because we will be delegated serious responsibility, so why wait till then to start learning about what we will be required to do?????*

In this regard, Daniel and Joseph serve as primary examples of ruling among and from within earthly kingdoms with the authority of God Almighty.

For example, as God's personal representative to Babylon, Daniel clearly communicated the reality that God is ruler over All the kingdoms of the earth, and THAT was the position from which Daniel ministered and conducted himself, in the presence of the earthly king Nebuchadnezzar.

Notice that Daniel's throne was exercised through prayer and consecration to God....Which is precisely the position that we rule from Now; "And God raised us up with Christ and seated us with Him in the heavenly realms in Christ Jesus," (Ephesians 2:6).

In fact, the book of Daniel is probably THE training manual for believers who understand the coming reality of the Millennial Reign.

We too will be representing the Lord to fallen kingdoms and fallen world leaders, with the reality of the Government of all governments—the Kingdom of God having come to rule over the earth.

That is a REALITY; it is not a fairytale; it is not a children's bedtime story; it is a Coming Reality, *and we as believers need to immerse ourselves in understanding this Now.*

Virtually all of the Old Testament prophets spoke in great detail of this coming reality, and yet we as Western believers haven't even bothered to dip our little toe in the waters of this subject, *a reality that Old Testament prophets gave their lives and died for!*

What a profound and tragic shame! **We seem to have little to no comprehension of what Western churchianity has cost us in terms of living in True scriptural realities,** versus the man-made teachings that have bound the so-called church of the West forever and rendered it impotent, weak, and irrelevant.....I pray the Lord will make the Reality of His Coming Kingdom something we can see continually before us, like a mighty mountain that eclipses all worldly tribulation........

Hebrews chapter 11 gives us the theme of Overcoming Tribulation and Suffering, *by seeing the invisible realities of God's Kingdom and God's Promises.*

Literally, this whole chapter states that All of those who acted in faith and stood in faith, **were doing so based on Gods unseen realities being more real to them than anything they could suffer.**

It is my wholehearted, relentless desire to help my brothers and sisters move into this type of holy mindset, where we will be immoveable, unshakeable, and profoundly empowered to minister hope and faith toward one another.

That is my all-consuming passion and drive till Jesus comes back.

CHAPTER 17

THE SPIRITUAL EQUIPMENT OF THE ENDTIME NEW TESTAMENT BELIEVER

realize, dear reader, that the title of this particular chapter might seem fairly straightforward to you at face value.

I'm sure the phrase "spiritual equipment" probably brought to your mind the passage where Paul talks about the armor of God, or perhaps the passage regarding the weapons of our warfare.

However, we are going to begin by focusing on something very basic and foundational to being a Spirit-filled believer that is consistently able to receive from and cooperate with the Holy Spirit—Because even though your first two impressions are completely correct, in regards to spiritual armor and spiritual weapons, you will notice that the operative word there is "spiritual".

*That means we must have a true understanding of what "spiritual"
actually means to us as believers.*

Simply put, "spiritual" means "of the Spirit"

That means if you are a believer in Jesus Christ, everything that you will ever need as a believer to function in the Lord here on earth is already provided for in the Holy Spirit, *but you must learn how to access what has been provided.*

First, you must truly understand from a spiritual viewpoint that you are no longer just a physical person living on this earth.

This is what I mean. The truly spiritual man and woman perceives the forces at work in the Invisible, BEHIND the forces operating in the physical realm, operating in the children of disobedience (Ephesians 2:2).

We in North America are not accustomed to dealing with these things in the spirit realm First, but rather, we have primarily reacted in the physical, and this must change Quickly......

The price to be paid, however, is also something we are not accustomed to.

Regardless, the Church of this Endtime must be led by those who HAVE paid the price to be vessels of the Holy Spirit.

- They have been Broken, and so have No confidence in the flesh.
- They have come to the end of Themselves, and so do Nothing out of vainglory.
- They know they have no power in & of themselves, and have been Baptized in the Holy Spirit & Power from on High.
- They know that our battle is not against flesh & blood, and, having had their spiritual eyes opened, cast out demons and war with a Heavenly prayer language.
- They come Not to be served, but to Serve....

It breaks my heart that, after walking with the Lord for over 44 years, there are fewer truly Spirit-led, Spirit-informed, Spirit-taught Bible teachers than there have ever been in my life.

The apostle Paul tells us the difference between those who teach the Word of God from their mind and their human reasoning, as opposed to those who teach with the Holy Spirit—The Teacher—living on the inside of them (And trust me, someone can say with their mouth they've received the Holy Spirit, but if they are still teaching from the human intellect and reasoning, I truly have to question that).

"We have not received the spirit of the world, but the Spirit who is from God, that we may understand what God has freely given us.

"And this is what we speak, not in words taught us by human wisdom, but in words taught by the Spirit, expressing spiritual truths in spiritual words.

"The natural man does not accept the things that come from the Spirit of God. For they are foolishness to him, and he cannot understand them, because they are spiritually discerned." (1 Corinthians 2:12-14)

One primary thing I have learned in discerning those who teach from the Holy Spirit versus those who teach from their mind is this:

Someone teaching from their mind can tell you all the things that are available to you as a believer, and they can expound on the meanings of different words and phrases, but there is One thing that they Cannot do—

They cannot tell you, dear believer, how to Access those spiritual provisions.

I have observed firsthand those who try to display great expository skills, and give the Greek meaning of this and that—but at the end of the day, all the wonderful things of God they've been expounding upon, **they cannot tell you how to ACCESS them—And yet Paul the apostle explains this very thing over and over by the Holy Spirit in almost every letter that he writes.**

The reason that these pontificators do not clearly see that, is because they are not teaching by the Spirit, and that is because they have not allowed the Holy Spirit to take up residence within them in His fullness.

That is not me speaking by way of criticism or condemnation; that is me speaking by way of over 44 years of close & careful observation, plainly seeing what is going on…And caring enough about my brothers and sisters in the body of Christ to take the time to point out the crucial spiritually life-saving difference....And trust me, the life-saving nature of this reality is going to be presenting itself very soon, and the Western professing church is not even near ready—in fact, it's in a whole universe away from being ready. We are right back to the wise virgins vs. the foolish virgins scenario.

Paul makes it abundantly clear, in almost every single letter he writes, that *the spiritual blessings we have received in Jesus Christ have to be appropriated Spiritually*, as they are in the Heavenly places (i.e., they're not accessible to us physically or even mentally).

This is the critical mistake that most all in the Western professing church make:

They fail to understand that Spiritual things can only be appropriated Spiritually—And they never seem to bother to ask HOW we do that.

If something is physical, you can pick it up with your physical hand.

If something consists of sound, you can receive it through your ear— your sense of hearing. Do you see what I'm getting at here???

The nature & composition of a thing dictates how it may be received and appropriated.

We apply this principle every single day we live, even though we don't stop to think about it, in the realm of our five senses.

Spiritual things (things that are of a spiritual substance) can only be appropriated spiritually, or via your human spirit working with and cooperating with the Holy Spirit.

That is why the Holy Spirit manifests Himself *in spiritual ways, but all of those ways consist of one category heading: Revelation Through (or Via) your spirit.*

The manifestations may be through a vision, a dream, a prophecy, a word of knowledge, a word of wisdom, a gift of healing, etc., *but they all come via Revelation by, of, and through the Holy Spirit to your spirit.*

And THAT is how you receive spiritual provision—From the Holy Spirit through Your spirit.

So, the teachers and preachers that expound all day long on the spiritual blessings in Christ sound wonderful, but they never tell you HOW you can appropriate those spiritual blessings, which means they're just speaking words into the air *that will never bear fruit, and never give Life.*

Paul specifically states that he prays for the believers to receive *"a spirit of wisdom and revelation in the knowledge of God,* and he also says, *"We have received the Spirit from God so that we may know the things freely given to us by God".*

These two passages deserve our deepest attention on a daily basis.

Meditate on them and pray them over yourself at the beginning of each and every day. Trust me, you will be absolutely Amazed at the powerful spiritual benefits!

I will quote both verses here for you;

"I have not stopped giving thanks for you, remembering you in my prayers, *that the God of our Lord Jesus Christ, the glorious Father, may give you a spirit of wisdom and revelation in your knowledge of Him.* I ask that *the eyes of your heart may be enlightened*, so that you may know the hope of His calling, the riches of His glorious inheritance in the saints."

(Ephesians 1:16-18)

"We have not received the spirit of the world, but *the Spirit who is from God, that we may understand what God has freely given us."* (1 Corinthians 2:12)

Here we see, in black-and-white, clear as day, *the Only way we can know the things freely given to us by God, are through the Spirit of God, if we have received Him.*

This is precisely why it makes perfect logical sense spiritually why the apostles are seen in the Book of Acts taking supremely great care to make sure that believers received the baptism of the Holy Spirit!

They weren't enforcing a "doctoral statement", folks—*they were ensuring that the Church of Jesus Christ received the Spirit of Jesus Christ Whom was sent.*

People who get all squirmy and defensive over this clearly do not understand what's really at stake.

The baptism of the Holy Spirit is to not only empower believers, but to equip believers to walk with God in the Spirit, to discern and see and learn things from the Spirit dwelling within them.

"And as for you, the anointing you received from Him remains in you, and you do not need anyone to teach you. But just as His true and genuine anointing teaches you about all things, so remain in Him as you have been taught." (1 John 2:27)

Speaking in tongues/praying in the spirit is the gateway to allowing the Holy Spirit to move through you and within you, and the New Testament is monumentally sheer proof of this.

The apostle Paul said that the man without the Spirit cannot understand (receive, perceive, comprehend) the things that come from the Spirit of God (*i.e., the things that have their source in and their impartation from the Spirit of God*), *because they are Spiritually perceived/discerned/received.*

Now please realize that Paul is speaking very clearly and spiritually intelligently here—he is not saying the person "without **Christ**"; he is saying "the person **without the Spirit**".

Let's look at the **context** of what Paul is saying;

"We have not received the spirit of the world, **but the Spirit who is from God, that we may understand what God has freely given us.**

"And this is what we speak, not in words taught us by human wisdom, but in **words taught by the Spirit, expressing spiritual truths in spiritual words.**

"The natural man does not accept the things that come from the Spirit of God. For they are foolishness to him, and he cannot understand them, because they are spiritually discerned." (1 Corinthians 2:12-14)

This short but powerful statement by Paul right here further enlightens us as to **why the apostles took such great care to make sure that every new believer received the baptism of the Holy Spirit**—and I'll keep repeating that until the day I die, because far too many are not understanding the vital importance of that—And far too many are making too little of it.

If we truly grasped the reality that **we receive Nothing from God apart from the Holy Spirit**, maybe people would quit squabbling and quibbling over the issue of speaking in tongues and the baptism the way they do, treating it as though it is of some secondary importance.

It is ALL-important, and again **I point you right back to the actions of the apostles themselves which testify to this fact.**

The early church possessed, in spiritual reality, the presence and ongoing power and manifestation of the Holy Spirit in ways that the religious West can only dream about—or, as they do now, only Talk about.... endless talk, endless chatter, endless religious posturing, with almost Zero life and power—this is completely unacceptable to the Lord!

The apostle Paul made it crystal clear, that **words from and by the Holy Spirit are accompanied with spiritual power** ("My message and my preaching were not with persuasive words of wisdom, but with a demon-stration of the Spirit's power"; 1 Corinthians 2:4).

Again, something that the religious West is virtually completely void of, and I speak this to their shame, because while they profess to be speaking *for* God, they only speak from a religious mindset that does not set anyone free, and it does not bring the very life and power of the Holy Spirit to those who need it most desperately—And this is something we all should see so very clearly, and it should be enough to motivate us to hum-ble ourselves and ask the Holy Spirit to fill us with Himself, and sweep all of the religious debris out of our soul and out of our mind, because it's not benefitting Anyone.

If what's coming out of our mouth is not accompanied by the power and demonstration of the Holy Spirit in a life-changing, tangible way, then it looks to me like we don't have anything to say.

However, we don't have to let it remain that way.

We can choose to humble ourselves before the Lord, and ask Him to fill us with compassion for those who are desperately in need of the rivers of living water (which isn't US, by the way; it's the One who should be IN us, living and speaking through us).

There was one scripture that came to me tonight while I was working on this message, one that we have heard probably thousands of times—but I don't remember ever hearing anyone actually expound upon it in a way that made scriptural and spiritual sense to me.

I've heard tons of religious interpretations, but nothing that had the ring of Holy Spirit truth to it—And if someone is delivering a message based on the Word and you don't get that Holy Spirit ring of truth, just go find something else to do.

Sorry if that sounds blunt, but time is way too short, and we have wasted decades on religious, watered down Christianity, and there isn't a second left on the clock for that.

The verse that came to my mind was John 20:21;

"Again Jesus said to them, "Peace be with you. **As the Father has sent Me, so also I am sending you."**

Whenever I think of this verse, I understand why Jesus repeatedly acted so astonished at His disciples regarding their seeming lack of faith.

He fully expected them to understand that the things He did and said were derived from the very throne of God's authority—That is precisely why Jesus spoke what He did in John 20:21. He was conferring upon them delegated spiritual authority and dominion!

The saints mentioned in Hebrews 11 (the "Faith Hall of Fame") possessed a Faith that was unquenchable, that would not be denied—a faith that was ruthlessly intent on obtaining the things promised to them by God....A faith that enabled them to choose the Invisible Kingdom of God over the visible world around them....Faith that made them Overcomers in the face of impossible odds; faith that empowered them to perform miracles, and to victoriously walk out the calling of God on their life...and yes, a Faith that embraced even martyrdom, knowing that they would obtain a Greater reward at the Resurrection.

With all my heart, I believe in this hour that we are going to need a violent kind of Faith; a Faith that ruthlessly shuts out the voices of the world and the flesh, the voices of choosing comfort over sacrifice; choosing perhaps some easier path other than the one you know God has called you to.

A Faith that is so rooted and grounded in the reality of the Spirit, that the ground you walk on seems like a mirage...

Like the ocean did when Peter got out of the boat to walk to Jesus— the realm of the Spirit was actually more solid under his feet than the waves themselves...

And that is precisely the kind of faith that each and every one of us is going to have to possess; the kind of faith that we are going to have to begin growing in right now, and we cannot allow ourselves to lower the bar to accommodate fear or spiritual laziness.

What I'm saying to all of you right now, is where I start out at every single day, and I beg the Lord to keep me honest in my self-assessment each and every day—"Where am I not growing enough in my Faith? Where can I grow stronger? What weights do I need to lay aside that are holding me back from growing a living, powerful faith, that is a doer of the Word, and not merely believing the Word, but putting it to actual work".

The gospels are a picture painted by the Holy Spirit, of Jesus and his disciples being doers of the Word, not merely believing what scripture said, but they were putting it into action by the power of the Holy Spirit.

The disciples came to Jesus at one point and asked Him to increase their faith. *Notice they did not ask him to TEACH them about faith; they did not ask Him to teach them about some religious subject—they asked Him to* **Increase** *their faith.*

Why? Because they knew that it was faith that accomplished the miracles Jesus did; it was faith that raised the dead, healed the sick, cast out demons, etc.

Speaking of being "doers of the Word", I was very close to some friends in the mid-1980s who were all pumped up on the Word, baptized in the Holy Spirit, and together we had formed sort of an intercessory prayer/laying on of hands/demon-casting SWAT team.

Any time one of us came across a ministry situation, where someone needed prayer for healing or deliverance, or some other serious spiritual situation that required the power of the Holy Spirit, we would get on the phone and call the rest of the team, drop whatever we were doing at the moment, and go to it.

That was some of the best Holy Ghost training I ever had in my life—just going out in the Holy Spirit with fellow believers who were bold, led by the Holy Spirit, and not afraid to jump in and get their hands dirty, but were eager to be doers of the Word. I'm sad to say I haven't seen that sort of thing in a very long time now, but I believe that is precisely what God is after!

My friends and I in the 1980s were not a large group—maybe six or seven of us—and we didn't see anybody else out there doing what we were doing; most everybody was content to base their Christianity on going to church every Sunday, and maybe every Wednesday night if they're super dedicated, but that's the extent of it. Nobody was out there actually Doing the Word, because they assumed that merely believing the Bible was enough—they never really contemplated what it means to put it into real action—and that is an entirely different way of life; And it is a way of life that we are called to, each and every one of us.

James said, "Be doers of the Word, and not hearers only. Otherwise, you are deceiving yourselves." (James 1:22).

Most of our religious system is full of self-deception, because it is full of people who have told themselves that merely believing the Bible and giving mental ascent to what it says is enough to qualify as a Christian—that is not at all what the New Testament says.

Jesus said, "And these signs will accompany those who believe: In My name they will drive out demons; they will speak in new tongues;" (Mark 16:17); "Truly, truly, I tell you, whoever believes in Me will also do the works that I am doing. He will do even greater things than these, because I am going to the Father" (John 14:12), and yet I don't see very many out there doing those works.

Jesus said, "Why do you call Me 'Lord, Lord,' but not do what I say?" (Luke 6:46), beginning with preaching the gospel of the Kingdom and demonstrating the gospel of the Kingdom.

That's part of 'the violent take it by force'—those men and women who are not content with living a religious Christianity. They are determined to live the Word of God in word and in deed, by the power of the Holy Spirit, and they will not settle for anything less.

This brings us to the next point, one that the Lord vividly brought to my mind recently, when the Holy Spirit spoke a very specific phrase to me.

A few mornings ago, at about 2:30 a.m., as I was simply meditating on the subject of ministering the Word to unbelievers who might be receptive, especially in the light of current world events, where many are searching for truth, searching for an unknown something, an undefinable something, I heard the Lord speak to me this phrase;

"Faith to Demonstrate"

Suddenly, I envisioned myself speaking to a group of people, and I began imagining what I might say, and how I might approach them, and the first thought that came to my mind was discussing the reality that we are spirit, soul, and body, and that God wants to have an inner relationship with us through our spirit, not through religious programs or religious thinking, or religious believing—But as a very real spiritual reality.

My next thought was, as I envisioned myself standing there speaking to this group of people, *how to move from simply speaking words to them, words that they would have to then filter through their thinking and past experiences and personal prejudices.*...Why not just give them a demonstration of the reality and power of God's Spirit—That would certainly transcend merely speaking About Him, and would instead be an act of Demonstrating Him.

Then the scripture came to me, where Paul said to the Thessalonians, *"because our gospel came to you not only in word, but also in power, in the Holy Spirit, and with great conviction—just as you know we lived among you for your sake."* (1 Thessalonians 1:5), and that was God's confirmation on what I was already thinking and envisioning in my mind, as I played out this scenario.

So now I have this as a new focal point, because I believe that *unless I and others intentionally focus on developing our faith to become servants of the Lord, to demonstrate Him to others, then we will never truly be effective—And in the seriousness of This hour of time, we Must be demonstrators of the Spirit, not just speaking words only!*

As I have said elsewhere, *we must begin to think tactically in the Spirit like never before*—we cannot afford to hold onto religious thinking. It must be 100% spiritually tactical.

In other words, how would the Holy Spirit of God want us to move and act in this situation?

How can I develop faith in the ability and the power of the Holy Spirit to move in this scenario?

How can I effectively be open to and tap into the supply of the Holy Spirit for this or that situation????

In other words, we have to be completely done with theory and conjecture—we Must move into hard-core spiritual application of the power and the ability and the presence and the reality of God's Spirit!

We have to push for reaching the levels of Faith that those men and women of God had in the Bible—Raising the dead; feeding 5000 with one sandwich; walking on water if we have to when there's absolutely no other way to get to our God ordained destination, or simply being transported by the Spirit to another location when necessary—But what THIS will require, brings me to yet another vital step in each of us becoming the Endtime New Testament believer we will need to be.

We must each become "God inside minded"

Our focus must be not on ourselves, and not on our own ability to walk the Christian life out—*our focus must be on God who is working inside of us; the God who indwells us by his Spirit. "For it is God who works in you to will and to act on behalf of His good purpose."* (Philippians 2:13)

Remember, it is not Your strength, but it is God who is effectively at work in you, strengthening, energizing, and creating in you the desire AND the ability to fulfill your purpose for His good pleasure. You're not interceding in your Own strength; you're not praying for healing in your Own power; you're not preaching the word of the Kingdom in your own might—it is GOD WORKING IN YOU!

Remember the Holy Ghost SWAT team I mentioned? When we got a call to go lay hands on someone for healing, for deliverance, or whatever the spiritual emergency was, you know what we were doing while we were driving to go do battle???? We were boldly and loudly declaring the Word of God over ourselves!

- Greater is He that is IN us, than he that is in the world!

  ("You, little children, are from God and have overcome them, because greater is He who is in you than he who is in the world"; 1 John 4:4)

- God has qualified us ministers of the new covenant; God has made us able ministers of the Spirit: for the Spirit gives life!

  ("And He has qualified us as ministers of a new covenant, not of the letter but of the Spirit; for the letter kills, but the Spirit gives life"; 2 Corinthians 3:6)

- The words we speak are spirit and Life for those to whom we are ministering!

  ("The Spirit gives life; the flesh profits nothing. The words I have spoken to you are spirit and they are life"; John 6:63)

"Because everyone born of God overcomes the world. And this is the victory that has overcome the world: our faith.' (1 John 5:4)

"Behold, I have given you authority to tread on snakes and scorpions, and over all the power of the enemy. Nothing will harm you." (Luke 10:19)

And another thing about our SWAT team; we were Always praying in tongues. Some of these guys worked in lawn maintenance and construction, so while their hands were working, their spirits were praying.

The most powerful way to be "God inside minded"—the most powerful way to keep our focus on the God who is working within us—is by praying in the Spirit, because it engages all of our senses, and focuses them on the Holy Spirit who is indwelling us.

When you are praying in the spirit/ praying in tongues, your mind is not running all over the place, thinking about this and that. Your mind is basically submitting to your spirit as you're praying in tongues. *If your mind is doing Anything, it should be yielded to the Holy Spirit as you are praying in tongues, because automatically you are hearing yourself with your own two ears praying in tongues, so your mind is basically taking a backseat, so to speak.* In other words, your mental faculties are not doing the driving right now. If anything, your mind should be giving way to your spirit as you pray in tongues, and you should be sensing an inward receptively and an inward posture of listening to the Holy Spirit within you.

This is precisely where you are working **with** *the Holy Spirit to train your spirit to be receptive and yielded to His guidance, His leading, His prompting, His correction, His wisdom, His instruction*—Because the Holy Spirit speaks to your spirit first, not to your mind, not to your emotions, not to your intellect, but to your spirit. **Why?**

Because you are a spirit—you are not a mind; you are not emotions; you are a spirit, made in the image of God (those who worship God must worship Him in spirit and in truth; not in mind and in truth, not in emotions and in truth, but in spirit and in truth—*And "in Spirit" is where we must always begin, and must always proceed from.*

Jesus put it very succinctly and very bluntly, and this is where we should be anchored every day—"The Spirit gives life; the flesh profits nothing. The words I have spoken to you are spirit and they are life"; John 6:63.

So you begin with the Spirit, you stay with the Spirit; you walk in the Spirit, and you live and act from the Spirit.

That is precisely how Jesus walked out His entire life, saying, "For I have come down from heaven, not to do My own will, but to do the will of Him who sent Me" (John 6:38), and He did it every day of His life.

Now, we have been baptized in the Holy Spirit, and it is God's will that WE walk each and every day out just like Jesus did, because the Word of God says if we say we belong to Him, then we should walk as He walked ("Whoever claims to abide in Him must walk as Jesus walked"; 1 John 2:6).

Our thinking, our reasoning, all need to be yielded and submitted to the Spirit—our thoughts should not be preeminent; what we think or feel should not be preeminent; but what the Holy Spirit is speaking and leading should be pre-eminent, and that should be what we are living from every single day.

Praying in tongues trains us to keep the spirit in first place at all times; praying in tongues trains our entire body and mind and emotions to put the spirit first always.

Remember in the book of James, where James says if you can control the tongue, you can control the whole body ("We all stumble in many ways. If anyone is never at fault in what he says, he is a perfect man, able to control his whole body"; James 3:2)???

Well, what do you think praying in tongues is for???

It is for lining your triune nature up with the will of God.

Because you are spirit, soul, and body, as you pray in tongues you enforce God's order within your own being, by keeping everything lined up in that order: spirit, soul, and body.

The body does not come first; the soul does not come first; *the spirit comes first, and praying in tongues enables you to keep God's divine order within yourself, because you are the temple of the Holy Spirit, and you are not functioning as the temple of the Holy Spirit if you are putting your body or your soul realm first.*

These are basic fundamentals of walking in the Spirit. If you can keep them uppermost in your mind and heart every single day, then everything else will be built upon this foundation—And I do mean, Everything else.

Walking in Spiritual Liberty

The entire tone and tenor of the language of the New Testament boldly declares that the child of God has been given lavish opportunity to walk in spiritual liberty and freedom in the Holy Spirit.

New Testament declarations such as, "Behold what manner of love the Father has given to us, that we should be called children of God." That verse in and of itself is probably the most sweeping New Testament declaration of spiritual liberty that has been bestowed on us. ("Behold what manner of love the Father has given to us, that we should be called children of God. And that is what we are! The reason the world does not know us is that it did not know Him"; 1 John 3:1)

Very possibly the next verse to speak so directly to our spiritual liberty would be Romans 8:2; "For in Christ Jesus the law of the Spirit of life set you free from the law of sin and death." How's that for spiritual liberty??

Spiritual liberty is mentioned at least 23 times in the New Testament, but probably the two most mentioned verses regarding spiritual liberty are Galatians 5:1 and 2 Corinthians 3:17.

Almost everyone probably knows Galatians 5:1; "It is for freedom that Christ has set us free. Stand firm, then, and do not be encumbered once more by a yoke of slavery."

The other verse I honestly have not heard it quoted or taught on that much, but it is probably my favorite, and I believe the most comprehensive verse in the Bible regarding spiritual liberty; 2 Corinthians 3:17; "Now the Lord is the Spirit, and where the Spirit of the Lord is, there is freedom."

And yet if we are completely honest in assessing the spiritual landscape of North American Christianity, it's quite evident that spiritual liberty—True spiritual liberty—is a pretty rare thing. Why is that?

Well, again, leaning on my 44 years in the Lord, I would honestly have to say Public Enemy #1 to true New Testament spiritual liberty would be the Religious spirit, which is so profoundly pervasive.

I truly believe, with every fiber of my being, that wherever the New Testament is clearly taught—Simply and by the illumination of the Holy Spirit—the result will be spiritual clarity in the minds of those who are receiving that ministry of the Word, and its accompanying result, liberty in the Spirit.

The apostle Paul said, "And this is what we speak, not in words taught us by human wisdom, but in words taught by the Spirit, expressing spiritual truths in spiritual words." (1 Corinthians 2:13)

When the Word of God (and more specifically, the New Testament as it pertains to the believers life and walk) is clearly taught, and communicated by & under the anointing of the Holy Spirit, then the result is the seed of that Word being planted in the hearts, minds, and spirits of those who are listening or reading, producing spiritual life and spiritual liberty.

Remember, one of the Greek words for "Word" (as in, the Word of God) is "rhema", and we see this in Matthew 4:4, John 6:63, and Ephesians 6:17.

The "rhema" Word of God is the Spoken word of God, spoken through any Spirit-filled and Spirit-empowered believer ("But when they hand you over, do not worry about how to respond or what to say. In that hour you will be given what to say. *For it will not be you speaking, but the Spirit of your Father speaking through you*"; *Matthew 10:19,20)*

The New Testament also speaks very directly and aggressively against those things that rob us of walking in spiritual liberty—Galatians being a very powerful book that addresses that issue.

The ministry of Jesus, in which He repeatedly confronted the religious legalists of His day, is a very graphic picture of the head-on spiritual battle between the Spirit of liberty in Christ Jesus, and the spirit of bondage through institutionalized religion, cults, and pseudo-Christianity denominations that are void of the Holy Spirit—having a form of godliness, but completely void of the life and power of New Testament Christianity.

On September 11, 1993 the Lord ministered a prophetic declaration to me; a prophetic word if you will, and I will read it to you now.

I have saved that particular prayer journal all these years, and the word that He spoke to me has consistently proven itself throughout the years, and as He has put me in positions of ministering the Word, I always find myself going head to head with the spirit of religion and bondage— Probably the one spirit that I hate the most, and I know without a doubt that Jesus himself hates it far more than I ever will, because it robs His people of spiritual life and vitality, and it robs the kingdom of God of true Spirit-led, Spirit – empowered, fruit bearing disciples.

The word the Lord gave to me was, "I have broken the yokes of men and tradition off of you. I have removed the burden from your shoulder, and set you free to walk in My Spirit. Just as I have broken the yoke off of you, so you will do for others—you will clearly see and discern the yokes of men and speak against them and destroy them, and lead many into liberty".

Religious yokes of bondage are strongholds that are erected by the enemy in the hearts and minds of believers.

I truly believe, after 44 years in the Lord, that the degree of spiritual liberty a believer truly possesses will completely and totally dictate the quality of his spiritual life, and most importantly, the degree to which he has real fellowship with the Lord, and is able to be a fruit bearing disciple.

To the degree that a believer does Not have true spiritual liberty, they will be lacking in their fellowship with the Lord; they will be deficient in their Christian character, and they will be much less effective for the kingdom of God. Their experience of everything that Jesus has purchased for them will be far less experiential than it should be.

Purposing to Live from your SPIRIT is the Beginning of walking in spiritual liberty.

I had a very intense and involved dream, where the Lord was talking to me about the subject of the inner man, and I remember Him showing me a plaque with a verse from Colossians on it, and as I was waking up I was talking to the Lord about that verse—but when I was fully awake, I couldn't remember what the verse was.

But what the Lord was talking to me about in the dream was that Christians need to begin living from their spirits like never before—not their mind, not their emotions, and not their thoughts, but from their SPIRIT.

He emphasized that He has made full provision for us to learn to do this, especially if we have been baptized in the Holy Spirit.

He reminded me that "But he who unites himself with the Lord is one with Him in spirit" (1 Corinthians 6:17).

He reminded me of passages, like where Paul said, "I went up by revelation" ("*I went in response to a revelation* and set before them the gospel that I preach among the Gentiles. But I spoke privately to those recognized as leaders, for fear that I was running or had already run in vain"; Galatians 2:2). In other words, Paul made a trip to a certain city, not based on his own will or his own planning, but he went by revelation from the Holy Spirit who was directing him.

Also, Paul made the incredible statement—which I've never heard anybody preach on or teach on—when he said, "I serve God **with my spirit**" ("God, *whom I serve with my spirit* in preaching the gospel of His Son, is my witness how constantly I remember you"; Romans 1:9).

I've never heard anyone teach or preach on the ramifications of that.

I mean, consider who is saying this; the apostle Paul, who wrote most all of the New Testament, established more churches than any man who ever lived (in the power of the Holy Spirit) and endured more persecution, hunger, homelessness, beatings, imprisonments, than any man I've ever heard of, and the same man says "I serve God with my spirit".

Frankly, I think the Body of Christ in this hour needs to pay more attention to walking in the Spirit and serving God in the spirit than ever before—And we are quickly running out of time to do so.

2 Corinthians 4:16; "Therefore we do not lose heart. Though our outer self is wasting away, *yet **our inner self is being renewed** day by day*."

Ephesians 3:16; "I ask that out of the riches of His glory He may strengthen you **with power through His Spirit in your inner being**,"

Remember what we talked about in Chapter 8???? About the Supply of the Spirit???? And HOW we Access the Supply of the Spirit???? In Philippians 1:19, Paul said, "Because I know that through your prayers and *the provision of the Spirit of Jesus Christ*, my distress will turn out for my deliverance."

So, *as we Pray in the Spirit*, we *Access the Limitless Provision of the Spirit*, and then *Receive the BENEFITS of the Spirit. Pray, Access, Receive.*

So let's break it down to reveal from the Greek language how we Personally Receive God's Supernatural Strength in the very same way, because the Greek language says it so powerfully.

The word "**strengthen**" in the Greek is κραταιωθῆναι (krataiōthēnai), meaning, "to empower".

The word "**power**" in the Greek is δυνάμει (dynamei), and in every instance this word is used in the New Testament, it signifies "**miraculous power**". Here are just a few examples;

*Matthew 13:54; "Coming to His hometown, He taught the people in their synagogue, and they were astonished. 'Where did this man get such wisdom and **miraculous powers**?' they asked."

*Mark 5:30; "At once Jesus was aware that **power** had gone out from Him. Turning to the crowd, He asked, "Who touched My garments?"

*Matthew 14:1,2; "At that time Herod the tetrarch heard the reports about Jesus and said to his servants, "This is John the Baptist; he has risen from the dead! That is why **miraculous powers** are at work in him."

*Luke 5:17; "One day Jesus was teaching, and the Pharisees and teachers of the law were sitting there. People had come from Jerusalem and from every village of Galilee and Judea, and the **power** of the Lord was present for Him to heal the sick."

I truly hope that I am laying this out so very clearly; *God's Limitless Supply is Through & From His Spirit dwelling in your inner man— your spirit.*

SO, the Supply of the Spirit is Already within you.

Deliverance, Healing, Life, is not "out there somewhere" just beyond your reach—All of those things are in Him, in His Spirit, and He is dwelling in you…In your inner man, your spirit.

But you have to access His resources by praying in the spirit. "But he who unites himself with the Lord is one with Him in spirit" (1 Corinthians 6:17). Does that sound like you are lacking anything?

But we have not been spiritually educated to depend on Him, to depend upon His Spirit dwelling within us, as our Primary resource.

We are conditioned by religion to be ever looking outside of ourselves for the solutions to our spiritual & life needs. Rivers of living water shall flow from within you (See John 7:38,39). Not one river, but Multiple rivers.

Again, *we have not been spiritually taught to look to the Holy Spirit within us Continually, as our Ever-Present Resource in Everything. This must be our continual spiritual mindset—Greater is He that is Within us (1 John 4:4; "You, little children, are from God and have overcome them, because greater is He who is in you than he who is in the world.").*

Look at the Gospels, for example; Jesus continually demonstrated the Supply of the Spirit in Every single situation, now didn't He???? And, He rebuked His disciples for not having the same faith in that supply, even though He himself repeatedly demonstrated its total availability.

If that supply was something beyond their reach, He wouldn't have rebuked them, now would He??

The gospels are Jesus' demonstration of the full and abundant supply of the Spirit for every need, in the face of every single impossibility. We should spend time reading the gospels looking through new spiritual eyes at each instance where Jesus accessed the supply of the Spirit, and how those around Him responded with various levels of faith.

You will Notice how Jesus Never acted like it was something out of the ordinary, as you observe His actions and His demeanor. *In fact, He Always showed amazement at those who Lacked faith—He also Acknowledged those who Demonstrated their faith, now didn't He???*

I believe this is one major reason why Jesus was so very prolific in the working of miracles—He wasn't trying to impress anyone, and He wasn't just doing them to prove He was the Son of God. He said, "Do not be afraid, little flock, for your Father is pleased to Give you the Kingdom" (Luke 12:32), *and then He Demonstrated the Reality of that Kingdom over and over and over—And the Holy Spirit was sent to Continue that Demonstration Through Us to the World. Amen!*

CHAPTER 18

A SPIRITUAL WARFARE MINDSET; LETTERS FROM THE BATTLEFIELD

I used to drive with a little pewter sword on my keychain, to remind me every time I looked at it that the Word of God is the sword of the Spirit, and it is alive and powerful. If we do not look at the Word of God even subconsciously as a living thing, it's not doing us any good at all—it's a paperweight sitting on a desk or a table.

Whatever we have to do to get and keep and maintain that mindset, is what we have to do—*because we've never lived in a time like this before, a time that demands such a state of heart and mind and spirit.*

Recently, I woke up from a very prophetic dream about my brother Mike and I killing snakes. Before that dream, however, I had woken up several times during the night, and each time I woke up, the subject of continuing my podcast message on dealing with deliverance kept coming back to my mind. It was like the Lord was assuring me over and over again, that it was a subject I need to continue with, and each time I woke up, my mind would dwell on the subject for a few minutes and then I would go back to sleep.

In the dream with Mike, we were walking along a street that seemed to go on for blocks and blocks, and it was as though the rain had brought all of these snakes up from the gutters, like when after a heavy rain, snakes and other creatures start to come to the surface of the ground to escape the torrential downpour.

Mike and I were walking down the street, alongside the curbs and gutters, and there were snakes coming up out of the drains everywhere, and we were swinging our machetes and chopping them to pieces, and we made sure that every snake we saw, ended up dead. It was a very powerful feeling; *we were walking as though nothing could even hurt us, we had no fear whatsoever—in fact, it was quite the opposite; we were walking in a tremendous sense of authority and power.*

Now, the fact that my brother Mike was in a dream is very reassuring and comforting, and indicative of one thing—That the demons that tried to destroy his life while he was here on earth failed to succeed, because in the end, he did give his heart completely to the Lord before he passed.

From Heaven, he is truly victorious over all of satan's serpents.

The torrential rainfall that drove the serpents to the surface out of the gutters also is very prophetic to me—**The Lord is bringing the subject of deliverance to the surface, and exposing the works of the enemy for what they are, and exposing and revealing the work of demonic spirits for what it is and bringing it to the surface, where it can no longer be denied or ignored.**

The day of being a Christian who simply lives by stoic mental grasp of the Scriptures is over, because the spiritual onslaught will be so great that any believer choosing to live in ignorance or denial of the spirit realm will soon be overcome.

Speaking of the Endtimes, Jesus said, "Men will faint from fear and anxiety over what is coming upon the earth, for the powers of the heavens will be shaken." (Luke 21:26).

The willpower and mental and emotional strength of believers, apart from the Holy Spirit, will be no match for the spiritual forces that are overwhelming and engulfing the earth right now.

At some point, believers are going to have to admit that in their own strength, they cannot fight this battle—they will have to humble themselves and receive the baptism of the Holy Spirit in power, or simply be overcome.

The Baptism and Power of the Holy Spirit is the PRIMARY Emphasis of this Endtime Focus, and Deliverance is the Next. The intensifying of spiritual darkness, which is causing an upheaval in demonic forces, is something that no one will be able to ignore forever.

Our Western culture, which has emphasized the temporal over the spirit for as long as I can remember, has caused the institutional church to adopt the very same mentality. I am here to tell you, that road has hit a dead end!

This is a subject that every true Christian is going to have to embrace, and avail themselves of everything the Holy Spirit has—NOW. Obedience to the Holy Spirit and submission to Him is the Only ark of protection believers will have in this Endtime.

But make no mistake—the spiritual forces that are rising up and increasing, will be something that you will never be able to contend with on your own, so consider the outcome very carefully.

There is another spiritual reality that the Western church is almost totally clueless concerning, and that is **the *Reality of the Kingdom of God.***

We can say we 'believe' in the Kingdom of God—but *believing is not enough.*

It's one thing to say we believe in the Kingdom of God—*but if we never ever Demonstrate it's spiritual reality, then our 'belief' does us no good whatsoever.*

BELIEF WITHOUT DEMONSTRATION IS USELESS.

That's why it's called "The Book of ACTS", not "The Book of Beliefs"!

Mere belief is just religious dogmas; lifeless, powerless, and changes nothing. It imparts life to no one, sets no captives free, and does nothing to *Demonstrate the Present Reality of God's Kingdom.*

Here's another powerful thought, one I think we need to pay extremely close attention to.

There's only One message that Jesus preached; there's only one message that Jesus told his disciples to preach; there's only one message that was preached in the gospels and in the Book of Acts, and by the apostle Paul himself, over and over—the Gospel of the Kingdom!

Let that phrase sink in for a few minutes...."*The Gospel of the Kingdom*"....Let's be honest, in the Western church—how often does the phrase "Gospel of the Kingdom" even float up to the surface of our thoughts????

How about I ask the question in a different way:

How often does the word "Kingdom" float up to the surface of our thoughts, our Christian mindset????

How often do we even dwell on what it means to be part of a spiritual Kingdom???? A spiritual kingdom that is going to have its physical manifestation on the earth we're standing on right now!

To put it in a different way, how honest are we willing to be when it comes to admitting that *most of our Christian thinking revolves around the religious structures*, and *religious activities*, and *religious thinking* that we have made for ourselves, and *then we have tried to fit the Word of God into that box—instead of letting the Word of God stand on its own two Kingdom feet???*

What I'm trying so desperately to communicate is that *we have two conflicting mindsets here in the religious West.*

We have our *Western religious mindset*, set over and apart from the **Kingdom mindset of the Gospels and of the New Testament**—and those two views are completely at odds with each other, are in total opposition to one another, and can never coexist.

THIS is the issue of the hour that Western believers must absolutely, unequivocally get settled in their own hearts as quickly as possible— You cannot have a true New Testament/ Holy Spirit/ Kingdom mentality at the same time as the Western religious mentality—the two are completely polar opposite, and to be a true Overcomer in these Endtimes, the Only mentality that you have even a chance with, is that of the Kingdom.

In striving to speak from the Holy Spirit regarding subjects as vital as deliverance; as vital as walking in the Holy Spirit; as vital as hearing from the Holy Spirit; as vital as ministering in the Spirit, we have got to boldly confront the giant elephant in the living room—*the Western religious mindset that opposes all of this!*

We MUST understand that lives are at stake, as well as eternal destinies! But unless we truly understand what our Western religious mentality has COST us, there will be NO lasting change.

The Word of God tells us to be transformed **by the renewing of our minds**—so we must acknowledge the extent to which our minds have been conditioned by our Western religious culture, in a way that is Counter to the Kingdom of God, for any actual transformation to take place.

THIS is the most decisive issue confronting us in this hour, and we Must face it head on.

The testimonies I'm about to share will illustrate the magnitude of this problem, as well as demonstrate the profound importance of looking at Deliverance in its proper context—which is, Spirit-baptized believers exercising their God-given authority over demonic spirits in the name of Jesus.

The Holy Spirit has been very careful to see to it that there are enough examples of deliverance in the gospels and in the Book of Acts, so that we can see there's no place for excesses or sensationalism—it is strictly a matter of moving in the power of the Holy Spirit, and in the authority of Jesus Christ, and commanding them to come out.

I have been involved personally one on one in many deliverance sessions, and all I needed was moment by moment sensitivity in cooperation with the Holy Spirit, and much time in the Word and praying in tongues.

Now, to speak to the question that is most likely in some people's minds—"Why even talk about this subject??"

Let's bring it right back to Jesus Himself, and His purpose for being sent to humanity in the first place.

Yes, He was sent to be the sacrifice for our sins.

But the Word of God also boldly declares, "The one who practices sin is of the devil, because the devil has been sinning from the very start. **This is why the Son of God was revealed, to destroy the works of the devil.**" (1 John 3:8).

Most Christians in the West tend to think of Jesus Christ only in terms of what He has done for us in relation to Sin.

They never bother to spend any real time considering the fact that not only Jesus was manifested to take away our sin, but to destroy the one from whom sin originated in the first place.

Being our Sacrifice for sin—Our Savior—was only One part of the equation.

As our Redeemer, He goes so far as to destroy the effects and out-workings of what sin and evil have done—And a big part of that is in giving us His authority to eradicate evil influences, including demonic powers that are still a part of this fallen world which is still under the curse.

Remember, you may be born again and saved & full of the Holy Spirit, but you still live in a fallen, sin-cursed world with principalities and powers and evil spirits; they don't evaporate when you get saved—And any such notion is incredibly naïve, and completely unfounded in Scripture.

It is tragic, but yes, I am aware of the mindset of many believers who mistakenly believe that when you get saved, you don't have to worry about any problems with Demons. They feel that to believe otherwise, is to admit your salvation was somehow incomplete or inferior. This is nothing more than a lack of understanding of how the spiritual realm works. They do not care that there are thousands of testimonies of solid Christian believers being delivered from demons and set free and being restored to the joy of their salvation. They are just like the Pharisees of Jesus time, who were so angry they wanted to kill Him for healing and delivering people on the Sabbath. They have a heart set in cement, a religious mentality that simply will not budge, and simply will not be persuaded by the mercy of Jesus being manifested for His own children—And to anyone who cannot see the love and mercy of Jesus in giving us His full authority to set the captives free, captives for whom he died and bled, there isn't much I can say to you.

True ministry is only born from a heart of the love of Jesus for the humanity He sacrificed Himself for

My dear reader, you would be shocked at how many times I have shared the testimonies of precious children of God being powerfully set free from the most evil wicked spirits, and the cold, hard, dead religious Pharisees simply remain unmoved—they do not care, if it doesn't line up with their institutional Western churchianity mentality; they don't care Who gets sets free!

They see nothing but something that is an affront to their religious mindset—And their religious mindset means more to them than a million people being set free in the name of Jesus.

That in and of itself is satanic, and yet they think they are free.

It is the exact same spirit that Jesus confronted in His time—spirits that caused the religious leaders to hate Him and want to murder Him for healing and delivering on the Sabbath day. If that is not a reflection of the satanic power of religious spirits, nothing else is.

Now, at this point, I am going to share a couple of testimonies of situations where the Lord sovereignly placed me in the path of someone who needed deliverance—and please note, it was not something I went looking for.

The testimonies I am about to share are not to lift myself up, but to show you "textbook" examples of God sovereignly moving in a deliverance situation; being prepared spiritually and ready to cooperate with the Holy Spirit in such a situation; and being determined in your heart to see someone set free.

You must remember, you are not ONLY dealing with the person needing deliverance— you are dealing with the spirits afflicting and tormenting that person. That is the clear spiritual mindset you must have, no exceptions.

You must Know that you are dealing with unseen spirits—not the person, not their personality, but spirits.

There are so many in the body of Christ who need help desperately, but people want to counsel them, console them, sympathize with them, empathize with them—*everything but deal with the spirits behind the persons' torment and affliction.*

Religious sympathy never delivered anyone. Sadly, my first testimony is of that nature, and it grieves me to have to share it with you, but for the sake of others suffering similarly, I must.

My first story is of a young man named Jules, whom I met on the streets while I was attending Gold Coast Baptist Church in West Palm Beach back in the early 80s.

I don't recall the exact circumstances of how we met, but I do remember him as a young man who was desperate for spiritual help.

When I say "desperate", I mean face to the ground/ sack cloth and ashes desperate.

When I say "desperate", I mean that to this very day, 40 years after I first met Jules, I can still hear the sound of him weeping and weeping till I thought his heart would explode, because he was so desperate to be free from the powers of addiction and bondage that ruled his existence. He was into witchcraft, heavy drugs, and sexual addictions. God always seemed to have a way of bringing the most lost of the lost across my path, even when I did not know what to do.

And with Jules, all I could think of to do was to bring him to my church and try to get someone there who could help him—but it was all to no avail.

I still remember the one weekend when I had brought Jules to church to talk to a youth pastor, who was totally clueless as to what to do—And afterwards, Jules just collapsed on the floor in one of the hallways, propped up against the wall sobbing his poor heart out like he had just been told that his case was forever hopeless.

He was the most broken young man I've ever seen in my entire life—it's like he was living with a raging inferno that was eating him from the inside out, and no one had any water to extinguish the fire that was destroying him.

I felt so completely helpless, and I was completely bewildered that I as a Christian could give him no relief whatsoever.

I wish that you could even for a few brief seconds hear the sounds of this broken man sobbing—sounds that I still hear 40 years later...

I still see the tears pouring from his eyes, at the thought of him having to spend the rest of his life in this tortured state.

But, Jules did not have to spend the rest of his life in that tortured state—At 29 years of age, on January 15, 1990, just 9 years after I had last seen him, Jules ended his own pain and suffering...Because the Church of Jesus Christ was full of dead religion, and powerless to set this captive free...

And I have told Jules's story over and over and over, in hopes of waking up the Body of Christ to their God-given responsibility.

My second testimony is of a much more positive outcome.

The very first time the Lord used me in a deliverance situation was completely out of the blue, not something I had been looking for at all. I'm giving you the condensed version here.

It was 1985, and I was getting a ride home from church one Sunday night, from a friend who regularly volunteered to drive me. On the way to my place, she had to stop by her house first, and we sat in her driveway once we got there for a bit talking. Her conversation veered toward issues that she was having with her dad, and it was clear that there were some intense situations between them, as her voice became full of rage, and then her eyes rolled back into her head and she blacked out. I knew at that moment that demonic activity was present, and I actually felt very concerned for her well-being. I felt that the demonic manifestations could actually intensify, to the point of causing her physical harm.

The next day, I went to the home of the pastor of the church we were going to, only to find out that he had gone out of the state on an emergency situation, and no one else was available for prayer ministry of any kind.

I basically cried out to God and said, Lord, this is a desperate situation, you've got to find me someone to help here!

I felt His response immediately—You have the Holy Spirit, you know the Word; you're it.

So I called my friend up, and we arranged to meet the next day for prayer (although I knew it was going to take a lot more than that).

Now, it is impossible for me to put into words adequate enough to convey to you my listeners what it felt like going into this situation.

Imagine you happen upon a horrific car wreck, and EMTs will be hours getting there, and you are the only one on scene who can help, but you have no experience. You know that you have no choice, you simply have to roll up your sleeves and get in there and do whatever you can.

Fortunately, I had been baptized in the Holy Spirit at this point for two years, and had been in the Word of God very steadfastly for the same amount of time. I even listened to the Word of God every day when I would come home from work and shower—I drove my roommate nuts.

But for me, this was a situation where failure was not an option.

This was, to me, a reminder of Jules several years before—and I was not going to let the enemy win this time, now that I had the weapons! But I also knew that I was 100% dependent on the Holy Spirit to guide me through what had to be done. I stayed up the entire night praying in tongues and reading and rereading a little booklet by a man named Norvel Hayes entitled, "Jesus Taught Me How to Cast Out Demons".

The next morning we met at a place that afforded us total privacy, because I wasn't sure what was going to happen.

As I laid hands on her and prayed in tongues, one by one demons began to manifest in different ways—some were very violent, some simply wanted to try to make her go to sleep and short circuit the whole process (a delaying tactic that demons like to use).

After about six hours she was finally free, and went to sleep on a couch. I just sat in a chair elsewhere nearby, praying and worshipping the Lord and keeping the atmosphere spiritually light. When she awoke a couple of hours later, she was like a completely different person.

These testimonies I'm sharing of the deliverances that I was used in, were because nobody else was available. I didn't go looking for those situations; God brought them to me and he told me point blank, you're all I've got, there's nobody else!

And at some point in time, You will be all God's got because there's nobody else, and he's going to put you in that person's life who needs to be set free—will you be ready? Will you do what it takes Now to Get ready???

Get baptized in the Holy Spirit—and if you're clinging to dead religious teaching that has convinced you that you don't need the baptism of the Holy Spirit, May God help you....Because the time we're in right now, the battle's coming to your doorstep, ready or not.

There is a reason why the apostles themselves made sure that believers who were born again received the baptism of the Holy Spirit; *because they were born into a spiritual battlefield!*

Everybody knows the words of Jesus when He said, "He that is not with me is against me" (Luke 11:23). *But how many know that those words of Jesus were in the context of casting out demons???* Jesus was saying those who do not participate with Him in the ministry of casting out demons are working against Him! "He who is not with Me is against Me, **and he who does not gather with Me scatters**" (Luke 11:23, complete verse)

(Also See Mark 9:38-40; Luke 9:49,50)

As you read the Gospels and over and over, you see Jesus talking about one thing that He can reward and bless—those who are Doers of the Word; those who are obedient, those who do what He says.

We want to call ourselves Christians???

Then we have got to LIVE the gospels.

There is no way around it. That means you have to be led by, instructed by, and taught by the Holy Spirit—And you have to be empowered by Him to do the things that Jesus said we're supposed to do; **Set the captives free and make disciples.** If you aren't doing that, you're not living as a Believer. That's not condemnation—that is a spiritual reality check from Heaven.

There are thousands of people just like Jules out there that we walk by every single day—And when we lay our heads down on our pillows at night and go to sleep, they are waiting for us to come into their life, to cross their path with the power of Jesus residing in us to set them free...When will we show up??? Actually, the question is more like, **When will we be Prepared and spiritually ready for God to be able to use us???**

I met a young Christian woman a few years ago, who had just gotten saved and came to the Lord out of the New Age and out of witchcraft. She had a light in her eyes and a freshness in her spirit, and I had no doubt in my mind her salvation experience was completely and totally real.

As Shari and I visited, she mentioned that she was having demonic attacks at night, so we went through her house to gather up any leftover paraphernalia from her New Age and witchcraft days.

I took everything to another location where there was a safe place to burn all of it, went back and prayed over her house, pled the blood of Jesus over every room, and thought that was that.

Well, a few days later I found out that she was still having demonic attacks at night. She said that the leader of their witchcraft coven was actually materializing at the foot of her bed every night, telling her that she would never be free and that she would always belong to him.

Immediately, I felt the anger of the Lord at those spirits, and I told Shari I would spend time praying in the spirit and fasting for as long as I felt was necessary, and we would get it taken care of.

I was working at a men's Christian rehab and discipleship ministry at the time, and I had lots of free time during the day, so I spent every day for two weeks straight praying in tongues on our property, and fasting.

I remember walking around on the backside of the property one afternoon, and as I looked over the fence at the afternoon sky, I could feel those spirits watching me, and I pointed my finger at them and said, "Your time is almost up!"

Most Christians in the West, in this day and time, have so little understanding about spiritual warfare and their authority in Jesus Christ over evil spirits, because we are so busy using our minds and our intellect to understand the Bible with—but yet having no real connection with the Holy Spirit, so the demons get to run around rampant & unchallenged, and precious people remain held captive. This should not be!

Jesus said, "And these signs will accompany those who believe: In My name they will drive out demons; they will speak in new tongues" (Mark 16:17—And by the way, that was Jesus speaking AFTER He was resurrected, and commissioning ALL of His disciples—not just the 12— to go into all the world and preach the gospel, so this was not limited to just 12 apostles. He said, "Those who believe in my name"—that is future tense; that means you and me and all the rest of us who believe on his name).

As I was praying in tongues on a Thursday afternoon, I could feel the Holy Spirit in me suddenly give me the discernment that "today is the day".

I called Shari up to tell her to meet me at the church that evening where they were holding a service, because I knew the pastors were Spirit-filled, and my thought was that after the service was over, I would take Shari to them, and they would pray over her and cast the spirits out. I knew they were spiritually strong enough and were always led by God.

While everyone was singing the praise and worship songs, I was sitting in my seat, quietly praying in tongues under my breath, because I wanted to stay spiritually focused on the job at hand.

That is another aspect of spiritual warfare; because it is done in the spirit, it's very important to keep your mind and your thoughts focused and submitted to the Holy Spirit—especially when it is something critical involving someone else's life. You're like a spiritual paramedic or EMT— this is not a game; it is life or death.

As I sat praying in the spirit, I began to pray over Shari silently—so quietly that no one sitting in front of me or in back of me would have ever heard a thing I said.

I found myself praying, "Father God, I plead the blood of Jesus over Shari, from the top of her head to the bottom of her feet—", and even though my eyes were closed as I prayed, I knew in the Spirit that something had just happened.

I opened my eyes and looked over to where Shari had been sitting—and she was gone!

I knew instantly in my spirit that the demons had heard me pleading the blood of Jesus over her, and had driven her out of the church!

(Now, it is very evident from reading the Gospels to see how demons torment and drive people, so while I wasn't surprised, I felt a holy anger at these spirits that were tormenting my new Christian friend)

I walked outside feeling like I was wearing spiritual armor from head to toe, and I scanned the property for any sign of Shari.

Suddenly, I looked to my left to the far end of the church property, and saw her standing under the only tree, and when I got up close to her, she was standing still, with her head hanging down, and she was shaking like a leaf and whimpering like a wounded animal.

I took a couple of steps towards Shari, listening intently to the Holy Spirit as to what to do next.

I said "Shari, are you feeling tormented in your mind?", but she couldn't reply—all she could do was shake her head 'yes' as she continued to tremble and whimper.

Suddenly, without me even giving it any conscious thought whatsoever, my right arm shot out with my hand on her head, and I commanded, "In the name of Jesus, come out of her!!!"

Shari let out a shriek like I had never heard before, and crumpled to the ground like she was unconscious.

And that is the last thing I remember—

And when I shared the story with a fellow minister, and told him that I could not understand why I went blank after that happened, he explained that it was because the Holy Spirit had taken over in such a powerful way, that my conscious mind was not engaged.

I am happy to report that Shari has been serving faithfully and joyfully in her church to this very day, overseeing their hospitality ministries.

CHAPTER 19

DREAMS, VISIONS, & WARNINGS —
PREPARING THE LAST
DAYS BELIEVER

For every individual who is intent on having a biblically, spiritually prepared heart for the Endtimes, it is vitally important to remember One Thing concerning the last days events—Jesus' primary focus and the Holy Spirit's primary focus is on His Church, His people—Not on the institutional church, but His spiritual body of believers. We Must make that distinction, and keep it clearly in our minds—God is NOT preoccupied with saving the institutional religious system. Quite the opposite, it is already under His Judgement.

Now, as sort of a preface to everything else that I'm going to address in this chapter, I'd like to share a dream that I had around the end of last October 2021, as I believe it contains a very pivotal message that relates to our topic.

In this dream, there were two groups of believers that I could see on Earth.

The first group was shorter in stature, and seemed to be walking in a yellowish atmosphere that reached from the ground just to over the top of their head—they could not see anything above that.

It was actually as though they were completely unaware that it was possible to see above the yellowish atmosphere—it was like everything that they could see at eye level was all that existed. They had no concept of there being anything higher than them.

The second group of believers was quite a bit taller, and even though they were walking in the same yellowish atmosphere from the waist down, from the waist up they were walking in a crystal clear, blue atmosphere that was not cloudy at all, and they were able to see at much greater distances, with much greater clarity.

This meant that their reality was based on a much broader, clearer perspective than the ones walking below in the yellow atmosphere, who were completely oblivious that anything higher or greater even existed.

As the dream continued, the Holy Spirit began explaining to me that the believers in the yellow atmosphere were those who were completely earthly minded, and whose reality revolved only around their earthly existence and their earthly lives—they did not see anything beyond or above that, even though they called themselves believers. Their entire focus was only on what was around them or in front of them, but nothing Higher.

This rendered them completely separate from the other believers, who walked higher than their yellow atmosphere, because their perspectives were completely different.

The believers in the yellow atmosphere only thought about and spoke about things that revolved around their earthly existence—*they even interpreted the things of God & the Bible only in terms of how it affected their earthly life.*

When the Holy Spirit told me that, I understood why, even though the two groups of believers seemed to be walking in the same direction, they seemed so completely different from each other.

The believers who were taller, walking in the clear blue atmosphere, who had far greater clarity of vision, had a completely different spiritual perception, and so when they tried to communicate with the believers in the yellow atmosphere, it was like they were speaking a completely different language.

Then the Holy Spirit showed me that that was why Paul had to tell the Corinthians, "Brothers, I could not address you as spiritual, but as worldly—as infants in Christ." (1 Corinthians 3:1), and so many other scriptures as well came to me while I was in the dream, such as, "The mind of the flesh is death, but the mind of the Spirit is life and peace,"(Romans 8:6); "Set your minds on things above, not on earthly things." (Colossians 3:2).

There was an intense sense of urgency throughout the dream, and I realized later it is because God is making that distinction Now between these two classes of believers—and the intensity of the spiritual storm that is building all around us is making that distinction as well, and those who are earthly-minded will cling to their earthly lives, and those who are spiritually minded will be laying their lives down for their brethren, taking up their crosses and following Him, loving not their lives unto the death.

This distinction is going to become so pronounced, that there will actually come a rending of the two classes of believers, with the earthly-minded believers even coming to resent and hate and oppose those who are spiritually minded, and whose gaze is fixed on Eternity...

Revelation 3:6; "He who has an ear, let him hear what the Spirit says to the churches"

In that one short, concise sentence, our Lord Jesus Christ—Head of the Church in all generations—Gives each and every believer in the Endtimes one clear objective—and in the end, it will be the One clear objective that matters the most; Hearing what the Spirit is speaking to the churches.

And, as Jesus is speaking this directive in the singular, by saying "let him who has an ear", the greatest priority becomes each and every one of us having developed a clear, "open channel" relationship with the Holy Spirit.

In the dream I just finished relating, it is clear that earthly-minded, carnal believers will not be able to hear what the Spirit is speaking to the churches—They are minding earthly things, and have closed themselves off from receiving anything from the Spirit of God. This is clearly why Jesus spoke in the singular in this verse.

There are two scriptures that I would like to share with you, in connection with that one overriding priority—The priority of hearing what the Spirit is speaking to the churches.

"He went on to say, "Pay attention to *what* you hear. With the measure you use, it will be measured to you, and even more will be added to you. For whoever has will be given more. But whoever does not have, even what he has will be taken away from him." (Mark 4:24,25)

"Pay attention, therefore, to **how** you listen. Whoever has will be given more, but whoever does not have, even what he thinks he has will be taken away from him." (Luke 8:18)

So here, Jesus is giving us a two-pronged approach when it comes to hearing the Holy Spirit.

First, he is emphasizing to pay close attention to WHAT we hear.

Second, he is emphasizing the importance of HOW we hear.

In Luke 9:44, "Let these words sink into your ears: The Son of Man is about to be delivered into the hands of men."

We know that how we hear depends greatly on the degree of importance attached to the words we are hearing.

If someone is merely giving us instructions to a store, we might be only half listening, while thinking about something else at the same time.

If, however, we are calling 911 and being given life-saving instructions for someone, you can bet we're going to be listening with every fiber of our being.

In both instances, we are listing to words being spoken to us by someone else—but in one instance we are only listening very casually, whereas in the other instance, we are listening extremely intently because it's a life or death situation.

So, to the degree we are a casual listener toward the Holy Spirit, or a very determined, focused listener, determines to what degree we will hear his voice—and it also determines not only IF we will hear from him, it also determines how much. After all, if we're only casually listening for his voice, how much do you think he's going to speak???

From personal experience, I believe in most cases the HOW determines the WHAT.

In this case, that means your HOW will determine your WHAT.

Here is what I mean.

If you already have it firmly settled in your heart and mind that you Want to hear from the Holy Spirit, and the Holy Spirit Alone, then you are now narrowing down your WHAT.

That means, you are not going to be listening to every TV preacher and every self-proclaimed prophet that opens their mouth. You are switching to one station, and one station only; one channel, and one channel only—You have determined and made the quality decision that you are going to receive your spiritual input from one source, and one source alone—the Holy Spirit.

THAT Takes care of the WHAT.

Now that you have settled the WHAT, You need to be committed to the HOW.

This is where we take all of the mystery and all of the complications out of hearing the Holy Spirit, because it really only comes down to the two qualifiers that Jesus said out of His own mouth in Mark and Luke, which we've already quoted. *Even the believer with the newest experience with the baptism of the Holy Spirit, if you will just focus on these two things—the HOW and the WHAT, and stay focused on those two things, you will do just fine.*

Now, as for being committed to the HOW.

That is determined by your level of commitment and desperation—How badly do you want to hear from the Holy Spirit???

How indispensable is hearing His voice to you???

I will tell you this from personal experience—if you are committed to praying in tongues at least a half hour every day consistently, you will have no problem hearing His voice, because you are taking the time and effort to build up your spirit man, which is how He will be prompting you, urging you, and speaking His thoughts to you.

You will become receptive, sensitive, and responsive to His inward promptings very naturally, and you will find it easier and easier to recognize when He is speaking to your spirit, prompting you in a certain way. You will begin to perceive His presence, and His impartation of a sense of urgency in matters in a new way.

*Because **this is an inward relationship**, the Holy Spirit through the baptism of the Holy Spirit **is living within you as a real person, but because He is in your spirit and not standing outside of you, you must learn to hear Him inwardly with your spirit.***

In much the same way that you are sensitive to the moods and unspoken feelings of your spouse, you learn to develop the same inward sensitivity toward the Holy Spirit.

There's no mystery here—there's just a concentrated focus on developing your inward sensitivity to the Holy Spirit living inside you.

You will begin to feel what He feels; you will begin to feel when He is wanting to direct you in a certain way, or to prompt you to take a different course of action than what your mind might have planned—**Because this is the beginning of learning to live from your spirit, not your mind.**

Your mind is not omnipresent—it can't be everywhere at the same time. The Holy Spirit of God IS everywhere at the same time, and He knows things that you don't know; He sees things that you don't see, and *He is in you to clue you in, for your good, and for your benefit.*

Now, for what I call my Revelation 1-2-3 checklist:

*FAITH FOCUS: Is my inward attitude one of faith and trust, or is there a mixture of doubt, anxiety, wondering, and fear? Jesus said, "Whoever loves his life will lose it, but whoever hates his life in this world will keep it for eternal life." (John 12:25). So, *is there any part of me or my life that is yet unsurrendered?*

*Commitment and Consecration—Again, looking to Daniel as our example. His level of commitment and consecration was so profoundly on point, that even his enemies in the kingdom of Babylon could not find anything to slander him with. I know personally that *our level of commitment and consecration is going to have to Eclipse what we have been accustomed to getting by with.*

Revelation 1:1 begins with the declaration that this Book is addressed to His SERVANTS, "to Show THEM the things that must soon come to pass"—MEANING, This revelation is Not for the casual, the merely inquisitive & curious, nor for those simply giving Lip service to God. "This is the revelation of Jesus Christ, which God gave Him to show His SERVANTS what must soon come to pass. He made it known by sending His angel to His *servant* John…" (Revelation 1:1)

ONLY THOSE WHO ARE SOLD OUT TO HIM AS SERVANTS, NOT LOVING THEIR LIVES AS THEIR OWN, WILL PERCEIVE CLEARLY WHAT THE SPIRIT IS SAYING.

The very Fact that Revelation opens with this pointed & specific reference tells us very clearly that THIS Book is specially devoted to those who have the heart-attitude of being a bond servant to the Lord, having forsaken the world and all else. (Not coincidentally, the apostle Jude—in the last book just before Revelation—likewise refers to himself as "a bond servant of Jesus Christ")

Now, Daniel prayed three times a day, and I'm pretty sure that a major part of his time spent before the Lord was done in self-examination. "Search me, O God, and know my heart; test me and know my concerns. See if there is any offensive way in me; lead me in the way everlasting." (Psalm 139:23,24).

When Jesus was undergoing heavy trials and plots against His life, He said, "I will not speak with you much longer, for the prince of this world is coming, and he has no claim on Me." (John 14:30). In other words, the enemy is coming, but he has no legal hold on my life—there is no area of compromise in my heart that he could take advantage of and exploit.

I think that it would benefit us greatly to continually turn to our prophet brother Daniel as our inspiration, and as our example of what the Endtime believer must be made of, in order to survive and overcome in the last days. Let us keep in mind that it was Daniel who received prophetic revelation and angelic visitations concerning specifically what was going to befall Endtime believers. We won't go into that here, but please feel inspired to dig into Daniel and see what the Holy Spirit revealed to him.

*An Abiding Awareness of His Throne & Our Sharing in His Coming Rule—Rev. 1:4-7,9

If there is one thing that stands out to me about the book of Revelation, is that when you look at it as a whole, it is a panoramic expression of the boundless compassion, love, and majesty of our God toward us.

I mean, the very first chapter alone is like a cosmic red carpet welcome to all those that He has loved and redeemed by the blood of His Son, and the status to which He has elevated us with a view towards sharing in His dominion for all eternity.

That is how this majestic Vision begins—a vision that encompasses all of eternity past, present, and future—an eternity that we are all invited to share in.

And right up front, the risen Lord Jesus Christ Himself tells us exactly the price He has paid for us to share in this, as well as what will be required of us to qualify for the right to rule and reign with Him.

There are absolutely No challenges or battles hidden from us—He lays all of it out with absolute, unwavering, crystal clear honesty. As our Supreme Commanding Officer (as well as Redeemer), He shows us very clearly what He expects from His people, as He does His troop inspection with seven churches, commending them where they have earned it, and correcting them where they need it.

He ends each inspection and reprisal with specific rewards for those who overcome.

He shows incredible grace towards those who have clearly endured the most brutal, heated battles—But the way in which He addresses each of the seven churches clearly reveals Jesus Christ as the divine Head and Ruler over His Church—A reality that is tragically ignored by most of the prosperous, comfort seeking, self-preserving Western religious system.

But as Jesus plainly declares in Revelation 2:23, "Then I will strike her children dead, and ALL the churches will know that I am the One who searches minds and hearts, and I will repay each of you according to your deeds"—Words we can run from, but we cannot hide. (Not at all coincidentally, the words of Jesus here are a profoundly distinct echo of what the Holy Spirit did in Acts 5:1-10!)

There is one more reality shown in Revelation, that is seldom discussed among God's people on this earth.

In fact, in my 44 years as a believer, I do not remember a single sermon or message preached, or a teaching taught on this one profound Heavenly reality:

At the center of everything that exists in the universe, is the throne of the Lamb.

In fact, chapters 4 and 5 of Revelation are about nothing else but the Throne of the Father, and the Son, and the Lamb in heaven—His throne is the center of all activity in the universe, and is the origin of every event related after chapter 5 in the book of Revelation. And how often do we meditate on the reality that we have been chosen to sit with Him on His throne and to rule with Him????

Revelation 5:10 says, "You have made them to be a kingdom and priests to serve our God, and they will reign upon the earth."

Ruling and reigning throughout Eternity with Him is the dominant theme of the Old Testament prophets and the New Testament promises, and yet I dare say it is a subject that does not occupy the place in our hearts and minds that it so abundantly deserves.

Just take a moment to deeply pause and meditate on the fact that the Holy Spirit has been sent from eternity to this earth, to indwell each and every one of us; to live in each and every one of us, to transform and shape each and every one of us, and to make us fit to reign and rule with him throughout all eternity.

Consider that in the few places on this earth where there are still actual kings and queens, that no heir to the throne is simply placed on the throne by virtue of being an heir; *they are groomed and prepared from earliest childhood, so that they may be equipped and qualified to occupy the throne later in life.*

How much more so those who will be ruling and reigning with the Creator of the heavens and the earth????

Hebrews 6:4,5 tell us that we have been provided with divine equipment, with a view toward preparing us for our future position, and that we have been made partakers of the powers of the age to come—powers of the Age when we will rule and reign with him.

This truth is something that we must absolutely spend quality time meditating on and studying, and get a living vision of it on the inside of us.

The apostle Paul was quick to remind believers that they would one day judge angels as well as the world, so it is unspeakably vital that we raise our sights (1 Corinthians 6:2,3).

The first recorded martyr in the New Testament, Stephen, said as he was being stoned, ""Look," he said, "I see heaven open and the Son of Man standing at the right hand of God." (Acts 7:56).

Again, we must meditate on these things now more than ever before, because, my beloved brothers and sisters, times of darkness are coming—and the only thing that is going to give us backbones of steel and hearts of fire is having that heavenly vision within us.

The one passage that we should truly let soak into our hearts is that scripture I just mentioned a moment ago, Hebrews 6:4,5.

I dare say we should make it a part of our daily prayer time, by speaking it over ourselves individually;

'By the power of the Holy Spirit I have been enlightened; I have tasted of the heavenly gift; I have been made a partaker of the Holy Spirit; I have tasted the good Word of God, and the powers of the Age to come'.

I think that ties right in with what David said in Psalm 103:2; "Bless the LORD, O my soul, and do not forget all His kind deeds", and then David goes on to list each and every benefit from the Lord, covering every area of his life. I think it would benefit us greatly if we did the same.

I would say add to that daily confession over ourselves 1 Peter 1:3-5;

"Blessed be the God and Father of our Lord Jesus Christ! By His great mercy He has given us new birth into a living hope through the resurrection of Jesus Christ from the dead, and into an inheritance that is imperishable, undefiled, and unfading, reserved in heaven for you, who through faith are shielded by God's power for the salvation that is ready to be revealed in the last time."

And actually, speaking God's Word over ourselves is abundantly scriptural—did you know, for example, that the English phrase "to learn by heart" in the Hebrew means "to learn by mouth". In other words, the Hebrew manner of learning a subject—especially when it pertained to the Scriptures—was to recite them out loud to oneself, in order to get it committed to memory.

I believe one of the most potent ways to get the realities of the Word of God established in our own hearts, to where they begin to actually become a part of our daily consciousness, is by speaking them over ourselves, as well as speaking God's Word over others as we are praying and interceding for them.

I am a firm believer in speaking the Word over our situations, over ourselves, and most definitely praying the Word over those we love, and those that we desire to see changed for the glory of God. Sometimes the only thing that will change the situation or a person will be the Word of God spoken and prayed over that situation, and over that individual.

Remember now, we have *already* been made a kingdom of priests unto our God, and we have been given His Spirit, so that when we pray in the Spirit, we are speaking directly to God and not as unto men (1 Corinthians 14:2).

We have been given boldness of access to his throne of grace, we have been given the authority and power through the Spirit to intercede on behalf of others, and to represent the interests of the kingdom of God here on earth.

Now, I would like us to revisit the subject we were speaking about earlier, from Revelation 3:6; "He who has an ear, let him hear what the Spirit says to the churches". This is the closing statement that Jesus makes when addressing each of the seven churches.

This is Jesus Christ, the head of the church, speaking from heaven to the seven churches, with His very specific admonitions, rebukes, and exhortations—*And yet, after each instance of Jesus speaking to each specific church, He closes by saying "Let him who has an ear, hear what the SPIRIT is speaking to the churches".*

Did you catch that?

Did it register with you?

It was JESUS speaking to each church, and yet He says, "Let him who has an ear, hear what the SPIRIT is saying to the churches".

(There's a very significant and powerful point I'm making here, I hope you're catching it)

Go with me to John chapter 16 for a minute.

Jesus is talking to His disciples about the ministry of the Holy Spirit, and precisely how the Holy Spirit will operate on their behalf when He comes.

Now, hold your finger at Revelation 3:6, and look at John 16:13-15;

"However, when the Spirit of truth comes, He will guide you into all truth. For He will not speak on His own, but He will speak what He hears, and He will declare to you what is to come. He will glorify Me by taking from what is Mine and disclosing it to you. Everything that belongs to the Father is Mine. That is why I said that the Spirit will take from what is Mine and disclose it to you."

Did you catch that?

The Holy Spirit will speak to us what He hears Jesus the Head of the Church speaking.

So, when Jesus says to each of the seven churches, "Let him who has an ear hear what the Spirit is saying", **what that means is, everything Jesus said to each church, was to be relayed by the Holy Spirit speaking.**

Jesus is in Heaven, and the Holy Spirit is the representative of the Godhead to the Church here on Earth.

If we are going to know and hear what the Head of the Church is speaking to us, it will come via one channel only—the Holy Spirit of the living God.

And here's the kicker—just because we don't hear the Holy Spirit, is not going to be an excuse for not hearing what Jesus the Head of the Church was speaking to the Church in this hour.

There's a saying that goes, "ignorance of the law is no excuse", and nowhere is that more applicable than here with the Church.

The Holy Spirit has been sent; He is available for each and every one of us. He is speaking to the Church, with some very specific instructions and directions, but not everyone is listening, because we aren't tuned in to the Holy Spirit, who is taking what Jesus is saying to the church, and trying to reveal it to us, but our ears are closed.

There is one theme that runs throughout the whole of scripture, and that is one of divine order.

And God is not going to break His divine order to accommodate our ignorance or spiritual laziness. That is why he has been so painstakingly careful and kind to establish for us what His divine order is for the Church.

Jesus had already said that it was better for us that He go to the Father, because then Jesus would then send the Holy Spirit ("But I tell you the truth, it is for your benefit that I am going away. Unless I go away, the Advocate will not come to you; but if I go, I will send Him to you"; John 16:7).

In other words, this is the divine order that the Son and the Father and the Holy Spirit are establishing, and it will determine the way the Church will be guided and led after Jesus goes to the Father.

All through Jesus's earthly ministry, He walked according to the same divine order that we are required to walk according to.

"So Jesus replied, "Truly, truly, I tell you, the Son can do nothing by Himself, unless He sees the Father doing it. For whatever the Father does, the Son also does." (John 5:19).

How did Jesus SEE what the Father was doing?? The Holy Spirit was revealing it to Jesus one step at a time.

How do we know the will of Jesus and the will the Father?? The Holy Spirit Reveals it to us one step at a time.

That's why Jesus said, "He will glorify Me by taking from what is Mine and disclosing it to you." (John 16:14).

We have not been accustomed to following divine order, because the religious system that we have been tied to and programmed by does not operate by divine order, and is not subject to divine order—it is subject to the order of man and the control of man, so hence we have inherited all of this mess—*our spiritual thinking isn't lined up with divine order.* **Our daily lives are mostly patterned according to religious thinking, not divine order.**

But if the Kingdom of God was to come to earth Tomorrow, what would each of us be walking according to THEN???? DIVINE ORDER.

Well, why should that be any different right now at this very moment in time????

We are at the most critical time in human history, and it is absolutely non-negotiably imperative that we take it upon ourselves, each and every one of us, to learn from the Head of the Church, Jesus Christ, through His Word and through the Holy Spirit, divine Kingdom order.

It starts with Jesus and the Holy Spirit and His Word—you cannot lean on some pastor, or some deacon, or some Bible teacher; this is going to be on you individually when we all stand before Him and give account.

I simply cannot state it any more clearly than that—this is the worst possible time in human history for anyone to be leaning on another man. I don't care how anointed they are, how nice they are— they are not going to stand next to you before Jesus and explain to Him on your behalf why you didn't hear this or that or do this or that.

The good news is and has always been that He has made His Holy Spirit totally 100% available to each one of us full-time, 24 hours a day! So whatever it takes, avail yourself of everything the Holy Spirit has and is, and wants to make available to you. Flush, nuke, torch every ounce of religious reasoning that would try to dissuade you, because time is short. Settle it in your heart that if you were the only believer left on earth, you would be completely and totally sold out to the Lord, walking in His Spirit. And remember, He has said He will never leave us or forsake us, even unto the end of the age (Matthew 28:20, Hebrews 13:5).

CHAPTER 20

SERVING AS PRIEST & PROPHET OF YOUR HOME, THROUGH INTERCESSION & PRAYING IN THE SPIRIT FOR YOUR FAMILY

t's been on my heart for a while to minister on the subject of husbands ministering to their wives as Christ ministers to the church, as I experienced so much of that in my life with Roopa. I will be sharing my some of my experiences, and my shortcomings and failures as well, because I believe that we can learn from the things that we failed to do, as much as the things we did right.

I will say this, though—I wish I had allowed the Lord to give me the grace to humble myself much, much more than I did, in praying in the spirit with and over my wife. I allowed myself to get all hung up on the fact that her physical healing was not coming in spite of all my prayers, so I felt like a complete failure in the prayer department.

I was very reluctant to pray over her, thinking I'm only going to feel like a failure again.

But I failed to see her need of my prayers through HER eyes; she still needed my prayers in the spirit to bring her comfort in her emotions, and peace for her mind. All I could focus on was the physical healing—I failed to look at all of her other needs as my wife (her emotional needs, etc.)

The primary ministry husbands have to their wives is to love them as Christ loved the church, by serving them through prayer and ministry of the Word and Spirit.

From personal experience, it takes a real humbling of oneself to pray over your wife, especially in the spirit, because you are serving her in the most intimate way possible—And humbling yourself to pray with the one who knows you best, the one who is most intimate and closest to you, takes true servanthood humility. It takes a deep willingness to lay aside your comfort level, and all of the subconscious baggage that we may carry, to kneel down and pray in your prayer language over the woman who is bone of your bone and flesh of your flesh.

You are allowing the Holy Spirit to open up the deepest part of you, in order to minister to your wife in the deepest parts of herself—the deepest parts of her where the Holy Spirit dwells.

I am ashamed to admit that I badly failed in that area.

One of the things that made it hard for me to open up in that area, was my feelings of failure in the area of praying for her healing.

I felt that if I was not successful in praying for her healing, then my prayers were not going to avail much in anything else, so I kind of just gave up.

There were many, many times during our marriage that Roopa would ask me to pray in tongues over her, and I don't think I can remember a single time when my flesh felt like doing it, but I would eventually acquiesce because I knew she wouldn't ask me to pray if she wasn't in need.

Again, it was just such a battle to try and get past my sense of failure as a husband in the department of prayer.

I don't know of a husband out there who takes a sense of failure lightly, especially when it concerns his wife, and I was so accustomed in my single days to seeing prayer accomplish mighty things—healings, deliverances, and so on, so this was a mountain staring me in the face every single day, the mountain of my wife's infirmity.

It was a mountain that seemed to mock me constantly; "Look, you can do great on your sales job, you can have great success with your career, but you can't move ME!"

I remember nights I would be lying in bed for the longest time, praying in tongues quietly over my wife, believing God for her healing. There were so many times when I felt such a divine, powerful authority, that I fully expected to wake up the next morning with my wife healed. The next morning would come, and nothing—and again, a sense of failure. Now that Roopa has gone home to be with the Lord, I have had 19 months to look back and reflect on so many things. I have huge regrets about not pushing through and getting over my hang-ups to simply pray over her in the spirit, and allow the Holy Spirit to do whatever HE wanted to do—not necessarily do the things that I was expecting. And, I see more clearly than ever before that it is the husband's responsibility under Christ his head to serve his wife in the Spirit and through the Word—NOTHING else takes precedent over that, and if it requires a humbling of our minds, a humbling of our flesh, then so be it.

We are to gird ourselves with Christ's humility, just as He did when He washed the feet of His disciples.

Yes, we are head of our home, but *we are also chief servant of our home, and especially of our spouses.* Fail at that, and no other successes matter in the eyes of God. Succeed in that, and you will find that all other successes pale in comparison.

I remember all of the times that Roopa and I were so one in the Spirit, it was impossible to describe. I also remember all of the times that I humbled myself and set my flesh aside, and simply prayed over her in the spirit until the Holy Spirit Himself would take over, and she would feel her spirit and her soul being greatly ministered to with overwhelming comfort and peace. It will now be my lifelong regret that I did not do it every day.

If you are a husband reading this, you do not have to carry the weight of regret that I do, if you begin serving your wife through prayer in the Spirit today.

But serving your wife through the Spirit and with the Word goes beyond just praying—however, I would definitely say it begins with praying, and if you haven't started there, then that is where you need to begin.

In addition to serving and ministering to your wife through prayer (especially praying in the Spirit over her and praying the Word of God over her), *we men need to cultivate the fruit of the Spirit by spending much time praying in the spirit, because it is the fruit of the Spirit that will minister to your wife more than prayer itself sometimes.*

Of course, the key thing is to simply be open to and led by the Holy Spirit at all times.

If you are prayed up in the spirit and allowing the Holy Spirit to manifest His fruit of, for example, gentleness or longsuffering, then when your wife is needing gentleness and long-suffering, she will get it from the Holy Spirit through you—you don't have to work it up in your own emotional self.

If you have a wife who is suffering from chronic illness or other similar life challenges, *the one thing she needs the most from her husband is profound, endless gentleness, kindness and patience.*

She needs to know and feel that she is not a burden to you; that she is not holding you back; that She is still the wife that you always dreamed of, regardless of how difficult it might be for her right now to Be that wife that she dreamed of being.

One area where Roopa needed my prayers and intercession the most was in the area of emotional anxiety—because where her chronic health condition was concerned, life and our future was one big question mark.

She needed me personally praying over her in the spirit to allow the Holy Spirit to flow, and to wash over her with a sense of calm, peace, and assurance that you don't get from just a little pep talk. She needed the Holy Spirit to minister to her the peace that passes all understanding, not just a quick little emotional Band-Aid.

That's the other thing we husbands need to lay aside—we always feel like we need to fix everything, but some things you have to admit your flesh isn't able to fix, so you have to step aside and allow the Holy Spirit to do the fixing and healing through your prayers. This is where you humble yourself and set your masculine abilities aside (which will not meet these needs), and *humble yourself as a praying, interceding servant, and allow the Holy Spirit to meet her spiritual needs through you, as her loving servant/husband.*

Have you ever had a Bible verse that always seemed to be trying to tell you more than what you were able to receive at the moment? A verse that you knew contained an ocean of spiritual revelation, with so many implications that you knew you would never be able to exhaust it????

Well, one such verse that has stayed with me for years now is *Philippians 1:19.*

This particular verse, to me, has always spoken to the subject of intercession (as is the very context of this verse), and nowhere is intercessory prayer more vitally important than in the context of marriage—because through intercession, you are standing in the gap for *someone else*, and through prayer you are identifying in a very deep and intimate way with *their* needs, doing so before the throne room of God.

So Paul says, "Because I know that through your prayers and the provision of the Spirit of Jesus Christ, my distress will turn out for my deliverance." (*Philippians 1:19*).

This is a divinely empowered partnership between believers and the Holy Spirit—A partnership of intense, focused, concerted, ongoing prayers, supplications, petitions, on behalf of a recipient (in this case, the apostle Paul) needing deliverance from trouble, tribulation, distress.

The Greek word for "prayer" in this instance is "Deesis", and it occurs at least 18 times in the New Testament.

It is a multifaceted word that conveys anything but casual, off-the-cuff praying as you go. *This is heels dug in, face to the ground, "not going anywhere from my prayer closet till God moves" kind of praying.*

Remember in Jeremiah, when God said "Is not My word like fire," declares the LORD, "and like a hammer that smashes a rock?" (Jeremiah 23:29)?? Well, this is jackhammer praying, and you don't stop till you're through the cement.

Now, remember the rest of Paul's statement that *through their concerted prayers there would be a resulting abundant provision and supply of the Spirit, which would in turn move to uphold Paul and move circumstantially for his deliverance.*

This same intercessory partnership with the Holy Spirit is what resulted in the apostle Peter being miraculously released from his prison in the Book of Acts (Acts 12:1-17).

Now, here is where I want to take Philippians 1:19 and boomerang it back to what we were discussing a minute ago, in regards to husbands laying aside any and every sense of self-consciousness—feelings like 'I've gotta fix this', 'I've got to be the deliverer', I've got to be the healer, I've got to be the answer to whatever my wife's spiritual needs are right now".

Remember, Paul said, "I know that *through your prayers and the provision of the Spirit of Jesus Christ*, my distress will turn out for my deliverance" (Philippians 1:19).

You and me, the husbands, *we are not the Supply*—we are the vessel, the channel, *through which the Supply of the Holy Spirit will come through our prayers.*

This is where we lean hard on Romans 8:26,27—And if you don't know that passage almost by heart, spend as much time as it takes to get all of Romans 8 into your spirit, because this spells out your partnership with the Holy Spirit, and His partnership with you, when it comes to the arena of prayer and intercession, and Him ministering through you, the vessel of clay.

"In the same way, the Spirit helps us in our weakness. For we do not know how we ought to pray, but the Spirit Himself intercedes for us with groans too deep for words. And He who searches our hearts knows the mind of the Spirit, because the Spirit intercedes for the saints according to the will of God." (Romans 8:26,27).

The one basic truth of the New Testament, starting with the gospels, is that the Holy Spirit is available to each and every individual believer—all that is needed is someone who is thirsty and hungry for Him, Humble enough to ask the Father for him, and willing to believe that it is God the Father's perfect will for them to receive that same promised Holy Spirit.

You don't have to wait until you "feel like" the "right kind of Christian" to receive Him; you don't have to wait until you "feel holy enough"; all you have to do, according to Luke 11:13, is ask your Heavenly Father for the Holy Spirit, and He will give Him to you.

You ask your Heavenly Father as His child—a child does not go to their father asking for a gift expecting to be turned down, or expecting to be given something that they don't want.

So let's get that issue settled right away—that it is the Father's will for every single believer (man, woman, and child) to receive the Holy Spirit in abundance, so that they may have fullness of fellowship with Him, and bear fruit for the kingdom.

The ministry of the first person of the Godhead was to reveal the Father, as Jesus Himself said, and to accomplish the work of our salvation and redemption on the cross.

The work of the 2nd Person of the Godhead was to be present on earth for the entire Church in each and every generation, in every geographical location on the earth—something that Jesus in the flesh could never accomplish.

It is profoundly tragic to see how we have failed Him in treating the vital ministry of the Holy Spirit as something optional, or something spooky, or something controversial.

There is only One member of the Godhead on earth to divinely and supernaturally lead and guide the Church of Jesus Christ in the earth, and that is the Holy Spirit—there is no one else; it's either Him, or us leading ourselves in the flesh.

Now husbands, we are going to look at where the rubber meets the road, concerning ministering to your wife in the Spirit. Right away, I want to calmly encourage you to resist any feelings of being overwhelmed, or like you are suddenly out of your element. Again, ***the Holy Spirit within you is your "divine equipment" and provision for ministering to your wife spiritually—none of what she needs is going to come from you directly; it will come from the Holy Spirit.***

Where she needs physical or emotional healing, the Holy Spirit is the source of that, not you, so just relax. And trust me, I wish I had had someone to talk this way to me when my darling wife was still here, and to keep my dependency on the Holy Spirit and not on myself.

Now, just prior to Luke chapter 4, we see that Jesus was baptized in the river Jordan by John the Baptist, and was baptized in the Holy Spirit (John 3:21,22).

Luke 4:1, "Then Jesus, full of the Holy Spirit, returned from the Jordan and was led by the Spirit into the wilderness."

So, at the very outset of Jesus' earthly ministry, He was baptized in the Holy Spirit, and was led by the Holy Spirit.

That's God's answer to any professing believer who thinks that they are going to function as a believer without the Holy Spirit, much less minister for God without the Holy Spirit. *If Jesus is our pattern—and He most certainly is—then you aren't going to do anything without the same Holy Spirit, I guarantee you that.*

In verse 14, it says Jesus returned to Galilee in the power of the Spirit—

"Jesus returned to Galilee in the power of the Spirit, and the news about Him spread throughout the surrounding region." (Luke 4:14)

So here we are in Luke chapter 4, and we are not even halfway through this chapter, and *Jesus has been baptized in the Holy Spirit, led by the Holy Spirit, and is now walking in the power of the Holy Spirit.*

Anybody with two eyes and able to read black letters on white paper can see that we are observing **two members of the Godhead functioning Together—Jesus and the Holy Spirit**—*and in the context we are seeing it, Jesus is submitted to the Holy Spirit; He is doing nothing apart from the Holy Spirit at all, nothing of His own volition.*

This is a truth, a concept, and a spiritual Reality that we need desperately to have embedded deep, deep, deep into our thinking and our consciousness—*that we have no expectation of our own ability accomplishing anything for God.*

Depending on, leaning on, relying on, and looking to the Holy Spirit every single day should be like breathing to us.

I'm not speaking this to you as though I have arrived. I certainly do not glow in the dark yet, but this much has been real to me for over 35 years, and it is something that I continually strive for, and strive to stay focused on.

Now in Luke 4:18, we see Jesus declaring what the Holy Spirit was going to do *Through* Him:

"The Spirit of the Lord is on Me, because He has anointed Me to preach good news to the poor. He has sent Me to proclaim liberty to the captives and recovery of sight to the blind, to release the oppressed..."

Notice that Jesus very emphatically declares that the Holy Spirit is upon Him, that the Holy Spirit has anointed Him, and He states very clearly & specifically the things He was anointed by the Holy Spirit to do:

1. The *Spirit of the Lord is upon me*;

2. The *Spirit of the Lord has anointed me* to preach the gospel;

3. The *Spirit has sent me* (i.e., Jesus did not "send Himself") to proclaim release to the captives, recovery of sight to the blind, to set free those who are oppressed—so healing and deliverance (This coincides perfectly with Acts 10:38; "How God anointed Jesus of Nazareth with the Holy Spirit and with power, and how Jesus went around doing good and healing all who were oppressed by the devil, because God was with Him.")

Notice it does Not say that Jesus did these things because He was God (which He was), but because He was anointed by God with the Holy Spirit.

Now, I would like to take a closer look at the very passage of scripture Jesus was quoting from, which is found in *Isaiah 61:1-3*, because first of all, it brings out in greater detail the work and ministry of the Holy Spirit that was manifested through Jesus.

Secondly—and in keeping with the theme of this particular chapter of ministering to our families and loved ones—*if we carefully appraise this passage with the heart of the Holy Spirit in mind, then we are able to see with spiritual eyes the many expressions of His ministry to us.*

"The Spirit of the Lord GOD is on Me, because the LORD has anointed Me to preach good news to the poor. He has sent Me to bind up the brokenhearted, to proclaim liberty to the captives and freedom to the prisoners, to proclaim the year of the LORD's favor and the day of our God's vengeance, to comfort all who mourn, to console the mourners in Zion—to give them a crown of beauty for ashes, the oil of joy for mourning, and a garment of praise for a spirit of despair. So they will be called oaks of righteousness, the planting of the LORD, that He may be glorified...."

(Isaiah 61:1-3)

Verse 1 says, "He has anointed me to bring good news to the afflicted, and to bind up the brokenhearted", "to preach good news to the poor" (Hebrew word for "poor", עֲנָוִים (ă·nā·wîm), meaning, "afflicted, humble, meek".

Psalm 149:4 speaks so beautifully to this; "For the LORD takes pleasure in His people; He adorns the afflicted with salvation."

Isaiah 61:2 says, "To proclaim the favorable year of the Lord, and to comfort all who mourn". "to proclaim the year of *the LORD's favor*; "Goodwill, favor, acceptance" (Psalm 5:12; "For surely You, O LORD, bless the righteous; You surround them with the shield of Your favor")

And notice that it says *it's the Lord's favor—it is Favor bestowed by the Lord.*

So many people struggle with believing that they are truly accepted by the Lord—much less favored by Him—even though they may not have any such feelings towards other people. They might, on the surface, feel completely accepted by other people, but acceptance with the Lord is where their struggle lies.

This is where the ministry of the Holy Spirit comes in to minister to the deep heart issues of the person struggling with feeling accepted by the Lord, to let them know that they are beloved, accepted, and yes, even favored by the Lord.

I have actually been given words of knowledge by the Holy Spirit for those who were struggling with deep issues of rejection and even abandonment, which caused them to believe that God felt the same way about them as the persons who rejected them.

After ministering to them with the words the Holy Spirit gave me for them, that deep-seated pain of rejection and abandonment was healed, and replaced with the Holy Spirit's love, acceptance, and compassion. The person's sense of self-worth in God's eyes was supernaturally restored, and they were able to experience true spiritual freedom and liberty in their heart. *This is precisely why the gifts of the Holy Spirit are so vitally important to our overall spiritual health.*

As Paul said, the one who prophesies speaks to others for their comfort and their edification (1 Corinthians 14:3; "But he who prophesies speaks to men for their edification, encouragement, and comfort"), and I will tell you from very personal first-hand experience that there are hundreds of thousands in the Body of Christ who are in very deep need of spiritual encouragement and comfort. In addition to that, *as you open yourself up to the Holy Spirit's presence and ministry in your own life, He will not only encourage others through you, He will also encourage and speak to you personally for your own inner healing, and sense of spiritual liberty and freedom.*

Psalm 16:11 is a beautiful spiritual promise from the Lord to you; "You have made known to me the path of life; You will fill me with joy in Your presence, with eternal pleasures at Your right hand."

Isaiah 61:3 is even more expansive; "to console the mourners in Zion—to give them a crown of beauty for ashes, the oil of joy for mourning, and a garment of praise for a spirit of despair. So they will be called oaks of righteousness, the planting of the LORD, that He may be glorified."

To me, this passage from Isaiah 61 speaks to the healing of the deepest wounds and traumas, and it is here that the husband truly needs to trust in and depend on the supply of the Holy Spirit, as being sufficient to minister to his wife's deepest needs.

Some of the deepest emotional needs which wives can subconsciously look to their husbands to meet, without even realizing it, are rejection and insecurity, oftentimes resulting from early childhood traumas, brokenness in the family, etc.

But true liberty and healing for these things can only come from the Holy Spirit, and through a husband who is willing to be a yielded intercessor for his wife, and available to be a vessel of the Holy Spirit, who wants to pour forth His healing, His oil of gladness and joy, His healing for the brokenhearted, His healing for the losses suffered and experienced in early childhood. *The husband who truly gives himself to yielding to the Holy Spirit in the area of interceding in the Spirit for his wife will experience some of the most transforming miracles you can possibly imagine.*

*Intercession carries your loved one and her needs right into the Holy of Holies, before the Mercy seat, the throne of Grace, where the impossible becomes Possible....what was lost, becomes Found....what was broken, is fully Restored....what was dead, is given New Life....*But First, dear husband, You must Lay Down your self-life, on the altar of living sacrificially as an Intercessor. It is an unvarying principle of Scripture, that Life only comes when the seed falls into the ground and dies (John 12:24), and nowhere is the power of the Spirit manifested More through self-sacrifice than in the covenant of marriage (Ephesians 5:25).

Okay, Now, I want to spend some time laying foundation on *how husbands and wives can begin to flow with the Holy Spirit in ministering to each other.* And trust me, I completely understand how the phrase I just used, "ministering to each other", can cause an initial inward feeling of panic or unease, because it represents an area of the unknown, something that perhaps you've never done before.

But always remember, the Holy Spirit descended upon Jesus in bodily form like a *dove* (Luke 3:22), and that was to reveal to us *His nature— He comes as a gentle dove, not imposing His will upon us, but He comes gently, as our Helper, as our Comforter, our Intercessor—*And through His indwelling presence, as husband and wife you are now free to actually experience the promise of Jesus, when He said, "For where two or three gather together in My name, there am I with them." (Matthew 18:20).

The Holy Spirit is right there with you both, and IN you both, making Himself totally & freely Available to you as husband and wife, heirs Together of the grace of Life. AND, His resources are ENDLESS, which is why Jesus said, out of your Innermost being shall flow RIVERS of living water...Just take some time to close your eyes and Imagine all of the changes that His Life-giving water can bring to your marriage, to each of you individually, to the people that you minister to.

Now, we have spent some time on the vital topics of intercession, praying in the Spirit, and now we move on to ministering in the gifts to each other.

The exciting thing about that is that the husband and wife relationship in Christ Jesus provides the ideal environment for ministering in the gifts, and learning how to become proficient in ministering through the Holy Spirit to each other. Think about it—you're not in front of other people, so there's no need to be self-conscious; this is your soulmate.

If you both have the Holy Spirit, you can spend time praying separately at your leisure and according to your own comfort level, and when you have been edified and built up thoroughly in your own prayer time by praying in the Spirit, you can—at whatever point in time you both feel comfortable doing so—come together to pray in the spirit over each other, reading the Word of God together, and edifying each other through ministering the Word of God to each other.

Now, as you spend time, husband and wife, praying in the Spirit over each other, and doing the same in your own private prayer times, you will both begin to develop a sensitivity to the Holy Spirit—to what He is saying, leading, directing, what kind of impressions He is giving you about whatever.

Always keep in mind that the Holy Spirit is there to guide, teach, and edify both of you, and His desire is to build your faith Together.

Remember the scripture from 1 Peter 3:7, that says husbands and wives are heirs Together of the grace of life.

So, it is the Holy Spirit's express desire that you Both receive from Him, as heirs together of the grace of life—the divine life of God, the Zoe life of God.

Knowing that you are—according to the Holy Spirit inspired Word of God—called to both be equal heirs together as one of the grace of life should encourage your faith tremendously in the area of receiving from the Holy Spirit, being led by Him and taught by Him together.

I know I might sound rather repetitious right now, but I am trying to lay to rest any and all insecurities that husbands or wives might have when it comes to praying with their spouse, and being open and even vulnerable to this process.

I also want you to see that the Benefits outweigh any insecurities, discomfort, or self-consciousness you might feel, and the self-consciousness will dissipate as your Faith grows in ministering to your husband or wife by the Spirit.

The more you hear from the Holy Spirit in ministering to your spouse, the stronger you grow in your own spirit through praying in tongues, in building your own personal receptivity to the Holy Spirit, and the more confident you will be.

This would be an extremely profitable spiritual focus for any home group, or church fellowship that is focusing on actively moving with the Holy Spirit and cooperating with Him, because if every husband and wife in that home group, or fellowship group, is practicing this at home, then when the believers all come together for group fellowship, there is a much greater likelihood of all the individual members being able to minister to each other, since as husbands and wives they've been practicing this at home!

This gets more and more exciting as we go along, doesn't it?

The spiritual potential that can be realized, simply as husbands and wives grow in the Spirit together and minister to each other and even to their children, is limitless.

Husbands can prophesy over their wives and spiritually edify their wives through words of knowledge, words of wisdom—wives can do the same to their husbands and over their children, building their children's spiritual self-esteem, prophesying over them, speaking blessings over them that are inspired by the Holy Spirit—there is simply no limit to how much God can edify a family, and minister to a family through its individual members.

When this type of family gathers with the home fellowship group or a church fellowship group that is doing the same things in their homes, just imagine the spiritual fruit that could be realized.

Spiritual discipleship of other believers in these environments would be fantastic!

So, as husbands and wives are starting out in this, just meditate on and deeply ponder the amazing spiritual possibilities that can be realized through the Holy Spirit, through His gifts, through His anointing moving through each of you.

Now, to lay a little foundation on this, remember that the Primary spiritual gift the apostle Paul gave exhortation on was the gift of prophesying. He made the incredible statement that "For you can All prophesy in turn so that everyone may be instructed and encouraged." (1 Corinthians 14:31).

Evidently the gift of prophesying is the easiest spiritual gift to develop, and the most desirable spiritual gift for it's potential to edify and build up the Body—which is why Paul said, "Earnestly pursue love and eagerly desire spiritual gifts, especially the gift of prophecy." (1 Corinthians 14:1).

Elsewhere Paul says to prophesy according to the measure of your faith ("We have different gifts according to the grace given us. If one's gift is prophecy, let him use it in proportion to his faith"; Romans 12:6), *in which case moving in the gift of prophesying builds your faith, and at the same time builds your proficiency in operating in that much-needed spiritual gift.*

I'll close this chapter out by sharing some examples from mine & Roopa's life—this is an entry from my prayer journal, August 2020....

"There have been so many times in the last few months—especially when Roopa was still with us—that I would be in our living room praying, with some devotional music playing, kind of making our living room into a chapel in our home.

I would just be quietly walking around the living room, praying in tongues, worshipping the Lord—and there were many times when, after praying in tongues for a little bit, a prayer in English would come out of my mouth—but it wasn't anything that came from my own mind or my own reasoning, and I would know immediately that what I was praying in English, was the interpretation of what I had been praying in tongues.

The interpretation of what I had been praying in tongues was so powerful, so real and specific to our situation, that it could have only been inspired by the Holy Spirit Himself. One example that comes to my mind is when earlier this month, Roopa had fallen and broken her polio leg and she was in critical need of medical help, but could not be hospitalized.

There were so many heartbreaking issues confronting us, and as I walked in the living room praying in tongues, a few minutes later I prayed something in English that was more like a worshipful declaration.

The declaration that came to me was, **"You are enthroned over all that concerns us".**

The moment those words came out of my mouth, there was such a release from worry and fear, and I began worshipping and praising God with that declaration that was given to me by the Holy Spirit.

Another interpretation that came to me on August 17, which I wrote down, was, **"You are the God who rules and governs in our affairs".**

Although a week apart, those two interpretations of what I was praying in tongues— declarations that were given to me by the Holy Spirit—*both emphasized that the Lord was governing over everything that concerned us. His Lordship and His divine authority were overruling everything in our lives that could cause us stress, fear, and anxiety.*

Can anyone think of a better reason why we need the gifts of the Holy Spirit operating in our lives on a daily basis???

To keep our faith built up, to keep our spirits strong, and to keep our hearts steadfast in the knowledge that the Lord is governing over our lives as we walk in His Spirit.

CHAPTER 21

GUARDING & GUIDING YOUR LIFE BY THE PROPHETIC MINISTRY OF THE HOLY SPIRIT

A t this critical hour, I believe it is crucial to focus on the New Testament operation of the gift of prophecy and what it means to us right here and now at this point in time for our lives, and for our ministries in the Lord.

To begin to put the New Testament gift of prophecy and prophesying in it's God-given, Holy Spirit inspired context, I'm going to start with Paul's apostolic encouragement to his protégé, from 1st Timothy;

"Timothy, my child, I entrust you with this command in keeping with the previous prophecies about you, so that by them you may fight the good fight" (1 Timothy 1:18)

Allow me to paraphrase from the Greek, along with my decades-long understanding of prophetic ministry and how it serves to equip and enable those in ministry, to give this verse a somewhat more potent, real-world application;

{I commit this charge to you, my son Timothy, according to the prophetic words spoken over you, and that by those prophetic words, you would be encouraged and emboldened to fight a good warfare—My paraphrase}

From this we see that, according to this very context, a Prophetic Word is His spoken desire and will specific to you.

Now, when I speak of a prophetic word, the context I am speaking in is **not** that of a "word of wisdom" or a "word of knowledge"; *those have entirely different functions*, and we will touch on those at a later time.

The Prophetic Word always consists of 3 elements: *Purpose, Process, Promise.*

Every word that proceeds out of the mouth of God has a *Purpose.*

One thing I have observed is that the Word does the work. This we refer to as the *Process.*

Everyone wants to receive the Promise, but few understand that first *they must go through the Process (Hebrews 10:36)*

Typically, as people receive a word from the Lord, they will focus more attention on the Promise, than they will on any other part of the word.

But the Word of the Lord is Eternal in nature, **which means the words that He speaks to us are meant to have an impact that will last for eternity, and bear fruit that will remain for all eternity.**

Some might say, "Well, the prophetic promises that God spoke to me only concerns something I will be doing in this life", but remember, it says that the works of the righteous do follow them, so nothing you do here for the Lord is anything short of eternal in nature, not ever.

I will give you **Three Dynamics of a Prophetic word** from the Lord, which are intended to produce in you results that will carry over into Eternity:

First, a word from the Lord given to you, **tests your obedience**.

Second, a word from the Lord given to you **tests your faithfulness.**

Thirdly, a word from the Lord **tests your ability to bear fruit**, and thus, *Personal Prophetic words can be benchmarks of your spiritual growth and progress.*

The word of the Lord spoken to us, while specific in nature to us as individuals, is meant to Grow and Mature us in those three areas; *Obedience, Faithfulness, and Fruitfulness.*

THIS is what separates True prophetic words from the Lord, from the flaky garbage that we have been exposed to. Soulish, manipulative, Flattering words and divination does not require anything of us in terms of strong character and maturity—it's just meant to tickle ears, and THAT is how you can discern the false "prophetic" from the true word of the Lord.

This distinction is made by the Lord himself throughout the Old Testament, when speaking through Isaiah and Jeremiah and Ezekiel, calling out the false prophets who speak & divine lies and speak things that the flesh wants to hear.

A true prophetic word from the Lord will crucify your flesh, and is designed to bring maturity and Christlike obedience to your soul, and as you give yourself to that prophetic word by saying Yes to it and submitting yourself to it, you place yourself on the pathway of growing in obedience, faithfulness, and fruitfulness.

A True Prophetic Word is intended to bring you into obedient alignment with His personal will for you.

The Lord is the potter, and we are the clay.

His word—Again, **His spoken desire and will specific to you—** starts the Potter's wheel, and as it turns, so do our surroundings.

Change is not always easy under the hand of the Lord, as He begins to shape and mold us into what His word has already proclaimed.

The vessel has to be formed in such a way that *transforms the will of the servant, before the promise can be poured into the newly created instrument* (2 Timothy 2:21; Psalm 105:19; Psalm 66:10).

So, when the Holy Spirit Himself, or someone used of the Lord, speaks prophetically over your life, in terms of your calling, etc., now you'll understand that *there is a definite process you will go through, before you see the end result—because the Lord is far more concerned with the end result than we are,* and He's got all eternity to shape us and equip us. He's not working on Our clock.

And always remember: the giftings, the faithfulness, and the character that you allow Him to develop in you NOW, will be with you for all eternity, as you will be functioning in His Kingdom.

Remember Jesus and the parable of the talents? (Matthew 25, Luke 19)

Well, let me inform you of something very important—Jesus was not just being poetic or speaking figuratively; *He was making a direct reference to the Millennial Reign, and future rewards for faithfulness during that time, and thereafter.*

So, your obedience and faithfulness to a prophetic word from the Lord spoken over your life in the here and now, is something that will have a definite impact on your Future fruitfulness in His Kingdom, and the part you will play in it.

Yes, you can definitely see **how broad and far reaching this subject truly is!**

Again, this clear understanding separates the flaky false "prophetic" *from that which is True, and is designed to shape you for fruitfulness in God's kingdom for all eternity.*

The false prophetic always seeks to *fascinate, flatter, entice, appeal to one's sense of ego, and to the soulish desire for insight, wisdom, and revelation that doesn't cost their flesh anything.* Those that operate in this realm always try to position themselves as having access to a spiritual insight that very few others have.

On the other hand, out of all the things that Jesus warned of concerning the Endtimes (wars and rumors of wars, earthquakes, famines, etc.), there was only One danger that He warned of multiple times—and that was the proliferation of false teachers and false prophets. There were no other Endtime dangers that He warned of more than once, except for this.

I believe that Jesus' warning also serves as an Encouragement for the operation of the True prophetic in the Body of Christ.

Take a moment to remember now, the repeated exhortations of the apostle Paul throughout the New Testament—to covet spiritual gifts, but most of all to desire to prophesy.

Why???

Because he who prophesies, speaks to men for their encouragement, comfort, and edification.

Was there EVER a time in human history when the Body of Christ needs to be encouraged, comforted, and edified more than NOW????

Again, let me call your attention back to Paul's apostolic exhortation to Timothy, to remember the prophetic words that were spoken over him, and to draw strength and encouragement and courage from those prophetic words, while he tried to discharge his spiritual responsibilities in a hostile environment! (1st Timothy 1:18)

So, I am firmly and totally persuaded in the Lord that NOW is the time for us to become intimately acquainted with what the Holy Spirit wants to do with this particular operation of HIS.

That is why I am taking great care to lay the proper foundation that will give us a sound, scriptural, and spiritual perspective on what it actually means to move in the gift of prophecy and in the prophetic, and I hope to inspire the same pure devotion in all of my listeners; to covet what is truly from the Holy Spirit, so that you may in turn minister to your brothers and sisters for their encouragement, their comfort, their edification, and their strengthening in these end times.

If I do not accomplish that end, then I have fallen short of what God has called me to do.

Now, I also would like to exhort you to read Revelation 2 & 3 with our subject firmly in mind, and watch the perspective that you gain from it this time.

In each instance where Jesus is speaking to the churches, He first of all exhorts them as to Specific aspects of His nature that directly correspond to their situation—their hardships, their trials, the things that they are having to overcome, as well as their shortcomings and where they need correction.

He prophetically tells them where they stand in terms of HIS assessment of them (not MAN'S, but HIS assessment from Heaven! Heaven's perspective, God's perspective!).

Then Jesus says, "He who has an ear, let him hear what the Spirit says to the churches." (Rev. 3:6).

Did you catch that?

Did you see what just happened there?

Jesus did the speaking; He spoke His assessment and spiritual diagnosis of each church—but then says, Let him who has an ear hear what the Spirit is saying to the churches! The Holy Spirit, Whom we are supposed to be LED BY, and WALKING IN, and FILLED WITH.

Remember what Jesus said to the disciples in *John 16:13???*

*"However, when the Spirit of truth comes, He will guide you into all truth. For He will not speak on His own, but **He will speak what He hears**, and He will declare to you what is to come."*

If you want to hear from Jesus, then you won't do it without hearing the Holy Spirit.

Jesus is saying, if we the Church want to hear what Jesus is saying to the church, what Jesus' assessment and diagnosis of us is currently, then we MUST hear it from the Holy Spirit, because HE is the one who will take what Jesus is saying from heaven, and HE will relay that to us—If we have an ear to hear.

That means without an ongoing intimate relationship with the Holy Spirit, you are out of touch with Jesus—And that is out of the mouth of Jesus Himself.

So if you are living out of your intellectual grasp of scripture, your own thinking and reasoning, then you are disconnected from the living, abiding revelation Jesus wants to give you—because that will only come through the Holy Spirit (and again, that is Jesus's words, not mine).

Remember what James said????

"As the body without the spirit is dead, so faith without deeds is dead." (James 2:26)—and James was not referring to just a physical body.

Without the Holy Spirit, the professing Body is dead; **without the Holy Spirit, you are not connected to the Head.** You may have made a profession of faith; you may have experienced the new birth, but—listen carefully to all that the scripture has just said to us—without the Holy Spirit, you will not hear what the Head is speaking to the Body, of which YOU are a part.

Without the Spirit, you are continually fighting your flesh, trying to stay on the path of salvation, and it is a constant struggle for you, because you are the one doing it in your own strength & your own power.

I know what it is like to live that way, I did it for over five years, and it was excruciating! Your flesh never gives you a day off; you are constantly trying to crucify it, to stay on top of it; you're constantly crying out to God, because the reality is, **you cannot live the life of Jesus without His Spirit abiding within you.**

For those still stuck in the valley of religious confusion and indecision concerning the Holy Spirit, Please take to heart every word I've said, as someone who struggled and suffered greatly without Him in my life for the first five years of my Christian walk.

The fact is, that does not have to be the case with anyone. It is a continual burden in my heart to convey this one supreme message to every believer—That No one needs to go one more day without the power and presence and fullness of the Holy Spirit dwelling inside of you!

If you've been baptized in the Holy Spirit, praise God!!!

Pray in tongues every chance you get, stay in the Word, and develop an expectancy for Him to speak to you more powerfully, more specifically, more directly than ever before in your life!

For those who have not received the baptism of the Holy Spirit, go to God and His Word, and remind Him that Jesus himself said He will baptize you in the Holy Spirit, and tell Him that you don't want to go one more day without Him dwelling in you in all of His fullness!

Take it from a man who in his younger days was infected with some Baptist brainwashing that I had to repent of, and I had to humble myself and say, "Father God, your Word says in Luke 11:13, how much more will your Heavenly Father give the Holy Spirit to them that ask Him, and Father God I'm humbling myself and repenting of my religious pride, and I'm asking You for the Holy Spirit today!"

The next day, this young introverted boy was walking all the way to his job singing in tongues at the top of his lungs, feeling freer than I've ever been in my life! Two years later, the Lord was using me to help others get free, and to see them walking in the liberty of the Holy Spirit in our father's kingdom.

Now how could anybody allow a religious mindset to keep them out of that????

So kick the religious spirits out of your life, out of your thoughts, out of your mind, and realize that your Heavenly Father wants you to enjoy everything in His Kingdom, starting with the Holy Spirit whom He has sent—and then you can begin ministering that same spiritual liberty to those who are in bondage, those who are shaking with fear for what's happening in the earth—because religious dogma isn't going to help them.

Only you being a minister of the Holy Spirit is going to do them any good, so why wait another day???

CHAPTER 22

THE ABC'S OF WALKING IN THE SPIRIT

In over 43 years as a believer, I can say unapologetically and unequivocally that praying in the Spirit and walking in the Spirit are the two factors that will positively make or break a believer.

I spent the first five years of my life as a Christian without the power of the Holy Spirit—it was the longest, hardest five years of my life, and I would never want to repeat them. When I was baptized in the Holy Spirit on the third Sunday of April 1983, my life was forever changed, in ways that you cannot possibly imagine.

We are entering the close of human history as we have known it—spiritual forces are mounting that no Christian without the Holy Spirit will ever be able to withstand, and that is the sole reason for my relentless, untiring focus on the things of the Holy Spirit.

Jesus did not begin His earthly ministry until He was baptized in the Holy Spirit, and it was the power of the Holy Spirit that enabled Him to endure, all the way to dying on the cross.

In Revelation 2 & 3, we see that at the close of this age, going into the tribulation, before Jesus is to return, He says to each of the seven churches—very directly and emphatically—"He who has an ear, let him hear what the Spirit says to the churches" (Revelation 3:6).

"Says" is in the present and perpetual, ongoing tense—Which is in complete harmony with what Jesus said concerning the Holy Spirit in John 14, that the Holy Spirit would show us things to come, and would lead us into all truth. In other words, **it is the ongoing, continual speaking of the Holy Spirit to the Church in every generation that we must contend for, and apprehend spiritually.**

And this area is the Lords predominant calling upon my life: to aid and equip the Church in every conceivable possible way to do this very thing—To walk in the Spirit, hear from the Spirit on a regular, consistent basis, specifically with regards to what He is saying to the church in this time.

Everything else in my life takes second place to this.

One Major area that I feel I really need to emphasize and underline, to make sure that people truly get it ingrained into their consciousness, is that *praying in tongues IS praying in the spirit; they are one & the same thing. The Apostle Paul makes that clear in 1 Corinthians 14:14.*

The reason for emphasizing that, is because there has been so very little teaching on praying in the spirit as the Doorway to walking in the things of the Spirit.

In other words, without consistently praying in the spirit as a spiritual exercise that we engage in habitually, we will be extremely limited in our effectiveness in walking in the Spirit.

Our level of receptivity to the Holy Spirit, our level of sensitivity to the Holy Spirit, is dramatically affected by how much we spend time praying in the spirit.

I cannot emphasize that enough, and have proven it over and over and over again, during the past 39 years of my life as a Spirit-filled believer. Praying in the spirit and walking in the spirit are directly connected.

The other major area of the believer's life that is affected by how much time they spend praying in the spirit, *is their level of spiritual vitality and spiritual strength.*

Later we will spend time looking very closely at the Greek wording that pertains to the Scriptures dealing with spiritual strength, being strong in the Lord, being strong in the power of his might; ***all of these are derived from the divine life and the divine, supernatural power of God Himself—it is not strength of human origin or human nature.***

Therefore, this spiritual strength and life must be accessed by a spiritual means—*And the means that God has provided, is through praying in the spirit,* and we will be taking a closer look at these 2 major areas that Must become absolutely foundational to our daily walk, as we enter the most spiritually challenging times the church has ever seen.

Now, as we launch into chapter 22, The ABC's of Walking in the Spirit, I believe that it's vitally important that we do so against the larger backdrop of 2 all-encompassing Realities.

The first is the Kingdom of God, and the second is the Government of God's Church.

Now, to many this may already be evident, but for those who might be operating with a different mindset, let me make it perfectly clear that when I say the government of God's church, I am most emphatically not in any way, shape, or form referring to what is presently referred to by many as 'the church'—The man-made religious system which has, for the most part, imposed itself as a man-made counterfeit to God's True Church.

Gods True Church, as clearly laid out in panoramic detail in the New Testament, does not envision a top down business system where one man presides over a large passive group of people.

The one or two man Pastor system was never in the mind of God, and cannot be found in the New Testament.

What was and is clearly in the mind of God concerning HIS Church, is that of a Body of believers ministering in the Spirit to one another, admonishing one another and instructing one another in the truth, with each member supplying what the other members need as a body. THIS is the Church that I live to serve.

All right, so referring to the realities of the Kingdom of God and the Church as the primary backdrop for all that constitutes walking in the Spirit, the gifts of the Spirit, etc., let's begin by looking at **walking in the Spirit as it is connected to the Kingdom of God.**

I am starting with that reality first, because the Kingdom of God is the dominant theme all throughout the Old Testament and through the Gospels; the Church does not appear till the Book of Acts.

The one verse of Scripture that sums this particular reality up the best comes from the apostle Paul.

The apostle Paul says, "For **the Kingdom of God is not a matter of talk but of power.**" (1 Corinthians 4:20) The Greek word for 'power' is δυνάμει (dynamei) "dunamai"; force; 'miraculous power'.

So here, Paul is literally saying the Kingdom of God is not manifested by merely speaking about it, but in *Demonstrating* it with miraculous, supernatural power.

This is also why, when defending his apostleship as legitimately from the Lord, Paul said, "The true marks of an apostle—signs, wonders, and miracles—were performed among you with great perseverance." (2 Corinthians 12:12)

Interestingly enough, "12" is the number symbolic of God's Government among His people; 12 tribes, 12 apostles, 12 judges in the Book of Judges, there were 12 "minor" prophets, 12 gates of Heaven, 12 gates to the city of Jerusalem, etc.)

Now, when you set that side-by-side with the religious institutions that most have commonly referred to as 'the church', you can see that the two are polar opposites. *One functions on mere talk and idle words (and 'idle' means 'Non-performing, and Void of power'), the Other in Life-giving Power.*

This same stark contrast is seen clearly in the gospels, between the rigid Pharisees and the ministry of Jesus; "All the people were amazed and began to ask one another, "What is this? A new teaching with authority! He commands even the unclean spirits, and they obey Him!" (Mark 1:27)

So here we see in a very visual, explicit way how walking in the Spirit is directly connected to operating in the realm of the Kingdom of God.

Remember, this particular incident was before the church was even born into existence, in the Book of Acts.

To further illustrate this, Jesus himself said, "But if I drive out demons by the Spirit of God, then the kingdom of God has come upon you." (Matthew 12:28). There! So simple even a child can see it—the Kingdom of God is revealed as a current, all-encompassing reality when the power of God is in demonstration, especially against opposing spiritual forces.

The one Reality that most believers do not have an understanding of, is that the Church is God's instrument for Representing & Exercising the Reality and Authority of His Kingdom in the earth.

The Apostle Paul says in 1 Corinthians 6:2,3; "Do you not know that the saints will judge the world? And if you are to judge the world, are you not competent to judge trivial cases? Do you not know that we will judge angels? How much more the things of this life!"

Walking in the Spirit, operating in the gifts, growing in & exercising our faith and our authority through the Spirit, is how we train for reigning in His kingdom in the future, by exercising His authority now.

That is clearly seen in Hebrews 6:4,5. In describing those who have been regenerated by the Holy Spirit, *it confirms Spirit-baptized believers by 4 spiritual traits:*

1. As those who have tasted of the Heavenly gift,

2. Were made partakers of the Holy Ghost,

3. Have tasted the good word of God (and here, "word" is the Greek is "rhema", meaning, "the spoken word"),

4. Have experienced the powers of the Age to come.

I realize that the actual context is one of stark warning, but it clearly shows the mind of God in terms of the fullness that He has provided for His Church now in this age, *and connects that abundant spiritual provision to our future time of ruling and reigning in the next age, the Millennial Reign* (As indicated by the phrase, "powers of the age to come").

> *Every time you lay hands on the sick, cast out demons, or operate in the gifts, you are demonstrating in real time here on earth, the existence and the reality of God's supreme Kingdom. And as the believer operates faithfully in this arena, they demonstrate faithfulness that will be rewarded in the Age to come.*

In fact, Jesus spoke to this very thing in what many assumed was simply a parable (referred to as "the parable of the talents"), *but in reality Jesus was referring to actual rewards to be given during the Millennial reign, to those who are faithful in the little things during this present age prior to the Millennium.*

The apostle Paul had this very perspective in mind in 1 Corinthians 1:7, when he said, "You come behind in no gift, *as you wait for the revelation of our Lord Jesus Christ".* Here, Paul makes the clear connection between the ongoing exercising of the spiritual gifts supplied by the Holy Spirit, to our anticipation of the coming day of the Lord.

One primary purpose that walking in the Spirit and in the spiritual gifts serves, is to keep us focused on the coming of our Lord Jesus and the setting up of His Millennial Kingdom.

As we maintain a consecrated, dedicated, and reverent stewardship of the Spirit and spiritual gifts, we are able to keep in sharp focus the Eternal Kingdom that we are going to inherit.

The most outstanding Old Testament example of our New Testament stewardship would be that of Daniel, and I think that it strongly behooves us to spend time looking at Daniel's life, taking careful note of his unwavering level of consecration to the Lord in spite of his circumstances, that allowed God to entrust him with dreams and visions, and opportunities to minister to those in high political offices.

The Book of Daniel truly gives the New Testament believer a visual picture of how we—now in this time—represent God's Kingdom here on earth, as consecrated vessels of the Holy Spirit, who will in turn be rewarded and promoted during the Millennial Reign, based on our current faithfulness.

My challenge is in wanting to paint a picture for my readers that—on the one end of the spectrum—clearly defines the smallest spiritual details of our daily walk in the Spirit, and leading all the way up to the Grand panoramic view of the Kingdom of Jesus Christ ruling and reigning over the entire earth, and our part in that...And painting the picture for you in such a way, that you can visualize how both ends of that spectrum are connected every single day.

In other words, our ongoing walk in the Spirit, and our operating in the spiritual gifts, is meant to keep us mindful of the Age to come, when we shall be partakers of that Kingdom, the power of which we are operating in Now. That is why the scripture clearly states that the deposit we have received of the Holy Spirit, is a down payment on our future inheritance in that Kingdom. (Ephesians 1:13,14)

Again, I think the prophet Daniel provides us with the clearest, most vivid picture of that—Of maintaining an inward focus on the coming Kingdom, while exercising the authority and power of that Kingdom *here in our present world and circumstances.*

Picture in your mind Daniel, kneeling in front of his open windows in his private room, facing the city of God, Jerusalem—three times a day he knelt before the open windows, facing the holy city, in prayer to God, the ruler of the heavens and the earth.

I truly believe that Daniel represents a type—or an example—of the Endtime remnant believer.

That is just my conviction over the last 30 some odd years, based on Daniel's level of consecration to the Lord; his understanding of ruling by prayer; and his prolific spiritual history of moving in dreams and visions, dream interpretation, and angelic encounters.

Not only that, but Daniel was shown much more graphically and vividly than any other Old Testament prophet I'm aware of, what was to transpire and take place in the endtimes we are walking out, specifically with regards to the tribulation and the antichrist.

All of these things taken together are what cause me to consider him as a living, breathing example that we may refer to.

As the king of Babylon's second in command, he was positioned in an earthly kingdom—*but on his knees before his open windows, facing the holy city, he was also occupying a Heavenly ruling position.*

Daniel was occupying two ruling positions at the same time: one in the natural realm, and one in the heavenly realms.

It is the same with us: we are seated with Christ in heavenly places, and yet in our earthly bodies we are here on this earth, "occupying until he comes".

Let's look at another picture of Daniel that visually illustrates our legal spiritual position.

Daniel set his heart to seek God with prayer and fasting.

Some 21 days later into the fast, the archangel Gabriel appears to him, Informing Daniel that he was dispatched to Daniel on the very day that Daniel set his heart to fast and pray. Gabriel had been delayed because of Satanic opposition in the heavenlies by the fallen angel who was over Persia. So, although Daniel was physically stationed here on earth, he had legal, divine authority that reached into the heavenlies, and set in motion angelic warfare.

Now, stop and consider for just a moment, that as powerful as Daniel's experience was, he did not have the ability that you and I do, with regards to being able to pray in the Spirit.

We might be tempted to be very envious of the encounter he had with the archangel Gabriel, but the reality is that as we pray in the spirit—as it says in 1 Corinthians 14–we speak not unto men, but unto God, *and in the spirit we are speaking mysteries to Him ("For he who speaks in a tongue does not speak to men, but to God. Indeed, no one understands him; he utters mysteries in the Spirit"; 1 Corinthians 14:2).*

This is a prayer language that goes straight into the throne room of God in heaven, as the Holy Spirit is not hindered or confined in any way. It says we are speaking directly to God from our spirit.

Our prayers in the spirit are very likely to set into motion a succession of events in the spirit realm, including the Lord dispatching angels to carry out things that we have prayed in the spirit, even though our mind may not understand what was prayed.

God knows, the Holy Spirit knows, and those things are communicated to whatever angelic servants are needed.

Now, Right here is where it would be worthwhile to mention that there were numerous angelic interventions in the Book of Acts, which fits in perfectly with our other focus, the Government of God in the Church.

There were numerous angelic interventions in the Book of Acts that reveals their ongoing partnership with the Church on earth as it carries out its heavenly Mission.

And as you read the Book of Acts, notice the situations in which they were dispatched—Angels were dispatched to a Spirit-baptized, Spirit-empowered, persecuted church of believers that were walking in the fear of the Lord, and were walking together as one—not as many denominations.

I hope you can see where I'm going with this. The God who rules from Heaven is not going to waste Heavens resources on man-made religious operations! The only church that can expect the backing of heaven and the full forces of God's heavenly armies and all other spiritual provision is the Church made up of those who love not their lives on to the death.

As it clearly states in Hebrews 1:14, the angels are ministering servants sent to minister on our behalf. This one spiritual provision of God (angelic intervention) is another area where we need to grow in our faith.

I don't know that Daniel was aware of any provision from God that allowed him to enlist angelic intervention, but the New Testament clearly states that we have that, And we would be wise to begin developing our faith in that area immediately, because we are going to need it in the days ahead.

You cannot release your faith regarding any spiritual provision, unless you are confident that that provision has been provided to you by God in His Word.

At this point, I believe I have (and I hope and pray that I have) successfully given all of you a clear picture of the panoramic backdrop of the kingdom of God and God's government in the church, as the supporting focal point for our daily walk in the Spirit.

I truly believe that we must strive to maintain that panoramic focal point in our spirits, in our hearts, our minds, and our imaginations every single day as a means to build and foster consistency in our spiritual walk.

Once again, our prophet brother Daniel serves as a tremendous visual aid in this context—Daniel displayed a lifestyle of spiritual consistency that I would imagine would be the envy of most in heaven (If envy was a spiritual quality to be found in heaven that is).

*Every single day, Daniels focal point was exactly what I'm striving to paint a picture of—he was focused first on the reality of God's ruling Kingdom; God's Kingdom that rules over the affairs of men on earth; all kingdoms, all kings, all governments. **That was Daniels springboard for spiritual service here on earth, as he was positioned in the kingdom of Babylon.***

He did not see himself as subservient to a Babylonian king—*he saw himself at the complete and total service and devotion to the God of heaven and earth.*

And I think that must be the starting point for each one of us, regardless of where we are in the Lord—how long we have been saved; how long we've been baptized in the Holy Spirit; if we've been praying in tongues and in the spirit for years, or if we just got our prayer language the other day.

We are all made kings and priests unto the Lord, regardless of how long we've been saved.

Now, Daniel set himself to pray three times a day through open windows—meaning, *he was completely and totally unashamed & unafraid of letting his spiritual position be known to all of the heathen in the kingdom of Babylon.*

Spiritual Purity begets Spiritual Boldness.

I believe he also prayed through open windows facing the skies in the direction of the holy city of God—Jerusalem—so that he could visualize the holy city in his heart and his mind as he prayed.

Facing the holy city of God reminded him of God's covenant with his own people; God's covenant to establish that city as the city from which the Messiah would one day rule over the world—In other words, every time Daniel prayed through those open windows, looking toward the holy city, he was ALSO looking forward to the day when Messiah would rule from that city. And that is where our focus must be every day; that as we pray in the spirit—no matter where we are, if we are working, driving, showering, whatever we're doing.

As we are praying in the spirit, we are inwardly looking forward to the day when Jesus Christ, Lord of lords and King of kings, sets foot onto this earth, and gathers us to Himself to rule and reign with Him during the Millennial Reign.

A major character quality of Daniel's that we should truly dwell upon, is his commitment to remain consecrated to the Lord, and to not defile himself. Now, one thought that came to me as I was meditating on this, was that the first area where Daniel was tested in regards to his commitment, was in the area of temptation to partake of the kings food.

It says he refused to defile himself with the king's food.

I think we would all be amazed (speaking to myself as well) at the amazing improvements in our spiritual health if we had the same dedication to refusing to defile our spiritual diet with too much TV, too much political news, too much natural reasoning, and instead decided to only eat what constitutes a truly spiritual diet, and what contributes to our spiritual health and vitality.

Jesus said, "The Spirit gives life; the flesh profits nothing. The words I have spoken to you are spirit and they are life." (John 6:63).

How much time are we devoting to feeding our spirit man the things that will make it powerful, full of faith and full of the Holy Spirit???

Part of the power of the early church was that they continued steadfastly in the apostles teaching, and they also broke bread together from house to house, sharing their lives together and having spiritual fellowship.

Notice that it was from *house to house*, not "church to church". These were not artificial, religious relationships—they were from "house to house", or home to home; *these were shared lives, with no religious activities, with no manufactured religious atmosphere.*

Another powerful thought to consider is, look at the times that Daniel was delivered and vindicated, in spite of horrific, life-threatening persecution from within his own government.

Do you think that he would've experienced the same deliverances and vindication from God Almighty if he had compromised in the area of personal consecration and devotion to God???

I would not want to roll the dice on that one.

I think the number one decision that every true believing Christian needs to make in this hour, is complete and total consecration and dedication to God, no matter what His requirements, and do not move off of that.

First of all, be determined that you are going to be committed to a steady diet of the Word of God and prayer.

Secondly, be committed to an absolute, all-out pursuit of building your relationship with the Holy Spirit.

Everything else comes after these two things.

These are the basics of walking with the Holy Spirit.

"Then my tongue will proclaim Your righteousness and Your praises *all day long.*" (Psalm 35:28)

What you use your mouth for the most, guides and determines the direction of your thoughts—*and the direction of your thoughts determines what you are most conscious of.* If you spend most of your time talking about sports, then sports is what will inevitably fill most of your thoughts and attention. You can apply the same thought to business, finance, politics, entertainment, etc.

But when you make a conscious decision to pray in the spirit/pray in tongues, the more you habitually do that, then the more your consciousness becomes more inward and more inclined toward the Spirit.

I must say, praying in the spirit is the doorway to everything else the Holy Spirit will do in your life—*There is absolutely a direct link between how much time we pray in tongues, and how much we are led by the Holy Spirit.*

Many years ago, someone asked a fellow believer, "What does praying in tongues mean to you?"

The young man's response completely amazed me, because he was actually a brand new believer, and had only been baptized in the Holy Spirit a few short weeks.

His simple but spiritually perceptive response was, *"Praying in tongues reminds me of the indwelling presence of the Holy Spirit"*—And I have never heard a more powerful explanation, ever!

For this young man, **the more he prayed in tongues, the more he became consciously aware and mindful of the Holy Spirit dwelling within him!**

Now do you understand why Satan hates this subject with all of his being????

Do you understand why there has been almost next to no sound teaching on the subject in almost 40 years????

Do you really think the most powerful spiritual enemy on the planet wants believers walking around who are consciously aware of the Holy Spirit dwelling within them, speaking to them and guiding them and leading them on a moment by moment basis, with his power and his anointing????

The enemy already encountered that once back in the Book of Acts, and he has worked overtime to make sure that Acts Part 2 doesn't happen again!

Now, dear child of God, close your eyes for just a moment, and picture Daniel kneeling in front of his open windows, facing the Holy City of God. *We too are looking for the City that is to Come* (Hebrews 13:14).

"So we fix our eyes not on what is seen, but on what is unseen. For what is seen is temporary, but what is unseen is eternal." (2 Corinthians 4:18).

It's so easy to skim over familiar verses with our minds, but it's like touching the surface of something with your fingers, and yet you don't grasp it in your hands, *like it **belongs** to you, like you **own** it.*

But when you see verses like the one above, and when you look at that verse and you can see your future inheritance in the kingdom in that verse, and when you begin to really grasp in your hands that you have a future inheritance in a very real kingdom, nothing on this earth can tear it out of your hands—And our spiritual inheritance has Got to become that real to us, to the point where if someone wants to kill our body, we don't really care, because no matter what they do to us, they cannot ever take our inheritance!

And when you have THAT reality down on the inside of you, you are a Very Unstoppable Christian.

BUT—how do you Get there?

In the natural realm, we exchange money for the things we want and need.

But in the spiritual realm, faith is what we exchange (Matthew 21:22).

The Bible tells us that when you pray, have faith, and you will receive it. Faith moves mountains. Faith pleases God. Faith is what opens doors. What is faith? It's believing in God and His goodness....It's knowing that He is a rewarder of those who diligently seek Him. Faith is believing that the promises of God are true.

Where does faith come from? Scripture tells us that everyone is given a measure of faith; that faith grows by hearing the Word of God.

Simply put, the more you hear the Word of God, the more real it becomes in your life and the easier it is to believe His promises.

Faith is what grows within you as you become more & more sensitive & responsive to the inner promptings of the Holy Spirit.

Each time you obey, by faith, the leading of the Spirit, your faith GROWS.

These are the ABC's of Walking with the Holy Spirit:

Confidence in your prayer language—"But he who unites himself with the Lord is one with Him in spirit." (1 Corinthians 6:17), so you are not merely on your own.

He has given you His Holy Spirit, so when the enemy comes to try to intimidate you make you feel like your efforts are useless or too weak to accomplish anything of spiritual value, remind yourself that you are joined to the Lord; you are one spirit with Him, and when you pray in tongues and in the spirit, you are speaking directly to God your Father, with nothing in between you and Him. You are able to come boldly before the throne of grace, praying in His Spirit directly to Him, with full access by the blood of Jesus.

In other words, when you take your position in prayer as a blood bought child of God, you do not do so with any confidence in the flesh (Philippians 3:3; Jeremiah 9:24). You take your stand based on your legal position in Jesus Christ, and the enemy cannot make any claims against you.

You come before the throne of God with boldness and confidence; washed in the blood of Jesus; filled and empowered by the Holy Spirit, and able to speak directly to God with your prayer language—this is a position of Sonship, anointing, authority, and power.

And when you are in this position to pray in the spirit (whether it's at home, or driving in your car, or wherever you are), my fullest recommendation would be to begin praying in the spirit, and do not stop until you are either feeling His praises pour through you, or worship, or tongues of authority.

Some of you will understand what I mean by this, and some may not—but what I'm trying to say is, you keep pressing in praying in your prayer language, until you know that you know that you know that it is the Holy Spirit praying through you, with a forcefulness and authority that is beyond just you.

Keep praying in your spirit until you feel His anointing and His power flowing through your prayer language, and then you will know you are accomplishing something.

*Building receptivity and sensitivity to the promptings and leadings of the Holy Spirit—*The more you yield and trust, the more He will lead and guide.

This means don't stress mentally about it; ***don't overthink it***. Simply have an inward posture of yieldingness and willingness, and then trust that the Holy Spirit will lead and guide and direct in His way, in His time, and trust that you will know it when He does.

He wants you to have confidence in trusting Him.

Remember, you are one spirit with the Lord, and He has put His Holy Spirit in you— *so **the more you pray in tongues, you are building your dependency upon your spirit**; not upon your mind, your intellect, or your emotions to lead and guide you.*

You are developing confidence in hearing the Holy Spirit in your spirit; you are developing confidence in being led by your born-again spirit, and taking the dominion away from being led merely by your mind, your thoughts, and emotions.

"For all who are led by the Spirit of God are sons of God." (Romans 8:14) —Not those who are led by their mind, or their emotions, or their soul realm.

Remember, your Mind must be Renewed by the Word of God, *and it is only reliable to the extent that it is Renewed. However, the Holy Spirit is ALWAYS reliable, which is why we must stay open, yielded, and receptive to His Wisdom, His Guidance, His Correction, His Instruction.*

CHAPTER 23

THE BODY MINISTRY OF THE HOLY SPIRIT THROUGH PROPHESYING

Prophesying is meant to be within the context of the Body of Christ, not an individual platform self-promotion "ministry".

Secondly, it is a ministry that originates from the Holy Spirit Himself, and so deserves to be treated accordingly, with the same respect and reverence you would give to the third person of the Godhead.

We are living in a moment in time right now where spiritual warfare is intensifying, and is only going to ramp up even more.

For my dear brothers and sisters who want to be grounded foundationally where this gift is concerned, I've got your back. I plan on going wide and deep with the subject, as *it was the primary gift that Paul the apostle exhorted the church to covet and exercise—and it is the only gift to come with such apostolic exhortation, because it had the widest possible benefit to the body of Christ at large.*

With that in mind, it's very easy to understand why it has been such a major target of the enemy, and I want to make sure that on my watch, I do the very best job spiritually to lay a solid, comprehensive, scriptural foundation for its use and exercise.

The gift of prophecy/prophesying begins in Genesis, and goes all the way through to the Book of Revelation.

The one foundational thing about prophecy/prophesying is that it is central to the nature of God Himself.

Why?

Because it is the nature of God to reveal Himself, and the primary way that God reveals Himself throughout the biblical record is the avenue of prophecy/prophesying. All throughout the Old Testament, we see God speaking His purposes to and through prophets, over and over again.

The expression of His sovereign will over all creation, over nations, over people, has always been primarily through prophecy—And once we truly grasp and understand that prophecy is central to God's nature, as the Creator who is continually communicating His Eternal thoughts, His purposes, His desires, His will concerning all that He has created, we will treat the subject of prophecy and the gift of prophesying with the utmost respect and care that it deserves.

The very fact that the gift of prophesying in the New Testament originates from the Holy Spirit of God Himself, should be more than enough to command total respect and sobermindedness from anyone and everyone who approaches the subject. To treat it as less than walking upon holy ground, is a sign that you are probably not ready to deal with the subject at all.

I state it that emphatically because the enemy has worked overtime to discredit this gift, he has worked overtime to see to it that there are those who will abuse it, misuse it, to bring it into further discredit and disrepute—And if we do not treat something as holy that originates from God himself, then we are setting ourselves up to fall into the same traps.

Another foundational thought to this entire subject is that we must first and foremost settle it in our minds that the upbuilding of the Body is by the direct and express will of God. Not man, not denominations, but God Himself.

That means that Every provision that God has made for the upbuilding of His body, is by HIS decree and under His authority—And I pray that every individual who ever speaks a word against any of it is confronted one day with that fact.

One very critical thing that our democratic culture has undermined is our view of the New Testament, especially as it pertains to the Church.

Contrary to popular culture opinion, the Church of Jesus Christ is NOT a democracy— it is a Theocracy, under one Head, one Ruler, the Lord Jesus Christ. We have told ourselves that God is perfectly OK with us splintering the body into thousands of different denominations, and hundreds of thousands of different little church buildings, with everybody pretty much calling their own shots—fortunately, God isn't bending to that wind.

Spend some time looking through the epistles, and notice how many times the apostle Paul makes statements as direct commands to the churches....Does it sound like the deacon board was allowed to vote on it????

The surest way to be grounded in the Word of God, is to accept it in that spirit—that it is the Authority of God Himself, and we are not given the slightest license to change or alter even one speck of it. The sooner every individual believer can truly embrace that mentality, the quicker you will be on your way to being fully established in the Word of God, and immovable in your Faith.

After all, you have to honestly admit that as long as there's any aspect of the Word of God that you think is up for discussion, or subject to somebody else's interpretation, you're going have a hard time having absolute rock solid faith in that part of God's Word.

But the Psalmist said, "Your word, O LORD, is everlasting; it is firmly fixed in the heavens." (Psalm 119:89)—So what we think or feel doesn't matter at all, except insofar what we think or feel lining up with the Word of God. As they say down South, if the cat doesn't like the way it's being rubbed, then let the cat turn around.

If there's one thing that Western churchianity is notorious for, it is having the mindset that there are many interpretations to many subjects in the Word of God. I'm sorry, but that's just flat out ridiculous, and is a denial of the very nature of God Himself—Why would the Holy Spirit inspire the Word of God, and then hand it to us so we could treat it like a jigsaw puzzle and interpret it anyway we see fit. The Word of God given by the Holy Spirit actually states that the scripture is not by any private interpretation—And that should settle that! We're not doing ourselves any favors by playing God with His own Word, *and the sooner we understand that, the sooner we can start growing into maturity and really moving and functioning in the Spirit.*

The believer who will walk in true spiritual authority and power, is the one who is fully submitted to the full authority and power of the Word of God!

Why do you think Satan has worked absolutely overtime to undermine and water down and dilute every part of scripture he can???

So that you will never walk in it's full authority and power over HIM!

And every area in the Word of God in which you compromise, or waffle, or refuse to take a solid stand, or remain wishy-washy, to that degree you lose spiritual authority and power.

Jesus walked in total submission to the Father, therefore the power and authority He walked in was absolute, because His Submission was absolute—And you aren't going do it any other way.

I'll state it another way so that it's crystal clear—The only believers who are going to walk in absolute authority and power in this Endtime, are those who are fully submitted to the power and absolute authority of the Word of God, and the absolute authority of the Holy Spirit. Your total submission will have the full backing of God's authority and power. He will not be anointing any halfhearted part-timers.

Some things are made clear in the Word of God by their very absence, and one thing that we do not see anywhere in the New Testament is a platform ministry for anyone calling themselves a prophet—Attracting followers to themselves, with no direct, ongoing relationship with the Body, where they are submitted to the Body.

What we have today are packs of self-proclaimed prophet's running around with each other, all supposedly supporting each other, but there is no direct, ongoing, submitted relationship to any segment of the Body of Christ. Because there is no existing precedent in scripture for that, I would say avoid it completely.

What we DO have, and what we DO see revealed clearly in the Word of God, is that God's priority is the Body of Christ, Not individual platform ministries.

The apostle Paul taught more on the gifts and on the nature of the Body of Christ itself than any other apostle—and his teaching and directives he said were by the authority of Jesus Christ himself.

So, with the primary focus of Jesus Christ being on His Body, anything trying to operate independently of that Body needs to be marked and avoided.

Remember, much of what we have in existence right now with American churchianity is by our own hand, and our own creation, not by the mandate of God himself—And guess what? He's not obligated to acknowledge anything that we have built in the flesh, or out of presumption or self-will.

And That settles the issue as far as independent platform "ministries" is concerned, and if you're wise, you will take heed to that and shift your focus to that of Jesus Christ's—the Body.

Again, to make it perfectly crystal clear, we are not judging based on how nice a person is, or how charismatic they are, or how popular they are—we are judging based on God's design for His Church and His Body, and since it's His Church and His Body, we do not get to make the rules, and we do not get to pass on exceptions.

This is where submission versus self-will comes in, and our American independent entrepreneur spirit does not have anything to do with how God runs His Church or operates His Body—and if there's one thing American churchianity is absolutely choking on, it is self-will and presumption—Just look at how fiercely we defend our favorite teachers and pulpiteers! We have them on the same pedestal as Jesus Christ himself!

Well, I have news for you—those who are going to go on with God in this hour are going to be the ones who strip away everything that American churchianity has tacked onto the Bible....Everything that we have substituted for God's design, everything that we have added to the Word of God because we like it, or it's convenient, or we just want it that way—That day is over, and it's over right now.

The good news is, once we see things the way He does, and where we are out of line and out of joint, we can make the decision to repent and lay aside everything that we have presumed, and assumed, and grasped out of self-will, and start over— start fresh, and say Father God, we're doing it your way 100% or we're not doing it at all. We are not going to come to your altar any longer offering our sacrifices, when stubbornness and rebellion and self-will are on the throne of our hearts.

This is now the perfect starting point for the subject of ministering in the gifts of the Holy Spirit...Because once we have dethroned all of our idols, and have clean hands and pure hearts, the Holy Spirit is free to do as He wills...And isn't that what we really want?

This is the endgame folks, and we are going to need our brothers and sisters more than ever before, and they are going to need us more than ever before, So let's clean house with absolute ruthlessness so that we can be vessels of the Holy Spirit, with a rock solid foundation of the Word of God under our feet that will withstand whatever storms come— Because it wouldn't do any good to teach, for example, on the subject of prophesying, if our foundation isn't spiritually structurally sound, and if our heart motivations aren't thoroughly purified. I would just be setting you up for disaster, and myself.

Okay, now I want to "set the stage" for each & everyone to be able to come into a Place of Expectation where the gifts of the Holy Spirit are concerned, and the doorway into that place of expectation is one word: "GRACE".

The Greek word used for the gifts is "CHARIS", meaning, "Grace".

A Simple but profound explanation would be this;

Just as we are saved by grace through faith through Jesus, We are equipped by grace through faith through the Holy Spirit.

The first one is an accomplished work (Saved by faith), the second one is a present tense, ongoing work (Equipped by Faith).

Both are from the Lord, and neither one can be earned—In the first, we Trust in the Lord Jesus by faith for the grace of salvation, and then in the second one, we Yield to and trust the Holy Spirit to equip us by faith through grace. Both our salvation and our equipping are by faith in the operation of the Holy Spirit.

However, in the first one—our salvation—we do not tend to be overly caught up in trying to earn that salvation or become deserving of it.

But for whatever reason, when it comes to operating in the gifts, we subconsciously get caught up in believing that somehow we have to be "deserving" or "worthy" of operating in the gifts, or there's something undefinable that we must first "do to qualify" for operating in the gifts— When they are freely given by grace through faith in the operation of the same Holy Spirit, who distributes freely to everyone so that everyone may benefit and be edified (1 Corinthians 12:11).

Just as we look unto Jesus, the author and finisher of our faith, trusting in Him to perfect our salvation, in the same manner we look to and yield to and trust the Holy Spirit to manifest His gifts through us in His way, in His timing, for the benefit and good of the Body—Without us feeling we have to make a human effort to work these things up, or get these things to manifest in our own strength, our own power, or worthiness.

The only thing we must do, is simply believe and trust that the Holy Spirit wants to move through us individually to bless and edify our brothers and sisters, and He knows exactly how, and when, and where to do that. That's as mysterious as it ever will get.

Now, here is a heavy duty thought that, if you will open your mind to it (and this is born out completely in the New Testament), it will completely revolutionize the way you think about gathering with other believers.

If you have your Bible (because I want you to see this in front of your own two eyes, and try to visualize what it says), turn to 1 Corinthians 14:26.

This is where we take the Western churchianity model of everybody sitting on a pew facing forward and listening to a pastor—here's where we take that model and turn it upside down on its little pointy head.

Here is where we get a crystal clear, plain as the noonday sun picture of what the apostle Paul taught the churches was the God-ordained way to gather together—And it was anything but passive and spectator-based!

"What then shall we say, brothers? When you come together, Everyone has a psalm or a teaching, a revelation, a tongue, or an interpretation. All of these must be done to build up the church." (1 Corinthians 14:26).

It doesn't look to me like there's any space in there to fit a pastors 45 minute sermon, does it???

Why not????*Because gathering together is about the Body ministering to itself,* **where every member is expected to receive from the Holy Spirit something to strengthen the rest of the body**. It's not a one-man show! Such a thing was never ever in the mind of God!

This is how believers grow in grace and grow in faith, because they assume mutual responsibility for one another's spiritual well-being in the Spirit—we are all equipped to be our brothers and sisters keeper! THIS is the very language of the New Testament, and it is born out in every letter Paul wrote to the churches.

Here are just a few examples that clearly show that the apostolic churches did not sit in rows of pews passively waiting for papa bird to feed them—rather, **they were spiritually developed enough to actively teach & instruct one another,** *and THAT is what we must return to!* The overwhelming seriousness of the Hour demands it.

Romans 15:14; "I myself am convinced, my brothers, that **you yourselves are full of goodness, brimming with knowledge, and able to instruct one another.**"

1 Corinthians 1:5; "For in Him you have been enriched in every way, in all speech and all knowledge"

Colossians 3:16; "Let the word of Christ richly dwell within you **as you teach and admonish one another with all wisdom,** and as you sing psalms, hymns, and spiritual songs with gratitude in your hearts to God."

Ephesians 5:19; "Speak to one another with psalms, hymns, and spiritual songs. Sing and make music in your hearts to the Lord."

Let Today be the day that you set yourself free from the pulpit prison that has kept the Body of Christ in a spiritually dwarfed and malnourished state—The Western pulpit prisons that we must break free from if we are ever going to minister to one another as the Body, building ourselves up to the place where we will be spiritually strong enough to face the things that are coming upon the earth—Because I guarantee you, the passive pulpit system will only serve to ensure massive spiritual casualties if corrective and evasive action is not taken immediately!

Now, as with any benefit or blessing of the Lord, the gateway to receiving is always by Faith. We are not looking to our own efforts, or our own worthiness, or any other such thing—*Rather, we are inwardly positioning ourselves by faith to receive from the Lord, and in the case of the gifts of the Holy Spirit, we are positioning ourselves to receive from the Holy Spirit whatever particular gift He wishes to manifest through us for the benefit of someone else.*

Now, I would encourage my readers to practice this expectancy by faith on a daily basis—don't wait until you know you're going to a home meeting or a Bible study to do this; practice it on a daily basis, and you will find that your faith will grow, and your sense of expectancy to receive from the Holy Spirit will grow as you deliberately exercise it on a daily basis.

In other words, just try to consciously maintain a sense of expectancy on a daily basis that you are yielding to the Holy Spirit, that you are available and your heart is willing, and He is free to speak to you or minister to you at any time he wishes.

Speaking from personal experience, ***praying in tongues on a daily basis is the primary way to stay in that place of expectancy and yieldedness to the Holy Spirit***, and you will actually find yourself going through your day feeling like your spiritual radar is turned on, and inwardly you are watching for signs that the Holy Spirit is orchestrating something, or moving in a particular way—And when it comes to moving in the gifts of the Holy Spirit, your inward sensitivity is everything.

Just as in any interpersonal relationship, there are many components to building that relationship, and keeping communication flowing. For example, much of our communication with someone we are close to is non-verbal (body language, a change in mood, an inward change in openness & warmth, etc.), and the success of that relationship depends on our being aware of our partner's non-verbal cues, and our responding appropriately.

The Holy Spirit is just as much a Person as Jesus, and as the Father— but since we cannot see Him or physically interact with Him, then we must develop and maintain a very high level of sensitivity and responsiveness to Him.

This means, first and foremost, our perspective & focus must be on spiritual things, and our inward "posture" must be "pointed" in a reverent & submitted attitude toward Him—so much so that even when we are occupied with work or activities, we maintain an awareness of His presence.

In much the same way as we can set a thermostat or a compass heading, we can "set" our inner man on the "fear of the Lord" setting. Praying in the spirit is the primary way we keep our inner man attuned to the promptings of the Holy Spirit, and keep our soul realm yielded and submitted ("to be spiritually minded is life & peace"; "You will keep him in perfect, unbroken peace whose inward man is anchored in You").

Also, developing an awareness of the ways in which the Holy Spirit speaks to us (Dreams and visions, thoughts, impressions, quickening a verse or passage of scripture to our heart, word of knowledge, word of wisdom, prophecy, a strong sense of peace in our heart, or a sudden sense of feeling grieved or distressed in our inner man, etc.).

Here is where I would encourage all of you to use journaling as an ongoing part of your journey with the Holy Spirit. Journaling will serve to greatly enhance your sensitivity toward the Holy Spirit, and to learn how the Holy Spirit communicates with you personally. *Journaling will also train you in how to Perceive, Discern, and Cooperate with the presence of the Holy Spirit in your Everyday life settings, not just when you are in a religious setting.*

Journaling will also guide you to focus on the various ways that you personally perceive & respond to the moving of the Holy Spirit in your life, *so that your spiritual growth is an outflow of the Holy Spirit's inward activity*—as opposed to simply absorbing head knowledge of Scripture, or reading books about Bible subjects.

You come into an appropriation of the experiential reality that TRUE spiritual growth comes from a daily, Living cooperation with the Holy Spirit who dwells within you, and Who guides you from within. *That is the difference between a believer who is living & operating solely from Head*

Knowledge, to living from Inward, Relational Guidance from the Holy Spirit (1 John 2:27). In this case, Knowledge does not always equal Guidance.

Now, I'm going to quote two passages to you, but before I do, I want to make a statement that I was actually going to save until after I share these two passages—but I think if I make the statement First, then read those two passages of scripture, they will take on a whole new fresh meaning for you, so here goes.

As a member of Christ's Body, when you are consciously cooperating with the Holy Spirit from day to day, hour to hour, and moment to moment, **you are walking in a real-time connection to the Head of the church, Jesus Christ.** You are then actually experiencing a living, real-time connection to your Head, Jesus Christ. That is something that probably 98% of the religious institutional system does not do.

So here is the first passage I was going to share with you. And I'd like you to take the time to look it up in your own Bible today, because it is full of power if you'll just spend some time meditating on it.

"And He is the head of the body, the church; He is the beginning and firstborn from among the dead, so that in all things He may have preeminence. For God was pleased to have all His fullness dwell in Him, and through Him to reconcile to Himself all things, whether things on earth or things in heaven, by making peace through the blood of His cross.

"Once you were alienated from God and were hostile in your minds, engaging in evil deeds. But now He has reconciled you by Christ's physical body through death to present you holy, unblemished, and blameless in His presence— if indeed you continue in your faith, established and firm, not moved from the hope of the gospel you heard, which has been proclaimed to every creature under heaven, and of which I, Paul, have become a servant."(Colossians 1:18-23).

The second passage I want to share with you is very much connected to the one I just read in Colossians;

"So I fell at his feet to worship him. But he told me, "Do not do that! I am a fellow servant with you and your brothers who rely on the testimony of Jesus. Worship God! *For the testimony of Jesus is the Spirit of prophecy.*" (Revelation 19:10)

In other words, it is the Spirit of prophecy who bears testimony to Jesus, which agrees with what Jesus taught about the Holy Spirit in John 16:13,14; "However, when the Spirit of truth comes, He will guide you into all truth. For He will not speak on His own, but **He will speak what He hears**, and He will declare to you what is to come. **He will glorify Me by taking from what is Mine and disclosing it to you.**"

That completely agrees with the words of Jesus to the seven churches in Revelation, when He said to each of them, "He who has an ear, let him hear what the Spirit says to the churches." (Rev. 3:6).

Now, look at those passages together when you have time, and look at them very, very prayerfully, and very meditatively and very closely, and see if you can see the main reality that is revealed in those passages.

Remember, this chapter is regarding the Body ministry of the Holy Spirit through prophesying. *The primary reality that all of these verses, when taken together, communicate to us is that our basic focus as believers is to abide in our Head, Jesus Christ, by walking in and hearing from the Holy Spirit, who in turn completes the cycle by speaking to us what He hears from our head Jesus Christ.*

Revelation 19:10 and John 16 tell us that the Holy Spirit bears testimony to Jesus, and reveals and unveils to us what Jesus our Head is speaking and directing.

And Jesus our Head exhorts and admonishes the churches and each of us individually by saying, "He who has an ear, let him hear what the Spirit says to the churches." (Rev. 3:6)

To me—especially with Jesus breaking it down to the individual level by saying "let him who has an ear" which is singular—the highest Endtime priority is for each believer to maintain living contact with the Head of the

Church on a day-to-day basis, which is the same thing as Jesus' exhortation in the book of John to abide in Him.

The apostle John said the same thing; "And now, little children, *remain in Christ*, so that when He appears, we may be confident and unashamed before Him at His coming" (1 John 2:28). ***And we abide in Him, our Head over the Church, by walking in the Spirit and hearing from the Spirit continually.***

It is a tri-fold relationship, if you will, that is dependent on no one else but us individually.

It doesn't matter how many believers you fellowship with, ***it is your individual responsibility and mine to maintain this threefold cord relationship with the Holy Spirit and with Jesus Christ our Head on a daily basis.***

To take this daily overriding priority one step further, I want to tie this into the main subject again (the Body ministry of the Holy Spirit in prophesying) by showing you that ***as we function in the gift of prophesying—as per Paul's instructions, with prophesying being the primary spiritual gift that edifies the body—when we function in that toward our brothers and sisters, we are enabling them to abide in their Head Jesus Christ, and hear what the Spirit is saying to the churches.***

In other words, by functioning in the gifts that edify our brothers and sisters the most, we enable them and strengthen them to abide in the Vine—the Vine is where the Life is, and Life is continually flowing through the Vine, which is descriptive of our walking in the Spirit.

Now, one final passage comes to mind, that ties Everything together;

Ephesians 4:15,16; "Instead, speaking the truth in love, we will in all things grow up into Christ Himself, who is the head. From Him the whole body, fitted and held together by every supporting ligament, grows and builds itself up in love through the work of each individual part."

So, as we are ministering in the gifts to one another, for the edification, building up and strengthening of our brothers and sisters, we are in real-time fulfilling and living out this passage, and literally functioning in our connection to our head, Jesus Christ.

To me, that is some amazingly powerful stuff! That here we are, in time and space in 2022, living by the Spirit and being connected to our Head Jesus Christ, who is in Heaven at the right hand of the Father, and we are functioning in a real-time, living connection with Him in heavenly places!

I believe the Holy Spirit wants to raise our sights even higher, as it concerns ministering in the gifts to one another.

I want you to see something so glorious and amazing concerning what Jesus Christ our Head gets out of us ministering in the gifts to one another—**His ultimate, Eternal benefit that He derives from us walking in the Spirit and ministering in the Spirit to one another**—watch this!

Back in Ephesians, this time in chapter 5.

Ephesians is the one letter in the New Testament where Paul really expounds on our position in Christ Jesus in the heavenly places, and the preeminence of Jesus as Head of the Church.

So, Ephesians 5:23-27;

"For the husband is the head of the wife as Christ is the head of the church, His body, of which He is the Savior. Now as the church submits to Christ, so also wives should submit to their husbands in everything. Husbands, love your wives, **just as Christ loved the church and gave Himself up for her, to sanctify her, cleansing her by the washing with water through the word, and to present her to Himself as a** glorious church, without stain or wrinkle or any such blemish, but holy and blameless."

So, part of our ministering to one another by the Spirit through His gifts, contributes toward presenting the Church to Jesus Christ in the spiritual condition that He is seeking; Presenting the Church to Him in all her glory, having no spot or wrinkle or any such thing, holy and blameless.

In other words, **when we are truly functioning in administering the gifts of the Holy Spirit to one another, we are as a natural byproduct helping to produce the fruit of the Spirit in one another—And that, in turn, contributes to maturing the Church into the pure and holy bride Jesus is waiting for.**

This, I believe, puts the gifts of the Holy Spirit in their truest light, by highlighting their Highest, Eternal purpose—The perfecting of the Saints, the Body of Christ—And perfecting the Body, making the Bride ready, happens on THIS side of Eternity!

THAT means that whatever we are doing that does NOT contribute to maturing & perfecting the Body & making the Bride ready, must CEASE.

ONLY the Body-focused activities that are Sanctioned by the Lord & Directed by the Spirit have any merit whatsoever. NO MORE RELIGIOUS BUSY WORK, NO MORE MAN-DRIVEN ACTIVITY. The Day of Decision is NOW.

CHAPTER 24

NO PLACE TO LAY HIS HEAD; NURTURING NEW TESTAMENT MINISTRY

I think it's very significant that our Lord, who was baptized in the Holy Spirit and anointed by the Holy Spirit, is the same Lord who said of Himself, "The son of man has nowhere to lay his head".

Now honestly, can you even begin to conceive of someone today having a ministry as powerful as the one Jesus had, and yet being homeless and at the mercy of whoever would let him stay for a few days or nights????

This is the same Lord who, when He was ascended to heaven, imparted ministry gifts for the building up, maturing, and edifying of the Body.

It has been my sad observation over the past 35 years, that those who have been true ministry gifts to the body of Christ have likewise had no place to lay their head.

Of course, if I take a step back and look again at the environment in which Jesus lived and ministered in, the answer becomes all too apparent.

Take a look at the Gospels and tell me, can you see even one instance in which Jesus—after being baptized in the Holy Spirit and walking in ministry —was actually welcomed into and made a part of the religious establishment???

That's right—He was not. In fact, the religious establishment was His biggest opponent and avowed enemy.

By its very nature, the religious institution exists for itself, to perpetuate its own ends.

Regardless of what it professes, it does not exist to truly honor, worship, and serve God—only the gods of its own making.

Your walk and ministry in the Spirit is a direct affront to the system, and that is why it reacts with such anger, hatred, and blind prejudice—and they are blind because of their refusal to receive the love of the Truth; they only want their own version of the truth.

In a nutshell, the religious system is anti-everything that God truly is.

Where the Spirit of the Lord is, there is liberty and there is life.

Where the religious system is, there is legalistic ritual and deadness.

If you want to have a clear visual of just how hateful and despicable the religious system is, just take a look at every instance in which Jesus healed or delivered someone in a synagogue—do you see the Pharisees rejoicing and praising God???

No—they only became more hardened in their determination to kill Jesus...And that is all you need to know about the religious spirit.

The religious system is all about control—controlled location, in a building controlled; set times; controlled, established rituals and formats; and controlled leadership who are divided from those who just sit and listen and do very little else.

This is clearly anti-Body of Christ—Only the most delusional would believe that this is an environment and description of a freely functioning autonomous body.

There is clearly no way that what we see with our eyes today as the religious institution, matches up to what we see in Ephesians 4 and 1 Corinthians 12 & 14.

One is a System, and one is a Body—and there's no way those two are ever getting married or coexisting.

So the only viable conclusion, then, is that for us to be a functioning part of the Body, we will have to come out of the religious system—there's no compatibility there.

"There is one Body and one Spirit, just as you were called to one hope when you were called; one Lord, one faith, one baptism; one God and Father of all, who is over all and through all and in all. Now to each one of us grace has been given according to the measure of the gift of Christ. This is why it says:

"When He ascended on high, He led captives away, and gave gifts to men."

What does "He ascended" mean, except that He also descended to the lower parts of the earth? He who descended is the very One who ascended above all the heavens, in order to fill all things.

And it was He who gave some to be apostles, some to be prophets, some to be evangelists, and some to be pastors and teachers, to equip the saints for works of ministry and to build up the body of Christ, until we all reach unity in the faith and in the knowledge of the Son of God, as we mature to the full measure of the stature of Christ.

Then we will no longer be infants, tossed about by the waves and carried around by every wind of teaching and by the clever cunning of men in their deceitful scheming. Instead, speaking the truth in love, we will in all things grow up into Christ Himself, who is the head. From Him the whole body, fitted and held together by every supporting ligament, grows and builds itself up in love through the work of each individual part" (Ephesians 4:4-16).

Those gifts are ministry functions intended to be empowered by the Holy Spirit, directed by the Holy Spirit, and under the Lordship of the Holy Spirit.

Those gifts were given by the ascended Lord Jesus, and those gifts were never recalled, and have not expired contrary to the deluded traditions of men, and the horrific misconceptions sown by the enemy. The function of those gifts is to bring the Body of Christ into a state of maturity which culminates in unity and submission to the Head, who is Jesus Christ.

Since this end result has not yet been achieved, it is more than reasonable to believe that these gifts, given by the Lord Jesus Christ to the Body, are still profoundly necessary and vital for the well-being and the health and the maturity of His Body.

In the context of Ephesians 4, it is apparent that the Major spiritual obstacles these gifts are designed to combat is widespread dysfunction, division, disunity, and deception (Ephesians 4:14).

It's quite obvious from the context that Without these gifts functioning in the Body as God intended, the above stated negative conditions will prevail—And I believe that it is readily apparent in the Western professing church that these conditions have been prevailing for quite a long time, and growing even worse.

But I believe that help is on the way.

Nowhere in the New Testament do we see any sign of those ministry gifts being recalled by Jesus, or being sent back to heaven from earth by the Holy Spirit, simply because the enemy was making too many inroads and these gifts weren't doing the job.

To the contrary—as long as the Body of Christ is here on earth, those ministry gifts are needed, and are still part of God's intention to mature and develop the Church, the Body of Christ.

Of course, Satan already fully understands Heaven's organizational structure, and he knows that these gifts will not be recalled—so he must work overtime to distort and pervert them, so that the Body of Christ holds these ministries in contempt and disrepute—and from where I stand, he has succeeded overwhelmingly for the last three decades. Satan has been very prolific in raising up self-promoting apostles, prophets, and evangelists over the last 25 to 30 years, and it's only getting worse.

And here's the catch: when Satan is successful in raising up—for example—a false prophet, he succeeds in prejudicing those in the Body against the TRUE prophetic gift and office itself, thereby conditioning those in the Body against Any prophet or prophetic gift, so it's a win-win for satan—He has used a counterfeit ministry to successfully inoculate the Body of Christ against the TRUE prophetic ministry....Thereby robbing the Body of Christ from the growth and maturity it could have experienced from true prophetic ministry, which was the stated objective in Ephesians 4.

I hope you see the Big spiritual picture here, and the spiritual warfare that is waged against the Body of Christ AND against the gifts that Jesus Christ gave to it.

We are just as responsible and accountable to Jesus to identify, guard, and preserve the TRUE ministry gifts in our midst, as we are to point the finger and identify the false—And so far, all I have witnessed in the last 30 some odd years is our tendency to only point out the false, without ever giving any thought to the TRUE....Without giving any thought to the incalculable benefit of what the Lord is wanting to bless us with....A ministry gift with its origins in the Heavenlies, designed by the sovereign grace of God to equip us and strengthen us...A ministry gift that—in its truest sense—has its origins not from this earth, but from Above....a ministry gift designed to keep our hearts and our affections Focused on what IS above....

And we have as our examples the fatherly apostle Paul, Peter, James and John, who pointed us heavenward, and whose apostolic ministry gifts serve even to this day to strengthen and ground the body of Christ—And it is through this lens that we should perceive the ministry gifts He still wishes to bestow upon us....While clearly keeping in focus these *past* ministry gifts as *the Divine template* for all *Future* ministry gifts to the Body....
Ministry gifts that were free from all selfish ambition, from all self-seeking

and self-serving tendencies…ministry gifts that were only content to lay their lives down for the Body, and to endure all things for the sake of the elect….to serve and guard the flock at whatever cost. THAT is the heart of any True ministry gift.

If it does not smell like a shepherd, then it is very likely a wolf.…

In the meantime, satan's principalities of religious spirits have been feverishly at work, raising up a huge segment of professing believers who are completely brain-locked and not Spirit-led in the least, to stand up and point the fingers at all of the false ministries that Satan has raised up, and proclaiming, "See, we told you the gifts have passed away, there are no more apostles and prophets!" *But to use the presence of the false as an argument against that which is true, is simply flawed logic, at best.*

In fact, Jesus was very quick to tell the parable of the wheat and the tares, stating that Both the wheat and the tares will be here until Both reach maturity, and then his angels will come, and the reapers will gather the wheat into the barn, and the tares will be burned;

"Jesus put before them another parable: "The kingdom of heaven is like a man who sowed good seed in his field. But while everyone was asleep, his enemy came and sowed weeds among the wheat, and slipped away. When the wheat sprouted and bore grain, then the weeds also appeared.

The owner's servants came to him and said, 'Sir, didn't you sow good seed in your field? Where then did the weeds come from?'

'An enemy did this,' he replied.

So the servants asked him, 'Do you want us to go and pull them up?'

'No,' he said, 'if you pull the weeds now, you might uproot the wheat with them. Let both grow together until the harvest. At that time I will tell the harvesters: First collect the weeds and tie them in bundles to be burned; then gather the wheat into my barn." (Matthew 13:24-30).

The presence of the false, according to Jesus, is clear indication that the True still remains—and That is what Satan is fighting against!

And as long as we allow that which is false to completely cloud our vision and color our perception, we are playing right into the enemies' hands, and unwittingly serving his interests.

> *So rather than just curse the tares, we need to look for the 'wheat ministries' that Jesus has already planted, and help those ministries reach maturity, so they can help US reach maturity! Because as Ephesians 4 states, we will not reach maturity without them.*

Now, I want to be very emphatic and clear, when I say that this is not a doctrinal issue—not in the least, and for anyone to take the approach that it IS, just means you have fallen for another diversion of the enemy.

Again, the only Correct approach to this subject, is understanding that these ministry gifts were given by Jesus, the Head of the Church—THAT is your starting point.

If you don't begin with the revealed intentions and provisions of Jesus Christ as Head of His Church, then you are starting off on the wrong premise, and you will never come to the correct conclusion.

Now, to provide some spiritual light for those who are still stuck on the false and the Counterfeit.

Let me show you from the Word of God that *if the True ministry is allowed to mature and function, then by its very nature, it should expose and confront the false.*

What do I mean when I say "by its very nature"?

Allow me to explain.

Again, as we camp out here in Ephesians 4, we are keeping in mind that the revealed intentions of Jesus, in giving these ministry gifts to the Body of Christ, is for the sole purpose of maturing, edifying and protecting the Body of Christ, as we ALL grow up Together into Him who is the Head—"As we all" includes those who are ministry gifts, *who are also part of us, the Body. They are not separate from us, and they do not ACT as though they are separate from us or above us.* They live and breathe and act as one of us—in other words, their function does not become a lofty ministry title that elevates them above the rest of us—*And if their actions and their personality speaks otherwise, then you know you are most likely dealing with a counterfeit ministry, and not the real thing.*

The apostle Paul described his heart and demeanor as that of a loving father towards children, not as a mighty apostle before whom everyone must bow down…And he vehemently opposed false apostles who had the opposite attitude and motives—***And that right there is a clear sign of a true ministry gift, when it rises up to protect the Body it serves, from those who are false.***

A true apostle seeks only the good of the Body, and will vehemently oppose and call out false apostles. A true prophet will likewise earnestly protect the Body from false prophets, out of its love for the Body.

In other words, each of these ministry gifts also has the responsibility and the heart of the great Shepherd, because they know that they have been set as a blessing to the flock, to feed the flock through their ministry gift.

A hireling only seeks to benefit from the flock at the flock's expense— Jesus made it clear the hireling cares nothing for the well-being of the flock, and will desert if there is any danger.

What I am trying to do is give you a broader spiritual perspective of the intentions of Jesus in providing these ministry gifts, and what they should "feel like" to us spiritually.

Virtually all we have seen so far is Satan's counterfeits, although there have been many manifestations of the true.

Of course, we are used to seeing the bright, shiny, glossy packaging of the counterfeits, so we're not looking for a baby in a manger, or Moses in the bushes, or Joseph the ruler in a prison or as a slave—*In other words, the true ministry gifts will never look like something high and mighty, or lofty or deserving of special recognition*—And again, if they pose as such, then you know who they're really working for.

A REAL ministry gift apostle or prophet or evangelist is probably going look like some regular person in blue jeans and a shirt, laboring and motivated purely by love, and a heart that swells with compassion and even sorrow over the Body of Christ, aching to minister where needed…. aching to bring relief, clarity, healing, wherever needed, at no cost, with no price—and with no fanfare, or parade, or glossy shiny advertisements…

And if you spot such a one in your midst, gather around them, love them, pray for them, because all they want to do is be His vessel of life and blessing to you.…

"While they were worshiping the Lord and fasting, the Holy Spirit said, "Set apart for Me Barnabas and Saul for the work to which I have called them" (Acts 13:2).

Notice it is the Holy Spirit Who has the authority and privilege of calling whom He will, when He will.

However, we must also be spiritually responsible to have an environment that is conducive to hearing the Holy Spirit, and fostering true spiritual growth in one another, so that when the Holy Spirit's appointed time for releasing Ministry gifts to the Body takes place, we are sensitive and responsive.

I am convinced that just as evil as abortion is in the natural, it's just as evil to the Lord in the spiritual, and I am convinced there are untold numbers of ministry gifts that were intended to bless the Body of Christ that were aborted, or that died prematurely because they were not allowed to come to full term in an environment that would nurture them into maturity, and then release them to the Body to edify and equip us.

Most people are familiar with the passage in the Bible that states, "As it is, there are many parts, but one body. The eye cannot say to the hand, "I do not need you." Nor can the head say to the feet, "I do not need you" (1 Corinthians 12:20,21).

Well, that passage is in 1 Corinthians 12, which outlines the gifts of the Holy Spirit and their operation within the Body—*and let's keep in mind that the gifts of the Holy Spirit also include the ministry gifts which Jesus gave in Ephesians chapter 4.*

When you take 1 Corinthians 12:20-22 and Ephesians 4:11-13 together, then it becomes crystal clear that the Body's members include those who are ministry gifts to the Body—so, to slightly paraphrase, the eye cannot say to the prophet, I don't need you; the hand cannot say to the apostle, I have no need of you, etc.

Furthermore, when we understand that ALL of the parts of the Body are ordained by God Himself, and each part of the Body is essential to the rest of the Body, **then we can focus on having a Body mentality, and a Body perspective.**

What I mean by that is that **our spiritual focus and mindset becomes much broader,** and *we begin to think of the Body as a whole,* and not just ourselves, our little family, our little group, but we begin thinking beyond those tiny confining little borderlines that we have maybe drawn for ourselves, and we start seeing things from Heaven's perspective—because Jesus is coming back for a Body, not pieces of a Body scattered all over the earth.

And if we will begin to cultivate and nurture this mindset in ourselves individually, it opens us up to a much deeper and broader ministry of the Holy Spirit to us personally, because now we are seeing things from His perspective, not our own.

I believe this is a major focus of the Holy Spirit in this moment of time that we need to acclimate ourselves to and adjust ourselves to—And I believe that *the FIRST place we can exercise our renewed spiritual mindset is our own home group gatherings and fellowships, where we can develop and exercise spiritual sensitivity to those in our midst that the Holy Spirit is cultivating as ministry gifts to the Body.* This does not mean promoting anyone or giving them some sort of a ministry title, by any means.

This simply means being open and receptive to the Holy Spirit's leading and guiding as to whom He may have His hand on, as one He has chosen to be a ministry gift, and simply being spiritually aware of that person and their calling, while maintaining an atmosphere that everyone can grow spiritually within and develop in their giftings.

Ephesians 4:16 gives us the True spiritual focal point for *balance* in this area:

"From Him the whole body, fitted and held together by every supporting ligament, grows and builds itself up in love through the work of each individual part."

So, every one of us is needed, and if the Body is to receive the full spiritual benefit of each one of us, then each one of us must be fully equipped and walking in our own individual calling, as ordained by God, in order to be of maximum benefit to the rest of the Body.

If I am called by the Lord to be an intercessor, I am not much benefit to the Body if I don't spend time praying and interceding.

If I am called by the Lord to be a prophet, informing the Body what of the Lord is speaking and saying to the Body at this time, I'm not much benefit to the Body if I don't spend time listening and hearing the voice of the Holy Spirit in that area.

If you are called to be an apostle, but yet you don't give the Lord the time to teach you how the Body is supposed to function, and the areas in which the Body may be deficient or lacking, or areas where it needs to be built up, then you will likewise not benefit the Body in your calling.

We all need one another, so it is of extreme importance that each one of us is deeply sensitive to the Holy Spirit with regards to what He has called us to do and be specifically.

If you are a hand and I am an eye, I will never be able to do your job—you must do it. And as a hand, I'm not really going to be very well-versed on what the job of an eye actually is.

That is why Paul said every one of us is given a measure of grace and faith to operate in our own individual Callings, whether it be teaching, whether it be prophesying, whether it be some other ministry—*so let us then exercise our faith and make it operational in the sphere of our calling.*

"We have different gifts according to the grace given us. If one's gift is prophecy, let him use it in proportion to his faith; if it is serving, let him serve; if it is teaching, let him teach; if it is encouraging, let him encourage; if it is giving, let him give generously; if it is leading, let him lead with diligence; if it is showing mercy, let him do it cheerfully." (Romans 12:6-8)

By faithfully doing this, we create an atmosphere where other ministry gifts are able to be nurtured and cultivated, and come to a place of maturity, so that they can be recognized by the Holy Spirit in our midst, and released to the Body, for further edification of the Body. THIS is a Primary Focus Point for the Lord's purposes as we gather together.

This, in a nutshell, is in fact New Testament Christianity, and the entirety of the New Testament supports this and expresses it very clearly, and in a very detailed fashion—

We just have to read the New Testament through the lenses of Spirit-filled Body life ministry.

In closing, I'd like to offer some final thoughts inspired by the Holy Spirit as I was driving through a major construction zone tonight.

"For it is God who works in you to will and to act on behalf of His good purpose" (Philippians 2:13).

Now unfortunately, when we read scriptures like this, most of the time it doesn't register as deeply as it needs to—and that's not our fault; that is largely a result of our Western religious conditioning.

We have seen certain Bible verses so many times that they become one dimensional to us.

Well, this verse became very three-dimensional to me tonight.

As I was meditating on Philippians 2:13 tonight, I was driving through section of highway with all the road construction crews working on it, equipped with all the signage, the heavy equipment, and so on.

That is something very easy for all of us to picture in our minds, because the first thing that you think about is you're going have to drive much slower or you'll get a ticket, because construction zones cannot be driven upon like every other roadway.

There are existing conditions that dictate a more acute awareness of your surroundings as you are driving.

You go slower; you're more aware of obstacles, barriers, moving equipment, and things that are not normally a consideration in your typical driving day.

You have to adjust everything about your driving to accommodate the special working conditions.

This is a spiritual reality as well, when you are spiritually tuned into the Holy Spirit doing an inner work in you, such as is conveyed in Philippians 2:13.

The reality is that the Holy Spirit is always present, and completely willing to work in us on an individual basis—But, *the key is being sensitive to that reality, and maintaining a sensitivity and a yieldingness that* allows the Holy Spirit to build in us individually what He sees is needed in our innermost being.

The more sensitive we can be to His inward presence, the more we are able to consciously cooperate with the Holy Spirit, *even allowing Him to give us an understanding of what it is He is seeking to accomplish and why*, which further enables us to cooperate with His process.

The "road work crew analogy" works really well for me, because *it underscores some key elements in cooperating with the Holy Spirit as He is working in us.*

The first thing is that reducing our speed in a construction zone, *speaks to consciously slowing down our pace of life when we become aware that the Holy Spirit is seeking to do an inward work.*

This may mean making more quality time to be still in His presence, taking prayer walks, or something of that nature, that puts you inwardly in a more relaxed, meditative state where you are listening for the Holy Spirits prompting's, etc., and giving Him the space and the time to speak to you when He is ready.

That is known as *"waiting on the Lord"*; you are setting aside your own personal agendas in favor of attending to His.

This is a spiritual habit that we absolutely must make the time to cultivate Now, before the Endtimes get more fully intense.

Again, the parable of the wise virgins versus the foolish virgins speaks very directly to this. You are not going to be in a position to develop a truly deeply sensitive, inward relationship to the Holy Spirit when persecution and tribulation are exploding all around you—NOW is the time if you're ever going to do it.

Furthermore, *determining to get positioned in this place of inward yieldedness to the Holy Spirit is going to allow Him to begin building in you and fortifying in you the calling that He has placed upon you, and that He has purposed for you to walk out—BUT, walking out what He has called you and gifted you to do is entirely dependent on your degree of commitment, consecration, and sensitivity....And those are things He cannot accomplish for you; you must provide the commitment, consecration, and the sensitivity yourself.*

And please believe me when I say that it is highly imperative that every one of us becomes sensitive and aware toward what He has specifically called us to do, because *walking out our calling in this hour—and in the times to come—is going to ensure that other believers are strengthened and built up by your gifting, and by what the Holy Spirit wants to impart through you to others.*

1 Peter 4:7,10; (*Please note that the exhortation to minister to one another according to the gifts we have been given, is against the backdrop of suffering and persecution*)

"The end of all things is near. Therefore be clear-minded and sober, so that you can pray.... *As good stewards of the manifold grace of God*, each of you should use whatever gift he has received to serve one another...."

Being able to minister to one another through our spiritual gifts is going to greatly contribute to our fellow believers being able to endure to the end—this is serious spiritual business, folks!

If you do not take the time to let the Holy Spirit develop you prophetically, evangelistically, apostolically, or in your teaching gift, others will suffer because of what you were not able to impart to them.

Remember, we are a body, and the hand cannot say to the other body parts "I have no need of you"—or conversely, "you have no need of me".

Each one of us is needed Now more than ever, to impart to our fellow believers what the Holy Spirit has already envisioned being needed, because of what we are going to be walking out—And I pray that the awareness of the times we are heading into is a monumental incentive for everyone to say, "Yes Holy Spirit, I want to get with the program, and I want to get with the program NOW!"

The apostle Paul made a very powerful and revealing statement, especially if we read it with this context in mind;

"For I long to see you so that I may impart to you some spiritual gift **to strengthen you**". (Romans 1:11)

Paul makes another very far-reaching and powerful statement (again, if we read it with this spiritual context in mind);

"Therefore you do not lack any spiritual gift *as you eagerly await the revelation of our Lord Jesus Christ.*" (1 Corinthians 1:7)

The apostolic mindset is that maintaining functionality in spiritual gifts is an indispensable means to enduring to the end until the return of Jesus Christ, and an indispensable means to maintaining our faith, our endurance, our hope, and our ability to encourage and strengthen one another.

I would say that puts it in the Number One slot of things deserving our utmost attention, commitment, and dedication.

CHAPTER 25

RECEIVING THE FULLNESS OF THE SPIRIT; EXPERIENCING THE PARTNERSHIP OF THE HOLY SPIRIT, ONE STEP AT A TIME

O ver the last few months, I have had a growing inner awareness that *the realm of the Spirit is a place we are going to have to become increasingly accustomed to and comfortable with as a part of our daily reality, no matter how many baby steps we have to take to get to that destination.*

At the same time, I fully understand why that is so—Because what is coming on this world is going to be spiritually malevolent beyond any of our current ability to comprehend, and those who are not spiritually prepared, will be completely overwhelmed.

Very much like what I felt in 1981, when the Lord was trying to draw me closer to himself, I feel the same gentle but insistent pull of the Spirit...A pull to go into places of the spirit that I have been in the past... places I remember going, but I know that it's got to be far deeper and far more intense than anything I ever knew before—deeper than any of the times of intercession and travail....deeper than any of that...I'm struggling to even give this new realm name—as if being able to identify it would help me to make the transition. And I am acutely aware of my responsibility and calling to help others enter that place as well....

I have had this reoccurring thought now for a little while, these past few months as I have navigated the completely unpredictable waves of grief and sorrow, and all of the other soul crushing that comes with losing the love of your life....

I have struggled beyond my ability to put into words, to just breathe on countless days....to the point where I had to fight the overwhelming urge to break down and cry, because I was afraid I might not be able to catch my breath, and suffocate on my own weeping (Seriously, there were quite a few times when I literally could not inhale to take another breath because of the convulsive sobbing—That was a new and terrifying feeling that I had never had before)

True love changes you so very, very deeply....And losing that true love, feels like your soul is being strip-mined and completely excavated.... You feel like you have swallowed a dark, cold, bottomless pit....

You weep and you sob from places deeper than you could've ever imagined....some unknown abyss in your soul has suddenly been opened up, and it is beyond any human power to close it back up....You are at the mercy of emotions that run deeper than you knew was possible....And an awareness washes over you, an awareness that you need God on a deeper level than you ever imagined—and you wonder if He's up for the task...

I have felt all of these things over and over the last several months, even on good days when the sun was out, the skies are blue, and I was beginning to feel alive again...and then, the smallest little thing sets off an avalanche (I wasn't paying attention to the sign on the side of the road that said 'watch for falling emotions')....

And out of this emotional maelstrom, has come an unexpected gift....a gift of heightened sensitivity to the heart of the Holy Spirit.... One thing I have discovered is that He wants to communicate with us on a deeper level than most of us will ever be comfortable with—And yet if we do not allow Him to have access to the deepest parts of our being, we will forever be at arm's length from intimacy with all that God is.

That recurring thought that I mentioned at the beginning of this conversation???

It is that the Lord has—for whatever reason—chosen me as His special test subject, for my brothers and sisters to learn from—And the lesson is, understanding what it takes to truly develop intimacy with the Holy Spirit, which is the gateway to deeper fellowship with the Father and the Son—but it has to be on HIS terms, because as deep as He wants (and Needs) to go with us, if it were left up to us, we would stay forever in our comfort zones....And the hour is far too late for us to go at our own pace with things of this nature.

Oh I wish I could convey to you in ways that would completely and totally grip your imagination and your focus, to communicate the profound sense of urgency I feel from the Fathers own heart toward His children in this moment of time, *how very desperately He needs us to have hearts of infinite trust and faith in Him...*

So, I am His "test subject" for you to learn from, as I am myself I am learning through all of this....

So what I am doing is relating to you, my brothers and sisters, things that I myself am learning for what feels like the very first time, with each and every step I take on this path from grief, Brokenness, and loss, into the very heart of God Himself—Yes, you heard me right, and by no means am I stating it that way for effect or exaggeration...

One thing that I have been experiencing very consistently over the last few months, is a very real sense of my Heavenly Fathers' compassionate patience with me....

But the one amazing thing that happened today, was actually the outcome of a conversation I've been having with the Holy Spirit for at least the last few weeks....I have been sensing the Holy Spirit wanting to communicate with me in a deeper, ongoing way than maybe I've ever known in my life—But I have been very honest with Him in saying that while I am open to that, I don't know if I have the strength to handle any emotions that might get triggered.

I mean, I'm still dealing with very deep grief, and that does not necessarily bode well if the Holy Spirit is going to—for example—initiate a spirit of travail and intercession in me; I don't really have the strength to keep on crying, and travailing in the spirit tends to do that. So, I'm being very honest and direct with the Holy Spirit about what I feel I can—and cannot—do about my emotional and spiritual limitations as I perceive them.

I know that He is well able to work within my current emotional condition, and I know He's not holding it against me. I did tell Him that I am open to Him doing a deeper work in me, as long as it doesn't trigger anything emotionally that I'm not strong enough for.

Again, this is the way we all need to communicate with our Heavenly Father and with the Holy Spirit—be yourself; be honest, acknowledge your limitations, and trust that He is compassionate and willing to meet you where you are at—but at the same time, be aware that He will be gently trying to grow you past your comfort level, even when you might not feel like you can—And He is able to do so in ways that you cannot imagine.

Take my breakthrough today, for example. For the first time in forever, I got up really early and started my day with prayer and worship. I began walking through the house praying in tongues, and speaking the Word over my daughter and myself, and at some point while I was praying in tongues, it was like the Holy Spirit himself began praying in tongues through me, and it sounded like an angelic warlord was speaking—It was so loud and forceful that I'm surprised neighbors didn't call 911 for noise disturbance. That has happened in the distant past, but never as powerfully as this morning.

So after about an hour, I felt things subside, and so I spent the next little while just quiet, making coffee, etc…

And yet the longer I went about the morning quietly, there was a nagging sense of something left undone...And then the thought came to me to put on some worship, so I put on an old worship CD of Roopa's, one that she played hundreds of times before we met.

And as I listened to this worship song—and there was such an absolute anointing on it —it was as though Roopa was here in the living room, singing it herself—and that deep, deep, deep place inside of me broke open again, and I began to worship and weep my heart out....but this time, the weeping was **not** from the deep recesses of **Grief**; it was from the same depths, but it was a depth of worship that I have never experienced or expressed to the Lord before in my life...And I suddenly realized that the Holy Spirit had used my grief to open me up to Him in a deeper way than ever before, *and this time I felt healing in my brokenness*, not just more grief, which was what I had been afraid of...

The Holy Spirit had been granted access to the deepest parts of my being—I guess you could call it the holy of holies—I honestly do not remember ever in my entire life a moment when the Holy Spirit was causing me to worship from such a deep place, where I experienced such a depth of release and where I experienced such a depth of oneness with him....

I truly did experience the promise from scripture that says the Lord is close to the brokenhearted, and He binds up all their wounds....The place where our deepest hurts and sorrows and griefs can actually be *the doorway for the Holy Spirit to go deeper in us than ever before, and bring true healing and oneness of fellowship with Him at the same time.*

So I encourage you, my dear brothers and sisters, to look at your griefs, sorrows, and heartaches, as doorways to let the Holy Spirit into your heart in a deeper way, and allow Him to bring healing through those very hurts, by allowing Him to go into those wounded places—and as you go before Him in worship (because I believe worship is what releases His presence into those deep places), and allow Him to touch you in the most loving, healing way, then you will never, ever be the same....

Our infirmities—whether they be emotional, mental, or otherwise— are not roadblocks to the Holy Spirit moving in our life, as we have perhaps been led to believe in the past by our own minds. *Does not Romans 8 itself tell us that the Holy Spirit lays hold with us "in our infirmities"????*

That means that in our weakness is when we truly experience our precious partnership with Him—and is that not when we need it the most???

We have here in the self-reliant, "pull yourself up by your boot-straps" West regarded our times of emotional, physical, mental distress as shameful, embarrassing weaknesses; "we should be stronger than that", "we should be braver than that", "we should be more resilient than that", and on and on the shame tape goes in our mind, Chastising us for being weak and frail and without answers and without strength...

And yet the apostle Paul said, "I glory in my weaknesses, for when I am weak, then I am made strong"....Right after the Lord told him, My strength is made perfect in weakness—meaning, His Holy Spirit partnership with you becomes most effectual when you are weak and depending on His strength!

"But He said to me, "My grace is sufficient for you, for My power is perfected in weakness." Therefore I will boast all the more gladly in my weaknesses, so that the power of Christ may rest on me. That is why, for the sake of Christ, I delight in weaknesses, in insults, in hardships, in persecutions, in difficulties. For when I am weak, then I am strong."

(2 Corinthians 12:9,10)

For the first time in my Christian life, I am actually aware that I am truly experiencing this as a living, breathing reality right now, in the midst of the worst heartbreak I have ever known in my life.

This is why I said earlier, I am the Lord's gracious test subject for you to observe and learn from—And most obviously, none of the glory goes to me, because I am learning as I go—but you get to be the recipients of learning from what I am going through (You're welcome for that, there's no charge).

So, it is as we make it a conscious point to lean on the Holy Spirit in our moments of weakness, in our moments of not knowing what to do next, in our times of perplexity, our times of lack, that our partnership with the Holy Spirit becomes the very doorway to experiencing God at work in us and around us in a very personal and profound way.

That scripture from Psalms 23:3, that says "He restores my soul; He guides me in the paths of righteousness for the sake of His name"?

That's not just a nice little verse—that's a Holy Spirit reality for us to walk out in our own experience! The only thing holding us back most of the time, is *our inability to inwardly hear Him* when He is trying to help us.

Here, I will share with you something by way of example that illustrates this point.

I was working at a hospital in North Carolina back in 1999, and I was experiencing a really blessed season of learning to hear the Holy Spirit in the littlest of ways.

Part of my spiritual education was in that I was always being tested by things that were chafing in my outward circumstances—and if I responded to the Holy Spirit in the appropriate way in each circumstance, I experienced a Breakthrough, and was able to see the Holy Spirit move in wonderful ways.

On one particular occasion, I was feeling really lonely for fellowship, because my shift hours at the hospital were at night, so that meant having to sleep all day so I could work all night, and so consequently, I never ever had the time for Christian Fellowship.

Well, there was one Spirit-filled Christian brother at the hospital who always working the dayshift, which meant he would be leaving when I was coming to work.

I remember parking in the parking lot and walking to the front entrance of the hospital, and telling the Lord, I'd really like to see David today, just to get some spiritual connection with somebody before I have to go all night long again."

As I was walking toward the entrance, suddenly it was shift change, and it was like hundreds of employees were pouring out of the front of the hospital to go home, and I thought, I'll never be able to find David in time before he leaves, not in this sea of people.

Suddenly, the Holy Spirit stopped me where I was, and I looked to my left and I saw a service door on the side of the building that I'd never noticed before, and He impressed upon me to wait by the door.

So I walked over to the side of the hospital building where the service door was, and I just stood there—within less than a minute, the door popped open and out came David; he almost ran into me because he was in a hurry to leave.

He looked surprised but happy to see me, and he asked me what I was doing there at the door, and I said, "I was waiting for you!"

He looked totally incredulous, and I explained that I had really been wanting to spend some time fellowshipping with him before I had to go onto my shift, and that the Holy Spirit had told me to wait at that door, that he would be coming out.

So we started having a Holy Ghost time right there, and then his darling wife pulled up in their car to pick him up, and David told her what had happened, she got all lit up in the Holy Spirit and started prophesying over me, and it was the most anointed 10 minutes I've ever had with any brethren!

It was a beautiful gift from the Holy Spirit, and it was a beautiful, anointed encounter that left me feeling spiritually empowered for my whole shift.

I was so completely in awe of how the Holy Spirit had orchestrated the entire thing!

And this was reflective of the entire season of my time in North Carolina—it was one Holy Spirit lesson after the other, teaching me to listen to Him and hear Him, and rely on His leading for everything…and That was the path that led me to meeting the woman who would become my wife, Roopa.

So, one huge lesson here is to pray for discernment and sensitivity as to the spiritual season the Holy Spirit has you in, so you can cooperate with him, and so you can learn the things He's trying to teach you— because learning those lessons is the doorway into the things He wants to do next in your life.

Each lesson the Holy Spirit brought me during that time in North Carolina was to encourage me to step out in faith a little bit more, step out in obedience a little bit more, and to step out in sensitivity a little bit more—and each step, when taken in obedience, led to the next step, and so on.

I shudder to think of what I would've lost out on if, at any point in time, I had just folded my arms and decided I didn't want to do that anymore.

It meant me being patient when I didn't feel like it; it meant me trusting when I didn't see any answers or breakthroughs forthcoming; it meant me being willing to trust Him when I did not see any good coming.

Remember the scripture that says, "Let us not grow weary in well-doing, for in due time we will reap a harvest if we do not give up"? (Galatians 6:9)

Well, *sowing begins in the spirit realm*: "The one who sows to please his flesh, from the flesh will reap destruction; *but the one who sows to please the Spirit, from the Spirit will reap eternal life*". (Galatians 6:8)

That's not just talking about salvation; *that is talking about the eternally living benefits from the Holy Spirit in the here and now*—so if you sow to the Spirit by being patient, then you will reap in due season His answer.

"Allow perseverance to finish its work, so that you may be mature and complete, not lacking anything", it says in James 1:4.

So, each spiritual lesson that the Lord brought to me in North Carolina was one where I had to be patient and trusting, knowing that in His time He would bring about the answer in His way.

Every test, every challenge, was an opportunity for me to walk in faith and obedience, and in looking back now all these years later, I can see how every step was almost in consecutive order, with each step requiring a deeper level of faith, a deeper level of trust, patience, but always leading to a greater reward and a deeper awareness of my fellowship with the Holy Spirit.

I tell you what, that was one of the most precious times of my entire life, and I really do miss it—it's just such an awesome feeling when you are truly aware that *each day is a day you are in the school of the Holy Spirit, and He is using your life circumstances, your circumstances on your job, in your surroundings, as His tools to train you and speak to you through and manifest Himself through in the most unexpected, miraculous ways*—sometimes in ways that seem so small, but when you join them to all the other little happenings, it's a miraculous thing to behold.

For example, in that little town in North Carolina, there was one little library, and there was a East Indian girl who worked there—that was the first East Indian person I've ever seen or met in my life. One night after I got off work, I went into the grocery store before they closed, and I saw the same Indian girl from the library (who was normally just wearing a

T-shirt and jeans) in the grocery store with her mom and dad, and they were wearing their beautiful east Indian outfits in this white redneck town in North Carolina, and I just thought, wow, what a beautiful culture, they look so sweet together as mother, daughter, and father.

But again, when you can look back and see how the Holy Spirit used every little thing to shape your path in this life, a path that will affect you for all Eternity, it makes you want to cooperate with Him as fully as you possibly can, because He truly knows what He is doing, and what He is putting together in your life. And quite frankly, *the biggest part of cooperating with the Holy Spirit is allowing Him to change the way we think.*

Here is what I mean by that.

Receiving is both the easiest and the hardest thing for Western Christians.

It is the fortress of our rational minds that must become like the walls of Jericho tumbling down, so that we can receive from our Heavenly Father with a childlike faith.

When we truly comprehend that everything we will ever need comes from our Heavenly Father by faith, it becomes easier to understand that our rational minds are no longer our friend, but our enemy, and must be made to bow their knee to Jesus Christ.

It's the rational mind that is the biggest hindrance. It has to have proof of everything.

I keep rehearsing in my mind how God moved in my life in 1983. In hindsight, it seems that receiving from the Lord should be the easiest thing for us to do. But in the flesh, because of the way our minds work in such a rational way here in the West, faith is something that does not come easily to us, unfortunately—it shouldn't be that way.

"Truly I tell you, anyone who does not receive the kingdom of God like a little child will never enter it." (Luke 18:17)

But our Western society demands that we work for everything and earn everything—however, in the Middle East, it is completely common to give gifts, especially from parents to children—and the child does not have to do a single thing to earn that gift, other than being the child of the parent who is giving it. Our minds simply have a very difficult time comprehending that kind of hospitality and generosity, because we think we have to deserve and earn everything. But that mentality will keep us forever outside of the kingdom, looking in, but never ever receiving.

But, the thing is, you will never, ever receive anything from God apart from you receiving it by FAITH.

Now, when I just made that statement, I could already feel the wheels in somebody's mind turning in a panic, going "What do I have to do to get faith????"

See???? That's the Western religious mentality—We always think we have to DO something to get anything from God.

We always think we have to "do something" to become more spiritual; we have to "do something" to become more complete in God.

The beast called "I have to do something" has to die—it has to be mercilessly, ruthlessly put to death, because as long as you think there's "something you have to do" in yourself, in and of yourself, in your flesh, then you will stay right where you are, mired in wet cement, & going nowhere fast.

Honestly, how much effort does it take to receive anything????

If you need something from the Lord, then Look to HIM, and KEEP looking at Him, trusting Him to get it to you—that is called FAITH.

I'm trying to help someone out there see that you've got to get out of your own way—and it's not that hard to do, if you remember that God the Father is the Giver—you are the receiver. Whatever you need that's covered in His promises, you can trust Him to get it to you.

That is why Jesus had to use examples like if you ask your earthly father for bread, he won't give you a stone, because the disciples' faith level had to be adjusted (see Luke 11:13).

We have to get out of our own way and understand that our Heavenly Father has already made the ultimate sacrifice of His own Son's blood to purchase for us everything that is stored up in heaven for us—So Why on earth would He be looking for an excuse to Withhold anything from us?????

Faith is simple when there is trust.

Where our trust in our Heavenly Father is shaky, faith is going to be a real complicated thing.

That is why Jesus said, "Do not be afraid, little flock, for your Father is pleased to GIVE you the Kingdom"—Not make you Work for it; not make you pay for it on the installment plan; not make you qualify for it by being "good enough", etc. (Luke 12:32).

Being baptized in the Holy Spirit and walking in Faith are the 2 biggest Basic Fundamentals, and you aren't going to go very far without those, I can promise you that. That means getting the revelation inside of yourself to simply RECEIVE from your Heavenly Father—*and the longer you allow your mind make it complicated, the more spiritually "Stuck" you are going to feel.*

Your Mind Does not have to Understand, in order for your Spirit to Receive.

In Fact, MOST of the time—especially those of you just beginning this walk of Faith in the Spirit—you are going to have to grab your mind by the collar and Make it submit to what the Word of God says. Take EVERY thought CAPTIVE, and make it OBEDIENT TO THE WORD OF GOD, WHICH IS ABLE TO TRANSFORM YOU—BE RENEWED BY THE SPIRIT IN YOUR MIND (2nd Cor. 10:5; Eph. 4:23; Romans 12:2)

Again, you MUST understand that *there Will be resistance from those areas of your mind that are not yet renewed by the Word of God, and those unrenewed areas will resist the things of the Spirit; those unrenewed areas will harbor confusion and unwillingness to change, to yield to the Spirit*—so YOU are Going to have to Determine just how much you WANT the Holy Spirit!

Do you want HIM more than you want to hold on to the indecisiveness of your mind???? Do you want HIM more than you want to hold on to your mind's need to "SEE BEFORE IT BELIEVES", like Doubting Thomas???? How much do you WANT the Baptism of the Holy Spirit?????

Do you want it SO MUCH, that you are willing to tell your mind to BE QUIET & BE STILL, I'm RECEIVING THE BAPTISM OF THE HOLY SPIRIT, AND I DON'T CARE IF YOU UNDERSTAND IT OR NOT.

Because brother, sister, I will stand before God and tell you right here & now, if you WAIT until it "MAKES SENSE" to your MIND, you won't receive even HALF of what God has for you.

The Spirit-Filled Life is a Walk of Constant Faith (Romans 1:17; Romans 3:22).

The mind that insists on PROOF, is the very opposite of childlike Faith, and it will Never allow you to enter into God's Treasury, where everything He has provided awaits. "And without faith it is impossible to please God, because anyone who approaches Him must believe that He exists and that He rewards those who earnestly seek Him." (Hebrews 11:6)

So let's remember who our God is, and be very, very, very slow to even let a crumb of unbelief fall to the ground in His presence…He has given us His Word containing thousands and thousands of promises made to His blood-bought children—please let us never respond to a single promise with doubt or unbelief.

Also, Consider This—the very one who said, "Father, I thank you that you have hidden these things from the wise and prudent, and have revealed them unto babes", the same one who spoke those words was born unto us as a babe in a Manger—the great, lofty Messiah, came in the form of a babe—and in doing so, he confounded the wise in their very own

341

conceits, and trapped them in their very own religious and worldly wisdom. He has NEVER changed His methods.

"At that time Jesus declared, "I praise You, Father, Lord of heaven and earth, because You have hidden these things from the wise and learned, and *revealed them to little children*" (Matthew 11:25).

CHAPTER 26

TEMPLES OF THE HOLY SPIRIT, PART 3; DRAWING CLOSE TO THE FATHER/ ADDRESSING SPIRITUAL WARFARE

Key Verses: "Now may the God of hope fill you with all joy and peace as you believe in Him, so that you may overflow with hope by the power of the Holy Spirit." (Romans 15:13)

"But you, beloved, by building yourselves up in your most holy faith and praying in the Holy Spirit, keep yourselves in the love of God as you await the mercy of our Lord Jesus Christ to bring you eternal life." (Jude 1:20, 21)

We are living on this side of all that is permanent and real.

Currently, we are on the side where everything is impermanent and passing away. "The world is passing away, along with its desires; *but whoever does the will of God remains forever*" (1 John 2:17).

So, as long as you and I are living to do the will of God, we are walking, living, breathing paradoxes to all of the impermanent, temporal things that surround us.

Furthermore, as we individually live to do the will of God, *We* become the Only truly permanent things in an impermanent world. The Word of God says so—if you live to do the will of God, then you will abide forever.

This also means that there is only One thing in the universe that can be allowed to stand forever, and that is the Will of God.

Why is it all important that we keep our focus on that one thing?

Because obviously everything that does Not serve the will of God must be shaken, until nothing remains But the will of God.

And that means that there is going to be a lot of shaking going on around us, and that is going to be great cause for alarm, disillusionment, and disorientation. *We are going to have to do everything possible to remain transfixed on the Word of God & the Spirit of God to maintain our emotional, mental, and spiritual equilibrium.*

To me, this is not an abstract subject—I watched my wife live this for well over 16 years, and I know she lived it for a lot longer than that.

It was her relationship to her Heavenly Father that saw her through years and years of sheer torment on earth, from her family and from life circumstances because of her disability.

As a believer of over 44 years, I can honestly say that I have never known a greater example of someone abiding in Him than my wife.

How did she abide in Him through years and years of physical chronic pain, emotional childhood abuse and cold lovelessness from her family, trapped in a body that did not want to do a fraction of the things she wanted to do???

I'll tell you how—her prayer journals from 1998 onward reveal a young woman who poured her heart out at His feet on a daily basis...she expressed to Him every raw emotion openly and honestly, as though He were her only trusted caring confidant: because He Was.

If she felt that there was any sin—even the smallest cloud—between her and Him, she asked Him for forgiveness and for help. But she literally poured her heart out to the Lord on a daily basis; it was not a religious habit—it was a matter of sheer spiritual survival.

So how do we abide in Him???

When we perceive it as a matter of sheer necessity on a daily basis, not a religious option.

And here is one point that I pray resonates with everyone, and I beg you to take it totally and completely to heart—*We abide in Him on HIS terms, not ours.*

I will say that one more time, and add this: the Western church for the most part does everything But abide in Him. We abide in Him on HIS terms, not ours. Virtually everything they do is derived from their own volition, and out of religious habit & traditions of men and denominations, etc.

Now, in addressing our second topic of importance, I'd like to discuss *Spiritual gifts as part of our weapons of warfare.*

Remember what Paul said to Timothy?

"Timothy, my child, I entrust you with this command *in keeping with the previous prophecies about you, so that by them you may fight the good fight.*" (1 Timothy 1:18)

The thing to keep in mind, is that *any spiritual endowment or spiritual gift* (which obviously is derived from the Holy Spirit Himself) *is in and of itself an empowerment against all that is of the enemy.*

For example, a word of prophecy/ a word of knowledge/ a word of wisdom by the Holy Spirit, *displaces the very opposite sown by the enemy*—Confusion and uncertainty, lack of understanding, are displaced by the vocal gifts of the Holy Spirit, which bring wisdom, spiritual knowledge and understanding that are Specific to the person's need.

For example, you might be ministering to someone who is extremely depressed and discouraged, thinking that their life is meaningless, and perhaps even on the verge of suicide.

The Holy Spirit rises up in you, and you prophesy over them concerning their future, with words that bring healing to their soul, to their emotions—now you have just effectively waged spiritual warfare that was attempting to take that person out, and you have done so through the operation of the gifts of the Holy Spirit.

So many times we have limited spiritual warfare to the arena of intercession and prayer alone, never ever stopping to consider that the gifts and operation of the Holy Spirit can operate at any time, through any means, and break the power of the enemy.

"Where the Spirit of the Lord is, there is Freedom"; that is the Holy Spirit's job—to bring spiritual freedom and liberty to those in captivity and bondage. ("Now the Lord is the Spirit, and where the Spirit of the Lord is, there is freedom", 2 Corinthians 3:17).

Be open, be teachable, don't put Him in a box—*He's not going to operate contrary to His own nature*, so let's get rid of this irrational fear (which is also, in many cases, by the way, just an excuse to do nothing).

Remember, Paul said, "The weapons of our warfare are not the weapons of the world. Instead, they have divine power to demolish strongholds. We tear down arguments and every presumption set up against the knowledge of God; and we take captive every thought to make it obedient to Christ" (2 Corinthians 10:4,5).

The gifts of the Holy Spirit work to achieve that very end.

In the context of which Paul was speaking, he said "the weapons of our warfare have divine power to demolish strongholds". That, in a nutshell, is spiritual warfare, because we are dealing with spiritual strongholds in the areas of the mind and the emotions.

The gifts of the Holy Spirit are manifestations of the Holy Spirit of God Himself, working to edify and build up the Body, and to dislodge, disarm, and displace all the works of the enemy.

Our Western problem is that we divide everything up into compartments, but you cannot do that with the Word of God and the operation of the Holy Spirit. The Word of God is a whole, not random assorted parts—meaning, God does not see spiritual warfare over here in a corner, and the gifts of the Holy Spirit over there in another corner, and intercessory prayer in still another corner; it is all part of one whole.

Furthermore, we do ourselves and our spiritual growth a grave injustice by allowing ourselves to see the Word of God and the operation of the Holy Spirit in divided little sections that somehow have to compete with each other, or are not entirely related to one another. Is my right hand not associated with my left hand? NO, they're part of the same body, the same whole unit.

The sooner we can understand that, spiritually speaking, the Word of God is a complete thing that is Alive, the sooner we will be able to receive much, much more of the Holy Spirit's wisdom and understanding, and many of the issues and problems, battles and roadblocks that we've been dealing with will be cleared up and resolved in very little time.

The Holy Spirit's wisdom is available 24 hours a day, seven days a week, but we have little log jams in our minds and in our perception that keep His wisdom from flowing through to us, and through us to others.

That is, **believers are subconsciously using human reasoning to try to comprehend and absorb spiritual language from the Holy Spirit, and it doesn't work—Which means the spiritual answers and wisdom you're crying out for, cannot get through the barriers in your mind.**

The apostle Paul explained **the starting point for every single believer on earth, for entering into the things of God and understanding, comprehending, and growing in them,** So listen carefully, and let this passage sink into the deepest recesses of your heart; "And this is what we speak, not in words taught us by human wisdom, but **in words taught by the Spirit, expressing spiritual truths in spiritual words**." (1 Corinthians 2:13)

Now, take that passage in conjunction with what Jesus said about the ministry of the Holy Spirit, which he elaborated on in John 14, and then read what the apostle John wrote;

"And as for you, the anointing you received from Him remains in you, and you do not need anyone to teach you. But just as His true and genuine anointing teaches you about all things, so remain in Him as you have been taught." (1 John 2:27)

That passage brings up two very vital points.

First, John said his reason for writing what he just said was concerning false teachers who were trying to deceive believers with false teaching. "I have written these things to you about those who are trying to deceive you"(1 John 2:26).

And what does the apostle John make absolutely clear, in terms of protection from being deceived by false teachers??? **The very fact that if you have received the baptism of the Holy Spirit, He dwells within you, and HE is your teacher.**

And that speaks very pointedly and directly to the problem we have here in the West, with so much of the professing church being so scared and terrified of being tricked into receiving a counterfeit spirit, that they have every door and window bolted and locked against the Holy Spirit.

The Western church has been so skeptical and opposed in their minds to the operation of the Holy Spirit, the third person of the Godhead, that they have created a gigantic spiritual vacuum (because remember, we are spirit, soul, and body— not just soul and body). The Church was intended from the very beginning to be empowered, instructed, comforted, and indwelt by the Holy Spirit. Now, just stop and think for a minute—what happens to the church when we remove the Holy Spirit from it????

All you have to do is look out the window and see the proliferation of false teachers and demonic spirits that have flooded the Western professing church over the last 20 years. It is worse now than it has ever been in my 44 years as a believer.

And we only have one institution to blame: the professing Western church that has deified its own intellectual grasp of the Scriptures, in place of being led and taught by the Holy Spirit, and in rejecting the Holy Spirit who was sent by the Father and the Son, we have condemned ourselves to delusion and to being prisoners of our own intellectual arrogance—and now, the principalities and powers over this earth are operating at peak fury, and spiritual battles and spiritual confrontation is coming which few can even begin to comprehend.

Now, let's take a very close look at the one passage in the New Testament that puts the arena of spiritual warfare in its proper context, looking at key words and phrases in the original Greek to bring out the fullest spiritual meaning, and how that will impact your spiritual life.

Ephesians 6:10-18;

"Finally, be strong in the Lord and in His mighty power. Put on the full armor of God, so that you can make your stand against the devil's schemes. For our struggle is not against flesh and blood, but against the rulers, against the authorities, against the powers of this world's darkness, and against the spiritual forces of evil in the heavenly realms.

Therefore take up the full armor of God, so that when the day of evil comes, you will be able to stand your ground, and having done everything, to stand. Stand firm then, with the belt of truth buckled around your waist, with the breastplate of righteousness arrayed, and with your feet fitted with the readiness of the gospel of peace.

In addition to all this, take up the shield of faith, with which you can extinguish all the flaming arrows of the evil one. And take the helmet of salvation, and the sword of the Spirit, which is the Word of God. Pray in the Spirit at all times, with every kind of prayer and petition. To this end, stay alert with all perseverance in your prayers for all the saints".

A. "BE STRONG"—ἐνδυναμοῦσθε (endynamousthe) "To fill with power, strengthen, make strong". From 'en' and 'dunamoo'—to empower".

The very same Greek word for "strong" here is used in Philippians 4:13, 2nd Timothy 4:17, 1 Timothy 1:12.

B. "IN the Lord"— - ἐν (en); A primary preposition denoting position, and instrumentality, i.e. A relation of rest; 'in, ' at, on, by, etc. (Variations of this in the New Testament include "abide IN Him", "remain IN Him", etc.)

C. "Power"— - ἰσχύος (ischyos); "Strength (absolute), power, might, force, ability". The very same word used in verses like 2 Peter 2:11; 2 Thessalonians 1:9; and Ephesians 1:19.

D. "Might"— - κράτει (kratei) and κράτος (kratos); "Dominion, strength, power"; Colossians 1:11; 1 Timothy 6:16.

When taken together, the words "might", "power", and "strength", in the Greek language, all signify "the power of a Supreme Dominion".

Why do you think that Jesus called His gospel "the gospel of the Kingdom"???

A Kingdom has Dominion and Authority and Power! THAT is precisely why Jesus said, "But if I drive out demons by the Spirit of God, then the kingdom of God has come upon you." (Matthew 12:28)

In speaking of the Endtimes, Jesus said, "And this gospel of the kingdom will be preached in all the world as a testimony to all nations, and then the end will come." (Matthew 24:14).

Neither Jesus Christ nor the New Testament recognizes any preaching of any so-called gospel unless it is the Gospel of the Kingdom that Jesus commanded to be preached, the gospel that He Commissioned to be preached.

Now, with all of this clearly laid out, I hope it is absolutely clear that this is the very reason why the Holy Spirit has been so opposed, fought against, maligned, ridiculed and mocked—*because Satan does not want the Gospel of the Kingdom preached!* And Satan knows that without the power of the Holy Spirit, he is under no threat of any such thing happening to him. Do you really think that he wants to live through the Book of Acts again????

I also hope that it is crystal clear that when you read your New Testament and you see words like 'power', 'strength', 'might', that you completely understand that that is derived from One source, and one source Only—the Holy Spirit of God.

Does not the Word of God declare that we have been translated out of the kingdom of darkness, and into the Kingdom of God's dear Son? ("He has rescued us from the dominion of darkness and brought us into the kingdom of His beloved Son"; Colossians 1:13)

Now, speaking to my dear readers as those who have been translated into the Kingdom of God's dear son, speaking to you as Kingdom citizens, can you understand your responsibility to represent the Kingdom of your God in the manner in which HE has prescribed?

I don't care what anyone's favorite preacher says; I don't care what their favorite Bible teacher says—all I care about is the God and Lord whose Kingdom it is.

And if our Lord and King spoke and said to wait until we receive power from on high, then you and I have no right to do anything but obey His divine kingdom directive.

THIS very issue is where the Western professing church is, whether it realizes it or not. It is the current spiritual reality, and everything else will revolve around it.

Every single pew sitting person, Every single individual who walks through the door of the building with a steeple on top of it this Sunday, whether they like it or not, the choice is coming, and they WILL have to make it—Is our complete and total allegiance to the King of Kings, or is our commitment to Him conditional upon what some denomination allows, or what some pastor in a shiny suit says from a pulpit????

When are we going to begin reading our Bible through Kingdom glasses, instead of denominational bifocals????

Do we understand that it is not a matter of some denominational belief or doctrine????

It is a matter of what the Kingdom of God has designated, commissioned, and prescribed, and That Kingdom has complete and total authority over every preacher, Bible teacher, and denomination on this planet. The question is, Are we willing to completely lay down every other religious allegiance, and give our total allegiance and obedience to the only King there is????

Do we understand that there is no room for divided allegiance or divided loyalties in a Kingdom????

As for ME, all I care about is what HE says, and if we are in His Kingdom, then we must understand that it is His Complete and Total right to insist that you and I function according to everything that He has prescribed.

The reason for the absolute seriousness of everything that I have just stated, is because here we are, looking at one of the most well-known passages in the Bible—that pertaining to our spiritual armor.

But that spiritual armor is reserved for those whose allegiance is to living for and representing the clearly defined Kingdom of God.

It is not for pew sitters; it is not for church goers; *it is for Kingdom citizens who have laid their lives down to serve the King of this Heavenly Kingdom.*

There are no weekend warriors, and the Kingdom of Heaven does not have National Guard reservists. You are either all the way in, or you are not in at all.

You don't take this armor and put it in a window so people can walk by and admire it—you wear it for active duty.

You wear it when you have decided that Jesus meant what He said, "Truly, truly, I tell you, whoever believes in Me will also do the works that

I am doing. He will do even greater things than these, because I am going to the Father." (John 14:12); "And these signs will accompany those who believe: In My name they will drive out demons; they will speak in new tongues;" (Mark 16:17); "Behold, I have given you authority to tread on snakes and scorpions, and over all the power of the enemy. Nothing will harm you." (Luke 10:19).

(Yes, by all means, read the job description before you start putting on the armor).

Now, as we are all aware, world governments all assign their military personnel specific uniforms that signify whose military force they are. No matter where the US military goes in the world, their uniform tells people on foreign soil immediately where they are from.

We are on foreign soil, but is it clear to those around us where we are from, and whose occupational force we are???

Well, one thing is for certain—if we are not carrying out the assigned duties of our Kingdom, then it's likely we look just like anybody else.

In just reading through the Gospels carefully, we see all of the mandates and assignments Jesus gave all of His disciples, and He was very descriptive in how they would stand out. Just take in the sweeping scope of this one particular passage:

"*You are the light of the world*. A city on a hill cannot be hidden. Neither do people light a lamp and put it under a basket. Instead, they set it on a stand, and it gives light to everyone in the house. *In the same way, let your light shine before men, that they may see your good deeds and glorify your Father in heaven*." (Matthew 5:14-16)

In fact, you could call the Gospels our mission statement—Because if we haven't even begun to do any of the things that Jesus commissioned, authorized, and empowered His disciples to do, we haven't even scratched the surface yet!

Again, the armor in Ephesians is to be worn by those who have committed themselves to be obedient disciples and servants of the Lord of lords and King of Kings.

And what is really heartbreaking to me, is that if this spiritual armor were visible to the naked eye, I'm sure that there must be hundreds of thousands of suits of spiritual armor still on the rack—because warriors don't just sit in the pews Sunday after Sunday, content to sing a few songs and shake the pastors hand and "thank you for a wonderful message today".

Spiritual warriors are out there seeking that which was lost, going after the one that left the 99; doing unto the least of these his brethren; setting captives free, binding up those who are broken, and bringing them to feast at the table of their Master...

In over 44 years as a believer, I can tell you that I was part of countless churches where I and a couple of others here & there visited the sick at hospitals, ministered at nursing homes, ministered on the streets, fed the homeless & gave them our clothes, our food....ministered to men with drug addictions, getting them set free and restored to their families and working in good honest jobs; ministering to those trapped in cults...And we never had enough fellow helpers in the Lord.

I'm not trying to guilt trip anybody, I'm just saying that the religious Western institutional church has Bibles all over the place—but we're just not doing anything with the contents of those Bibles.

Now, I have to say I am hugely blessed by so very many in our Vigilance group who are true prayer warriors and Intercessors, because they are the ones that are wearing that spiritual armor—And I will say from very personal experience, that being an intercessor, a prayer warrior, and a worshipper of the Lord in your prayer closet, is one of the most awesome spiritual assignments from heaven you will ever get!

You will be walking around in your house, or some special place that you go to to pray, and you'll be walking around with your hands raised up in the air, praying in tongues, walking in such a worshipful, reverent attitude, and the Holy Spirit will pour out so much revelation on you, and use you to break spiritual strongholds in people's lives, that when you get to heaven, you are going to have freight cars full of heavenly rewards!

And right here is where I will stop and address those of you who have been called of the Lord to intercession and prayer ministry, because many times the Lord will use your sensitive spiritual heart to minister one on one to people who are broken; who are damaged by life, and they need someone with a very deeply sensitive heart to the Holy Spirit, because He will guide you to minister to them in specific ways that will set them free.

If you'll notice, a very big part of using the armor in Ephesians 6 has to do with praying and intercession, and the sword of the Spirit is the Rhema of God—Rhema is Greek for "the spoken word", the Word of God that you will be speaking by inspiration of the Holy Spirit, by revelation of the Holy Spirit; the Word of God that you will be speaking and quoting in your time of prayer in intercession over people; scriptures that you will be claiming for peoples' deliverance and salvation and healing.

Now these are the kind of people I like to run with!

And trust me, you people are the very ones that God will use to cast out demons, because you have such an intimate connection with the Holy Spirit in your prayer times, He can trust you with that—and you are already open to His power; you are already familiar with and intimate with the power of His operation within you when you intercede and travail in the spirit.

I know I'm speaking to someone right now who has been contemplating this, and asking the Lord about this, and maybe the Lord's been putting it on your heart, but you just have not been sure, and you have not been ready to quite take that next step—but I'm telling you, trust the same Holy Spirit that guides you in prayer and intercession and travail, to be the Holy Spirit that teaches you how to cast out demons and set captives free—they need you!

CHAPTER 27

UNDER AUTHORITY

Everyone in the Body of Christ right now—regardless of your maturity level; regardless of your level of experience in the Spirit, etc.—every one of us has a very unique opportunity right now.

How long we will have this opportunity remains to be seen, so time is truly of the essence.

This opportunity is something that is highly prized in the business world, and the more competitive and powerful the business, the more prized this kind of opportunity is.

It's called *Positioning*.

We see examples of this played out in the gospels repeatedly, but I am not sure if you've noticed.

Tonight the Lord brought it very forcefully to my attention, and even though I have seen it in the past, I haven't until now seen it for what it Really is in the spirit.

All evening, a phrase kept coming to me, over and over again.

It was the words of the Centurion, to Jesus whom had offered to go to his house to pray for his servant, who was lying at the point of death.

After telling Jesus that he felt completely unworthy that Jesus should even come under his roof, he said something that has always resonated with me—but tonight the Holy Spirit brought it home to me with a force that I have never felt before.

The Centurion said to Jesus, "That is why I did not consider myself worthy to come to You. But just say the word, and my servant will be healed. For I myself am a man under authority, with soldiers under me. I tell one to go, and he goes; and another to come, and he comes. I tell my servant to do something, and he does it" *(Luke 7:7,8).*

I am sure that there are many men in the military who, even when they are not even going about military business, are able to recognize another person with military training and bearing, simply by the way they conduct themselves.

So this centurion recognized the spiritual authority with which Jesus was conducting Himself, and it was so pronounced that he was able to submit himself to Jesus' evident authority, and acknowledged that Jesus obviously had a higher rank than he did, so if Jesus exercised His greater authority, then the result would be that his servants illness would have no choice but to obey.

Once we begin to understand the principle revealed over and over again in the Gospels of Kingdom Authority, and how it works when we are rightly related and submitted to it, *then we begin to see operating in the Spirit in a brand new way.*

We've all read passages hundreds of times in the Gospels that revealed this very thing, but we didn't even realize what we were looking at.

Case in point— Luke 17:5,6

"The apostles said to the Lord, "Increase our faith!"

"And the Lord answered, "If you have faith the size of a mustard seed, you can say to this mulberry tree, 'Be uprooted and planted in the sea,' and *it will obey you."*

Isn't that exactly what the Centurion said to Jesus??? 'Jesus, if you will SAY, it will OBEY'.

"That is why I did not consider myself worthy to come to You. But just Say the word, and my servant will be healed". (Luke 7:7)

And what was Jesus' response?

"When Jesus heard this, He marveled at the centurion. Turning to the crowd following Him, He said, "I tell you, not even in Israel have I found such great faith." (Luke 7:9)

Wasn't that what the disciples asked Jesus to do?

They asked him to increase their faith— the very faith that the Centurion had possessed, but they did not.

So over and over again in the Gospels, we see that **the exercise of Kingdom Authority and Kingdom faith is contingent upon recognizing the authority of Jesus, and being rightly submitted and related to it.**

The disciples were with Jesus all the time, and yet they always seemed to be astonished and amazed at the authority with which He acted.

"You of little faith," Jesus replied, "why are you so afraid?" Then He got up and rebuked the winds and the sea, and it was perfectly calm. The men were amazed and asked, "What kind of man is this? Even the winds and the sea *obey Him*!" (Matthew 8:26,27)

(There is that combination again, of speaking to the opposing situation and it obeying—Saying and Obeying).

So tonight, as the Lord was stirring all of this up inside my spirit, the phrase that I kept hearing in my spirit was **"Under Authority"**.

And immediately, the awareness that I had was of the overwhelming urgency of the call of the Holy Spirit to every single member of the Body of Christ to *consciously come under the authority of Jesus Christ now, and begin to live and conduct ourselves individually and corporately under His Authority, because He intends to pour out His Spirit and His power in a profound and unprecedented way—But if we are not positioned as completely & consciously submitted to Him, in placing ourselves under His authority, then we will not receive that.*

It is an actual kingdom principal that we see demonstrated all throughout the Gospels—those who exercised authority over sickness and demons were those that Jesus himself had called and conferred His power to and upon. And in this regard, remember there was one seen going and casting out demons whom John wanted to rebuke because the man wasn't following the disciples with Jesus.

In other words, John only believed the man to be qualified to cast out demons if he was walking right next to them.

But obviously this was an individual who recognized the authority in Jesus, and so he—by the same faith of the Centurion—began moving in that authority, because he had recognized it and in some way submitted himself to it.

All of this ties in very directly to my last post that dealt with murmuring, complaining, and focusing on worldly concerns and worldly distresses.

If we are using our speech primarily to complain and murmur, then we are effectively neutralizing any spiritual authority that we could otherwise exercise.

You can't spend a large portion of your time murmuring and complaining about worldly situations, and then use the same mouth to exercise spiritual authority over spiritual matters.

Why do you think it is that in the very early parts of each gospel account, *Jesus spends time refocusing their minds from the earthly concerns, to their Heavenly Father who provides for their earthly concerns???* (*Matt. 6:25-34*)

Do you see that there is a very specific spiritual reason why Jesus framed things the way He did, when He did, and in the order that He did?

None of the things that Jesus did or said were haphazard or random—He was a man under authority—as the centurion recognized—because He said that He did nothing of His own will, and He conducted

Himself that way every single day, in word and in deed (see John 5:19; John 5:30; John 6:38; John 8:28; John 12:49,50; John 14:10).

He kept himself rightly related to His Heavenly Father and submitted to His Heavenly Father by spending time in prayer every single day, yielding Himself and submitting Himself to His Heavenly Father's will, which is why He had the authority to say, "So then, this is how you should pray: 'Our Father in heaven, hallowed be Your name. Your kingdom come, Your will be done, on earth as it is in heaven." (Matthew 6:9,10).

The very best way— the most effective way—to consciously come under the authority of Jesus Christ and all of heaven is to spend time every single day reciting the Word of God to yourself, and applying it verbally to yourself.

And when you are reading specific verses, I would recommend the passages that pertain to who you are in Christ, and personalize them because in so doing, you are applying that Word to yourself. You are not just reading a mere book; You are speaking the very Word of the living God over yourself, over your circumstances, over your situation, over your home, and over your family—and because it is God's Word, it has ultimate authority and ultimate power, and you are consciously, willingly, and verbally submitting yourself to that power and that authority.

You are literally building a spiritual fortress around yourself as you are speaking the Word of God over your being and everything about you— Or do we not remember that Jesus said, "The Spirit gives life; the flesh profits nothing. The words I have spoken to you are spirit and they are life."—it is not just a religious exercise.

Remember, the very things that Jesus was making real to His disciples, the very things that were real to that Centurion—if you are under His authority, you have the power to Say, and it will Obey!

CHAPTER 28

BECOMING AN APOSTOLIC PEOPLE; APPROPRIATING APOSTOLIC SPIRITUAL QUALITIES AS THE ENDTIME CHURCH

"Becoming an Apostolic People"—

This was a phrase that the Holy Spirit spoke very emphatically to my heart on the evening of May 18, 2022.

As such, I believe it is a prophetic word, and a prophetic exhortation for the Body of Christ at this time—*A prophetic focal point that needs to become our primary spiritual outlook, starting now and going forward.*

When the Holy Spirit spoke the phrase to me, "Becoming an Apostolic People", *the immediate sense that I got was that of the apostle Paul shaping the New Testament believers in a very specific way.*

Paul said he labored as a wise master builder. He was always very mindful of the spiritual materials he was using to build Christ's Church. The emphasis was on quality of an eternal nature, always with a view that what he was building was meant to last for eternity, and was worthy of divine rewards (1 Corinthians 3:10-15).

He was always very aware that his greatest rewards lie in building a people of God who would endure to the end, rooted and established in the faith (1 Thessalonians 2:19,20; Philippians 4:1; Colossians 1:28).

I believe that the New Testament reflects another spiritual quality regarding becoming an apostolic people, a spiritual quality that is echoed in all of the apostolic letters. There are three key passages that stand out in my mind, that I believe make this abundantly clear.

In Galatians 1:12, Paul says, "I did not receive it from any man, nor was I taught it; rather, *I received it by revelation from Jesus Christ*".

In 1 Corinthians 11:23, Paul says, "For *I received from the Lord* what I also passed on to you: The Lord Jesus, on the night He was betrayed, took bread".

The last verse is 1 Corinthians 14:37, where Paul, who has been setting things in order concerning operating in the spiritual gifts, says, "If anyone considers himself a prophet or spiritual person, let him acknowledge that *what I am writing you is the Lord's command*".

We here in the West have been operating for a very, very long time under a subconscious notion that everything Paul taught, and the teachings that the early church lived by, were all in some readily available Bible of some sort.

Now, I'm sure we don't come right out and say that to ourselves, but it is part of the religious conditioning that we in the West have been subjected to for decade after decade.

We assume that the believers in the early church were just like us— *living by words on a printed page.*

They, in fact, for the most part were not.

Yes, the apostle Paul wrote letters from prison that were circulated to the churches, but there is no way we could possibly assume that every single person who called themselves a believer in Corinth, Galatia, Thessalonica,

Ephesus, or Phillippi, etc., had their own personal copy of Paul's letter stuck in their pocket to read every day.

What I am saying is that the early church functioned and lived mostly by revelation from the indwelling Holy Spirit—the same Holy Spirit that provided Paul the apostle and the others with revelation concerning the body of Christ, and the things that the Holy Spirit wanted to have functioning within the church.

When we read the New Testament letters carefully, it becomes crystal clear that the early church operated by Revelation of the Holy Spirit on a constant and continuing basis.

In fact, Paul repeatedly makes reference to the believers receiving ongoing revelation from the Lord, pertaining to all the things that are freely given to us in Christ Jesus.

The prayers that Paul prayed over the believers in Colossians, Philippians, Ephesians, are all prayers that God would speak to the believers and minister to the believers via direct revelation by the Spirit.

*That is called living by your spirit—your inner man—*which is completely opposite of how we here in the West live, which is by our mind, and by what we can see, and by what we can read with our eyes, and assimilate with our mind—and hopefully, some of it gets down on the inside of us.

God's method, as revealed in the New Testament, is that He works completely opposite of the way we think.

God works from the spirit man *Outward.*

That is because God is working to Transform us, and that can only be done via the Spirit working in *our* spirit (2 Corinthians 3:17,18).

Spiritual transformation will never come through your mind.

One of the most long-standing difficulties in Western Christianity is the habit we make of focusing on something, and making it the Main thing.

We get fixated on a particular topic, and we make that our Starting point—when in reality, the starting point is something much bigger, and much different.

For example, the subject of faith. One could spend a week looking just at all of the references of the apostle Paul regarding faith—Two or three weeks altogether if you spend the time absorbing everything Jesus taught on the subject of faith in the gospels.

Now, in the mid to late 1980s, there was a huge movement that emphasized faith—and rightly so, because without faith it's impossible to please God.

But as happens with any Bible truth that is emphasized at the expense of other Bible truths, it caused a great deal of imbalance and extremism.

We have seen the same distortion when Grace is emphasized over other Bible truths.

However, when you closely read the apostolic letters, you will never find one apostolic truth presented to the exclusion of others.

That is the beauty of how God designed His Word.

There is a profound sense of harmony when all of the apostolic teachings are taken together as a whole. You never see the apostle Paul teach one thing, at the expense of everything else.

You never see him emphasize one spiritual attribute or quality, at the expense of the rest of them.

Instead, they are all presented by the Holy Spirit through Paul in such a harmonious manner, that just thinking about it gives me a profound sense of peace. I believe that is because all of it taken together as a whole, is a reflection of the very heart and nature of our God.

To refer to something in the New Testament as "apostolic" is simply to say that it is absolutely, immovably foundational—And it is absolutely, immovably foundational because it is derived from the very nature and heart of God. And this was the very heart and inward motivation of the apostles, who hungered and desired to see the very nature of God Himself reproduced in us.

It was never about just teaching on faith, or just teaching on the gifts of the Spirit; it was about seeing the very life and nature of God being formed within His people.

Another example; people focus on the spiritual gifts, which is a very good focus, *but then they make it such a large focus* **that the true intention and purpose for the gifts becomes completely lost.**

In order to recover God's full intention for ALL His spiritual provisions, such as the gifts of the Holy Spirit, praying in tongues, and things of that nature, we must Reframe those subjects within the context of God's larger intended purposes—which are of a much broader scope than we normally take into consideration.

We must refocus, in order to take into account God's Ultimate purposes for Everything He has provided spiritually—What are the end results and the Eternal objectives God has in mind, when it comes to the spiritual provisions He has made for us, and intends for us to avail ourselves of?

The highest, ultimate purpose in God's heart and mind is our union with Him. That is summed up in John 17.

Now, how does God intend to achieve that ultimate intention—our union with Him??

God spoke of this very thing when through Ezekiel He prophesied, "I will give you a new heart and put a new spirit within you; I will remove your heart of stone and give you a heart of flesh." (Ezekiel 36:26)

Actually, the 3 verse context is a profoundly Comprehensive encapsulation of God's ultimate intention for His people:

"I will also sprinkle clean water on you, and you will be clean. I will cleanse you from all your impurities and all your idols.

I will give you a new heart, and put a new spirit within you. I will remove your heart of stone, and give you a heart of flesh. *And I will put MY Spirit within you* and cause you to walk in my statutes and to carefully observe my ordinances." (Ezekiel 36:25-27)

Notice that God's full and comprehensive provision for us is designed to restore us to full, complete and unbroken fellowship with Himself.

The prophet Jeremiah, speaking the word of the Lord, *adds even more intimate detail to God's ultimate intention:*

"*I will give them a heart to know Me*, that I am the LORD. They will be My people, and I will be their God, for they will return to Me with all their heart." (Jeremiah 24:7)

When related to in this context, the gifts of the Holy Spirit, praying in tongues and in the spirit are now seen as an obvious, spiritually logical outworking of God's expressed desire to have an intimate, ongoing relationship with His people that is spirit to spirit-based.

In fact, when we truly comprehend the awesome nature of God's intention to have eternal fellowship with us as His people, *then all the provisions of the Holy Spirit—including His gifts—are a logical extension and outworking of that. As Jesus said, God is spirit, and those who worship Him must worship Him in and through the Spirit.*

By keeping God's ultimate intention in mind, we maintain a sense of strong spiritual balance, and thus avoid abuses, misuses, and excesses which lead into error and away from maturity.

THIS is the Essence of an Apostolic mindset.

Another very crucial aspect to the phrase the Holy Spirit spoke to me, in regards to "Becoming an Apostolic People", is the aspect of the supernatural, especially with regards to supernatural levels of faith, and agape love—the love corresponding to God's own nature that "endures all things, believes all things, hopes all things"....The God kind of love that never fails.

Clearly the word "apostolic" reveals a spiritual benchmark in the mind of God, in regards to the level of maturity and strength desired for His people.

I think that it will become all too apparent as to why the Western religious system is the disaster that it is—*because absolutely none of the apostolic benchmarks of the New Testament are emphasized consistently, and most of them are completely ignored.*

After 44 years as a very committed, Godward believer, it is clear to me that *we Must make the quality decision right now to pursue the apostolic qualities of the early church*, which I will outline shortly, if we intend to be Overcomers in the Endtimes—which are upon us right now.

STEPS TOWARD BECOMING AN APOSTOLIC PEOPLE

I have listed nine apostolic qualities that the apostles sought to impart and establish in the hearts of believers, but this is by no means an exhaustive list.

Also, what I have listed here is not in any particular order of importance.

In fact, I believe that they are all equally and vitally important to every believer. Now, I am pretty certain that we will not be able to cover all nine apostolic qualities I have discovered and meditated on, so this final chapter—Becoming an Apostolic People—will probably necessitate a follow up book.

However, I'll list all nine qualities here, with scripture references, and then I would wholeheartedly encourage you to prayerfully seek the Holy Spirit for further in-depth understanding and spiritual application, keeping in mind that this is not just a mental exercise. *Discovering and apprehending these apostolic qualities in your own personal spiritual walk will add new dimensions to your growth, stability, and fruitfulness in the Lord, and in the ministry to which He has called you.*

1. *Apostolic Empowerment (Key Scriptures: Colossians 1:11, Ephesians 6:10, Jude 1:20; Romans 1:11; 1 Thessalonians 1:5-10; 1 Thessalonians 3:10; Philippians 2:13; Hebrews 13:20,21)*

2. *Apostolic Vision (Key Scriptures:* 2 Corinthians 4:16-18; Romans 8:18; Colossians 3:1,2; Philippians 3:20; Romans 6:5)

3. *Apostolic Endurance (Key Scriptures: Romans 16:25; 2nd Corinthians 4:17; 2nd Thessalonians 2:16,17; 2nd Thessalonians 3:3; Romans 1:11—spiritual gifts serve to strengthen us; 1st Corinthians 1:8; James 1:12; Romans 5:3,4; Romans 8:25; 1 Thessalonians 1:3; Philippians 2:13; Hebrews 13:20,21)*

4. *Apostolic Devotion to Jesus (Key Scriptures: 1st Corinthians 1:7— spiritual gifts serve to enhance & undergird our "longing for His appearing; Philippians 3:20; Colossians 3:4; 1st Thessalonians 1:10; Philippians 3:9)*

5. *Apostolic Faith (Key Scriptures: Acts 3:16; Acts 14:9; Matthew 8:10; Matthew 13:58; 1 Thessalonians 2:13; Romans 10:17; Galatians 5:5; Colossians 2:12; 1 Thessalonians 1:3)*

6. *Apostolic Agape Love (Key Scriptures: 1st Peter 4:8-10; showing hospitality and serving one another through spiritual gifts is a powerful & strengthening expression of the God kind of Love; 1 Peter 1:22; Colossians 3:14; 1 Corinthians 14:1—the true apostolic focus is Always & Forever Faith Working Through & By Love; 1 Thessalonians 1:3)*

7. *Apostolic Hope (Key Scriptures: Romans 15:13; Romans 12:12; Romans 5:2; Romans 8:23; Romans 2:7; Romans 8:25; 1 Thessalonians 1:3)*

8. *Apostolic Grace (Key Scriptures: 1st Peter 5:10; Romans 16:25; 2 Thessalonians 2:16,17; 2 Thessalonians 3:3; Psalm 86:5,15; Romans 8:28-30; 1st Timothy 1:14; 1st Peter 4:10)*

9. *Apostolic Peace (Key Scriptures: 2 Corinthians 13:11; Hebrews 13:20,21; Philippians 4:6,7; Isaiah 26:3; Psalm 119:165; Proverbs 3:2; Isaiah 32:17; Psalm 29:11; Jeremiah 33:6; Galatians 5:22; Romans 5:1; Romans 8:6)*

Apprehending Apostolic Empowerment—Paul said, "I pray in tongues more than you all"—And he said this to a church that apparently spoke in tongues all the time, even when it was—according to his directives—out of order.

Remember in 1st Corinthians 14 where Paul said, "I thank God that I speak in tongues more than all of you"? (1 Corinthians 14:18)

One reason why Paul prayed in tongues more than the rest was what he stated in 2nd Corinthians 11:28; "Apart from these external trials, I face daily the pressure of my concern for all the churches".

Paul wasn't just bragging about praying in tongues more than anyone else—*it was out of sheer spiritual necessity, and that is the part we need to grasp.*

Continually praying in the spirit as a means of spiritual empowerment and strengthening is completely and totally indispensable, and it begins with every one of us making the decision to resolve to continually pray in the spirit, as a matter of spiritual habit, regardless of whether or not we "feel like it". In fact, I'm pretty sure Paul seldom had days where he "felt like" praying in the spirit.

In 2 Corinthians 1:8-9, Paul says, "We do not want you to be unaware, brothers, of the hardships we encountered in the province of Asia. We were under a burden far beyond our ability to endure, so that we despaired even of life. Indeed, we felt we were under the sentence of death, in order that we would not trust in ourselves, but in God, who raises the dead. He has delivered us from such a deadly peril, and He will deliver us. In Him we have placed our hope that He will yet again deliver us."

And yet this is the same apostle who said, "I thank my God that I pray in tongues more than you all".

As a man who has been enduring heart crushing grief for over 19 months, I don't think Paul would've ever made it without praying in tongues. If I had spent the last 19 months not praying in the spirit and not focusing on the Word, I don't know where I'd be right now.

*It was against the very backdrop of spiritual persecution and the onslaught of false teachers in their midst, that the apostle Jude's spiritual counsel was this very thing—**and I think that that alone places praying in the spirit at the very top of the list of our spiritual priorities.***

After all, if you go to the doctor for a critical health condition, and the doctor gives you his prescription, it would be most foolish to try to sidestep that which is prescribed to do something else to remedy your situation.

Now here's a little something free of charge, from someone who's been a believer and in the Word for over 44 years.

As I was working on this chapter, I was looking at a passage in 2 Corinthians 12.

What I was specifically looking at was one verse in particular—2 Corinthians 12:12. Now, I'm not sure how many are aware of this, but the number 12 is symbolic of the government of God—12 tribes of Israel, 12 disciples, 12 apostles, and so on.

So I find it very significant that Paul states here, in defending his apostleship (which is part of the government of God), that one of the divine marks of approval of his apostleship was fulfilling his ministry "with great perseverance".

"The true marks of an apostle—signs, wonders, and miracles—were performed among you *with great perseverance*" (2 Corinthians 12:12).

Many may have signs, wonders, and miracles attending their ministry, but if they do not have the ability to endure, then they will not fulfill their ministry.

The word "perseverance" here is also translated as "endurance" and "patience" in the King James.

We see that in Luke 8:15, where perseverance leads to fruitfulness ("But the seeds on good soil are those with a noble and good heart, who hear the word, cling to it, and by persevering produce a crop"); Luke 21:19 ("By your patient endurance you will gain your souls"); and finally, in Colossians 1:11, which ties in beautifully with our overall theme of this last chapter:

"Being strengthened with all power according to His glorious might so that you may have full endurance and patience…" (Colossians 1:11)

Being empowered by the Holy Spirit through praying in the spirit gives us access to His divine power and strength within our inner man, to enable us to have fullness of endurance and patience, and this was precisely how Paul walked out and fulfilled his ministry, by continually being empowered by the Holy Spirit.

In fact, Colossians 1:11 could be the key verse for what we're discussing right now.

2). *Apostolic Vision*—"These light and momentary afflictions".

Here are some of Paul's "light & momentary" afflictions:

"Three times I was beaten with rods, once I was stoned, three times I was shipwrecked. I spent a night and a day in the open sea. In my frequent journeys, I have been in danger from rivers and from bandits, in danger from my countrymen and from the Gentiles, in danger in the city and in the country, in danger on the sea and among false brothers, in labor and toil and often without sleep, in hunger and thirst and often without food, in cold and exposure. Apart from these external trials, I face daily the pressure of my concern for all the churches." (2 Corinthians 11:25-28)

Paul's response was derived from seeing all of these things from the Heavenly perspective of the Holy Spirit;

"Therefore we do not lose heart. Though our outer self is wasting away, yet our inner self is being renewed day by day. For our light and momentary affliction is producing for us an eternal weight of glory that is far beyond comparison. *So we fix our eyes not on what is seen, but on what is unseen. For what is seen is temporary, but what is unseen is eternal.*"

(2 Corinthians 4:16-18)

If our trials are perceived as Permanent or Never-ending, then we lose hope, and our spiritual strength is drained.

Paul also makes this declaration in Romans 8:18; "I consider that our present sufferings are not comparable to *the glory that will be revealed in us.*"

WHAT glory is Paul referring to?

"And if we are children, then we are heirs: heirs of God and co-heirs with Christ—if indeed we suffer with Him, so that we may also be glorified with Him. I consider that our present sufferings are not comparable to the glory that will be revealed in us. The creation waits in eager expectation for the revelation of the sons of God." (Romans 8:17-19)

The Glory that awaits us is that of our Heavenly Inheritance in Jesus, reserved in Heaven for us.

The constant challenge is to keep our eyes fixed on what is currently INVISIBLE, and to Not Lose Hope because of the trials that are VISIBLE.

One Key to maintaining Apostolic vision is to make sure "our inner self is being renewed day by day" by the Spirit, as Paul stated. The Invisible Holy Spirit, residing within us, in our spirit—our 'inner man'—empowers us to maintain an abiding awareness of our equally Invisible Inheritance in Heaven, and *His very Presence within us is the Guarantee that our Hope is not in vain.*

A new believer was once asked, "What does praying in tongues mean to you?", and I never forgot Danny's answer. He replied, "Praying in tongues reminds me of the Indwelling presence of the Holy Spirit". THAT is the very BEST explanation I have ever heard!

If we remain continually aware of the Holy Spirit's Indwelling presence, then we will be able to maintain our Heavenly perspective through whatever trials may come.

A major key to remaining continually aware of the Holy Spirit's indwelling presence, is by continually praying in the spirit.

Again, I personally believe that every one of us making the decision to resolve to continually pray in the spirit—even if we don't always hit that target—will be far more beneficial than we could possibly imagine, Especially in light of the Endtime events looming on the horizon.

Now at this point, I'm sure many of you can see that these particular steps toward becoming an apostolic people are all very much interconnected.

For example, one of the partial verses that I just quoted was also part of a passage that I just mentioned having to do with apostolic vision.

The truth is (and it should not be a surprise to anyone), all of these apostolic traits that were part of the early church—because the apostles embodied these traits, and imparted them—are rooted and grounded in unseen spiritual realities.

A truly apostolic people—which is what we are, and are striving to be more of—is simply, in its purest sense, a people who are looking for a City whose builder and maker is God.

The very fact that Paul supported himself and others by tentmaking is quite prophetic!

Jesus handpicked as a chief apostle *a man who MADE TENTS!*

In other words, *at the core of our being, we are meant to be a people whose true and enduring, primary focus is Never on the seen, visible things of this world, but on all the unseen eternal realities that we are going to inherit*—Unseen realities that are soon to become quite Visible realities in this present world, beginning with the Millennial Reign, a 1000 year age, where all of the unsaved inhabitants of this world who survived the tribulation will see that the God we always spoke of, and the Kingdom that we always testified to, is in reality the One True Kingdom—and they will see it with their unbeliever eyes as much as we have seen it with our Believing hearts all this time.

Quite honestly, it is that particular vision that strengthens my faith probably more than anything else—Knowing that at some point in time in the future, the very real Kingdom of Jesus Christ is going to be finally set up in Jerusalem, and from there He and all of us will rule over the nations for 1000 years....

Every single unbelieving nation, every single unbelieving king, queen, Prime Minister, president, governor, will finally see with their own naked eyes the risen Lord Jesus ruling from Jerusalem, over every man, woman, and child on the planet that survived the tribulation, and we will be ruling and reigning with him over the same presidents, Prime Ministers, governors, etc.—they will be answering to Jesus through us.

Personally, I think we would be profoundly well served to spend as much time possible meditating on that, researching it through the Word, and building a visual/mental/spiritual image of it in our hearts, because that is the reality that we look to inherit!

"Then the end will come, when He hands over the Kingdom to God
the Father after He has destroyed all dominion, authority, and power.
For He must reign until He has put all His enemies under His feet.
The last enemy to be destroyed is death."

(1 Corinthians 15:24-26)

ASHLEY WHITEHOUSE BUMGARNER
A PROPHECY TESTIMONY

A few days ago, I was walking around my neighborhood with my family. My daughter asked me, "Do you like ministering to people in public?" I told her, "I do, but I always get nervous beforehand." She expressed how she doesn't know how to approach people with Jesus, but desired to.

A few minutes passed, and we walked by a house where a woman, her husband, and her daughter were playing outside. I didn't think too much about it, but I suddenly felt compassion for this woman. My immediate, natural response was fear and not wanting to approach this woman, but I knew in my spirit the Lord wanted to encourage her. So, I told my daughter to come with me, so she could be a witness of how to minister. I said to the woman, "I'm sorry to bother you, but as I was walking by I felt the Lord highlight you to me. I'm not sure if you're a believer. Are you a believer in Jesus?"

She immediately replied with astonishment, "Yes, I am!" My heart leapt, and the Lord instantly gave me a word for her. I said, "There's something you've been asking the Lord for and you haven't seen it, yet. You've been faithful to pray every day, repeatedly, over and over, and He sees you. Don't be discouraged in well-doing, for in due time you will reap."

She was in awe and asked me how I could know this. I told her that it's the gift of prophecy from the Holy Spirit. She explained to me how she was saying, a week prior, that she doesn't understand why she "does everything right" and hasn't seen her prayers answered. She felt like giving up. She was teary-eyed and said she needed that word to keep her faith going.

Isn't the Lord amazing? He knows every heart. If I'm honest, I struggle every time the Lord asks me to step out in faith. It's never easy or comfortable approaching strangers, especially with matters of the heart. Some Christians might excuse themselves from these opportunities of ministry by believing only evangelists share their faith. But I am finding the Lord has no limits, and if you are a believer in the presence of someone whom He has prepared, He will ask you to reach out to them. He's so merciful that He would ask you to speak to the lost, broken, hurting, and abandoned. I'm growing in trusting Him, and every day, I see a little more why He is so trustworthy. I love Him.

BREAKING THROUGH HINDRANCES INTO SPIRITUAL FREEDOM, BY FAITH GUZMAN

Before Faith relates her story, I'll just share a conversation we had during the time preceeding her wonderful breakthrough from the Holy Spirit. I think Faith's experience just goes to show that the Lord meets us where we are, and His ministry is truly as compassionate as it is specific to our heart's deepest needs. Her story will bless you!

From Faith~~~

"Hey Mark, I wanted to share with you what happened to me today. Today was the women's brunch at my church. My mom spoke. After it was ending, our head of the women's ministry got up to close us out in prayer. She started to pray, and we all did as well. Women in the back started speaking in tongues. I got chills over my whole body and felt the presence of God. I felt something happening with my tongue and it started to come out, but it again did not last long. I know God is doing something, but I have to tell you that I felt like I was holding back, out of fear of "is this really you God?" Do I sound right? You know all these doubts."

My response to Faith~~~

My dear sister Faith, I feel the Lord is telling me that you are like Peter—you just have to step out of the boat onto the water, and Jesus will be right there to meet you. The next time you have that feeling, let the Holy Spirit take you by the hand, and help you step out onto the water, and Jesus will be right there with you, and the fear will be forever broken. Now, this may sound somewhat strange, but I feel the Lord impressing me to tell you, "Don't be afraid to be Loud". I'm confident that, at the right time, He will show you what that means.

From Faith~~~

"I just remembered what you told me the other day, that you felt God telling me to not be afraid to be loud. I was afraid, so I know I'm dealing with fear, and I know fear is not of God. I just want to say that I cried today, sharing with my husband all you spoke with me, and never have I felt so much like people are behind me the way I have with you and people you have praying for me. The support amazes me. I really appreciate your ministry and I know God is doing something in me, and I am just thankful for coming in contact with you, because your messages on Facebook are really challenging me in my walk with Christ, to desire more."

My response to Faith~~~

If your mother and those women are going to be gathering together tomorrow (which is Sunday) to pray again, I want you to be there OK? And I will be there with you in faith and in spirit, believing that you will get the tremendous breakthrough that you have been needing, and remember—Jesus is with you and so is the Holy Spirit, and that fear is going to be broken forever.

From Faith~~~My testimony for your book:

"So, I am nowhere near where I need or desire to be in regards to the manifestation of the Holy Spirit in my life. However, I have noticed God giving me more and more of a desire for it, which has started me on the path of pursuing a deeper relationship with the Lord in this area.

I have never believed in the whole "repeat after me" movement when it comes to speaking in our heavenly language. I have always pictured it coming out in deep prayer or worship.

Many times I have been prayed over to receive the Holy Spirit, but back in 2019 I finally was baptized in the Holy Spirit. It was a Wednesday night, and one of my Pastors called me up to pray for me, and he spoke regarding spiritual gifts that night.

He said, "I want to pray for you for Words of knowledge, but what gift do You want?" I said "I want to speak in tongues", and he said "Well, you're going to need that".

It came out, but not strong as I would have hoped. I think mainly because there has been a slight resistance on my part, and feelings of inadequacy, even doubt. I find myself questioning, "Is that you Lord, or is that me?"

Through the years, the times it has come upon me has been mainly in my sleep, or in waking up from my sleep. I never understood why that is, until I spoke to Mark, and he explained that God is gently trying to work in this area of my life when I'm most relaxed, and less resistant. I agree.

God has really worked on me in many areas throughout the years, and I know He is working in this desire I have as well, to walk confidently in the Baptism of the Holy Spirit.

As a young girl, I went through a lot of torment in my mind. The devil tried to deceive me at a young age regarding my sexuality, so much that I would sleep with my Bible to keep the enemy from attacking me in my dreams.

The Bible was my sword. The enemy for years tried to confuse me, but thanks be to God for parents who raised me in the truth and covered me in prayer.

Today, I am married and have a precious son. For years I could not lift my hands. I felt unworthy because of the battles in my mind that I was trying to conquer every day. I now lift my hands with no inhibitions, and just recently during a worship service, as I allowed myself to focus on my worship, I experienced more of my heavenly language coming out. It is nowhere near where I want it to be, but little by little I am seeing God work in this area of my life.

I look forward to being able to pray in my heavenly language more confidently as I draw closer to God through worship and prayer. I'm thankful for the ministry that God has given Mark Judy. If it was not for his convicting posts, I would not have been made uncomfortable in this area the way I needed to be. We have to get uncomfortable sometimes in our walk, or we are simply not growing."

* *

From Faith~~~

Apr 26, 2022, 8:01 a.m.

I got my first message from the Holy Spirit! He said, "To walk in the Spirit is to obey the initial promptings of the spirit"

"For if you are living according to the [impulses of the flesh, you are going to die. But if [you are living] by the [power of the Holy] Spirit you are habitually putting to death the sinful deeds of the body, you will [really] live forever. For all who are allowing themselves to be led by the Spirit of God are sons of God". Romans 8:13-14

HEALING IN HOSPITAL THROUGH PRAYING IN TONGUES, BY TIFFANY JAMES

've always had a deep interest in bringing healing to people, at one time as a physician's assistant, but now it's more spiritual than physical for me. I have had so many "divine appointment" situations relating to car accidents and trauma victims. In one of many incidents, I came upon a little girl involved in a car accident who was not speaking, and I prayed over her and then she began to talk.

One really notable event was even more personal. My husband was in the hospital for over 10 days, and staff had no idea what was wrong with him. I was very weak in faith at the time, but it was as if I audibly heard the Lord say, "Go lay hands on him".

I rushed into my husband's hospital room, prayed in the spirit in tongues, and the next day his white blood cell counts went up and his fever left, and he was released.

FROM ATHEIST TO BORN AGAIN, TO BAPTIZED IN THE HOLY SPIRIT, BY MATTHEW YOCKEY

I was brought up in church, but at age 13 I turned away after they mistreated my family. Like my father, I turned to atheism, built my life on facts, logic, believing the only realities were tangible ones.

At age 24, Jess and I had just had our miracle baby Isaac—born 15 weeks premature, weighing in at a measly 1lb. 3oz. You'd think his surviving would have been evidence enough of divine intervention, but not for me. "Modern medicine saved my child's life", I reasoned.

However, I wanted to instill Christian morals into my child, so we gave church a try again, going to a Baptist church. The pastor seemed like a genuinely nice guy, and was courteous when we discussed my beliefs. Jess and I began attending shortly afterwards, and around 6 months later (Christmas) I accepted Christ as my Savior, and was baptized a month later.

I tried to live my life in a Christ-like way and serve to the best of my abilities, but *there was always something missing. I never really felt connected to my Savior. I saw this version of the Church in the Book of Acts and in the Epistles, and I don't see how the early Church and what we call "Church" here in the U.S. can be reconciled.*

Then the pandemic hit, and more or less cooled any remaining fervor I had for finding a church home, and I just lost my desire to keep trying. I still believed in God, and Jesus' sacrifice, I just wasn't "trying" any more. Six months later, a nice lady on my mail route invited my family to join them for dinner. It a kind gesture, especially after the lockdowns and social isolation. I learned later that it was going to be a Bible study with some other families, and we began attending their monthly gathering. I really began seeking the Lord in a renewed way, listening to the Bible while delivering mail on my route. It really began stirring in me, but I was still torn between the Early Church and the Western church. During this same time, I saw a post on Facebook from a friend, in regards to how we receive teaching from a church. This triggered the same questions I'd been contemplating about the Early Church vs. today's "church". I commented on their post & asked their advice.

Mark happened to be one of Ashley's friends and saw my comment, and reached out to me about my questions. He turned me on to his podcast called "Vigilance for the End Times". His ministry has a singular focus of helping people receive the Baptism in the Holy Spirit and learn how to walk in the Spirit.

I began noticing repeated references to the often-repeated phrases "in the Spirit" and "in the Holy Spirit" in the Bible, coinciding with what I was hearing Mark speak about in his podcasts, regarding being baptized in the Spirit to have a truly intimate walk with the Lord.

I thought, "Maybe this is what was missing in the churches, and in my own walk with the Lord". So, that's what I began to seek with all my being. I began to live and pray in ways that I never had before. My prayer times were conversational, less like me trying to repeat the "Christianese" I've heard prayed in church. I described it to my wife before we began praying together every night, that it was like I was having a conversation with my Dad—my Heavenly dad, but my dad. I trusted in faith that God was doing a work in me. My time in the Word was more fruitful. The Holy Spirit was jumping out of nearly every page of the Bible.

By this time, I realized that I needed the whole filling of the Spirit. It was no longer enough to have the Spirit walking *with* me, I wanted Him in me. I wanted to be overflowed. I wanted a closeness I had never felt before. I reached out to my new pastor friends, with the express purpose of understanding this more clearly, and for a session of prayer and laying on of hands.

Again, this was another powerful session of prayer, but tongues were not manifest. I was reminded of Jesus asking the disciples to pray with Him in the garden ("Then Jesus returned to the disciples and found them sleeping. "Were you not able to keep watch with Me for one hour?" He asked Peter. "Watch and pray so that you will not enter into temptation. For the spirit is willing, but the body is weak"; Matthew 26:40,41)

There was something in my flesh that was preventing me from fully receiving the baptism. What could it be? I knew Ashley's prayers were led by the Spirit, because she prayed things over Jessica and I, things that we had not shared with anyone. Ashley was certain that I had received the Spirit and that it would manifest in its own time.

She was right. But, there was still a bit of the "old me" that resisted accepting anything that I couldn't prove or physically touch. I talked to Mark about this, and he recommended I go back and listen to his podcast, "Temples of the Holy Spirit Part 3. Identifying and Overcoming Hindrances to Fellowshipping with the Father"

One evening on my way home from work I was praying, when I "felt" this word in my mouth—mentally I tried to dismiss it, but it just lingered there. So I just let it go—it was words that my mind did not understand, as spirit began praying while I was driving. Shocked and surprised, I just tried to keep my car on the road! My mind was racing and I thought, "Did I just make this up? Did I want this so badly I just fabricated it out of my own mind?" When I got home I talked to my wife and we prayed. I decided to call Ashley from church to see if she could confirm if this was the Holy Spirit, or "just me". She laughed and rejoiced that I'd received the fullness of the Spirit!

The Baptism of the Spirit is not a "one and you're done" thing, as some teach. This is something that will change everything about you. You will be empowered, you will become bold, you will be in direct connection with the Father, getting your marching orders directly from the Source. But you must keep and cultivate it. The Holy Spirit is a gentleman, He's not going to force Himself on anyone, but He will nudge you, and encourage you to act in accordance with His plans and desires. It is up to you to submit and act. In turn, you will be rewarded with a closeness that grows greater with each act of faithfulness, and with time spent with the Holy Spirit. Now, if you are apprehensive, or feel unworthy, remember my story. I had turned away from the Lord, was a staunch atheist for more than half of my life, then spent the first decade of my walk with Christ absent from the Holy Spirit. God still chose me. He still acted. He will use you too, if you just accept His gifts and allow Him to work.

Powerful testimonies come from opening our hearts to the Power & Life in the Word of the Living God, the God who said, "No word shall return to Me void".

Here are some of the Scriptures breathed by the Holy Spirit (2 Timothy 3:16) that reveal just how Indispensable the Life & Power of the Holy Spirit is to the Family of God.

Matthew 3:11; "I baptize you with water for repentance, but after me will come One more powerful than I, whose sandals I am not worthy to carry. He will baptize you with the Holy Spirit and with fire."

Acts 2:1-4; "When the day of Pentecost came, they were all together in one place. Suddenly a sound like a mighty rushing wind came from heaven and filled the whole house where they were sitting. They saw tongues like flames of fire that separated and came to rest on each of them. And they were all filled with the Holy Spirit and began to speak in other tongues as the Spirit enabled them."

John 16:7-8; "But I tell you the truth, it is for your benefit that I am going away. Unless I go away, the Advocate will not come to you; but if I go, I will send Him to you. And when He comes, He will convict the world in regard to sin and righteousness and judgment".

And we can see from scripture that baptism in the Holy Spirit is a unique gift that is set apart from salvation, and from water baptism.

Acts 19:1-6; "While Apollos was at Corinth, Paul passed through the interior and came to Ephesus. There he found some disciples and asked them, "Did you receive the Holy Spirit when you became believers?"

"No," they answered, "we have not even heard that there is a Holy Spirit."

"Into what, then, were you baptized?" Paul asked.

"The baptism of John," they replied.

Paul explained: "John's baptism was a baptism of repentance. He told the people to believe in the One coming after him, that is, in Jesus."

On hearing this, they were baptized into the name of the Lord Jesus. And when Paul laid his hands on them, the Holy Spirit came upon them, and they spoke in tongues and prophesied."

Luke 11:13; "So if you who are evil know how to give good gifts to your children, how much more will your Father in heaven give the Holy Spirit to those who ask Him!"

Acts 8:14-17; "When the apostles in Jerusalem heard that Samaria had received the word of God, they sent Peter and John to them. On their arrival, they prayed for them to receive the Holy Spirit. For the Holy Spirit had not yet fallen upon any of them; they had simply been baptized into the name of the Lord Jesus. Then Peter and John laid their hands on them, and they received the Holy Spirit."

Acts 9:17; "So Ananias went to the house, and when he arrived, he placed his hands on Saul. "Brother Saul," he said, "the Lord Jesus, who appeared to you on the road as you were coming here, has sent me so that you may see again and be filled with the Holy Spirit."

ABOUT THE AUTHOR

Mark Judy is the creator of the cutting edge discipleship podcast, Vigilance for the Endtimes, which emphasizes building a dynamic relationship with the Holy Spirit for inward spiritual transformation. He was the creator of the Jericho Chronicle News Magazine, based in Austin, Texas, which focused on Endtime events with a prophetic perspective. He also served as Men's Discipleship Coordinator for the Regeneration Center in South Florida in the early 1990s. Raised in the Presbyterian Church as a young man, Mark's life took a profoundly dramatic turn when, in the Summer of 1978, he had a life-changing vision of Jesus Christ being crucified for him—A sovereign, supernatural encounter that took him from mere religious head knowledge of Jesus, into an unspeakably life-altering, personal revelation of Jesus as the living Lord of Lords and King of Kings. A short time later he was baptized in the Holy Spirit in Jacksonville, Florida, and began outreach ministry to the homeless, and to those in the New Age cults and witchcraft, seeing many delivered of demonic spirits and radically changed by the power of the Holy Spirit. His darling wife of over 19 years went home to be with the Lord in November 2020, after a 16 year battle with chronic illness, and during a period of prayer and fasting after Roopa's passing, the Lord called him back into full-time discipleship ministry—and thus, Vigilance for the Endtimes was born.

His book "Discipled by the Holy Spirit" is the First of a series of intensive discipleship manuals, born out of the Vigilance For the Endtimes podcast ministry that has already been used by the Lord to transform so many lives.